CHARACTERIZATION AND INDIVIDUALITY IN GREEK LITERATURE

Characterization
and
Individuality
in Greek Literature

EDITED BY

CHRISTOPHER PELLING

CLARENDON PRESS · OXFORD

*This book has been printed digitally and produced in a standard specification
in order to ensure its continuing availability*

OXFORD
UNIVERSITY PRESS

Great Clarendon Street, Oxford OX2 6DP

Oxford University Press is a department of the University of Oxford.
It furthers the University's objective of excellence in research, scholarship,
and education by publishing worldwide in

Oxford New York

Auckland Bangkok Buenos Aires Cape Town Chennai
Dar es Salaam Delhi Hong Kong Istanbul Karachi Kolkata
Kuala Lumpur Madrid Melbourne Mexico City Mumbai Nairobi
São Paulo Shanghai Singapore Taipei Tokyo Toronto

with an associated company in Berlin

Oxford is a registered trade mark of Oxford University Press
in the UK and in certain other countries

Published in the United States
by Oxford University Press Inc., New York

ISBN 0-19-814058-4

Preface

The 'individual' has always proved a slippery figure. He was discovered by the lyric poets, we are told; or in Athens, at the end of the fifth century; or by Plato, with his portrait of Socrates; or in the Hellenistic age; or by the Roman poets; or by the Antonines; or by Augustine. Perhaps he had been there all the time, lurking in Homer's Achilles and Odysseus. Still, he had evidently fled away again by the early Middle Ages, only to be rediscovered first in 1050-1200;[1] then, according to Burckhardt's famous analysis, in Renaissance Italy;[2] then again in the sixteenth, or seventeenth, or eighteenth centuries.[3]

It all depends what we mean. We may (as in most of those analyses) be concerned with self-consciousness, a clear awareness of one's own or others' identity as something which will involve definitions of social role, status, and responsibilities, but—at least in the Greek and later European context—will not be *exhausted* by those definitions: already in Homer, we can ask whether Agamemnon has the qualities to live up to his position,[4] and the question makes sense. But we may mean something a little different, more clearly introspective: a person's capacity to describe or analyse psychic events, or simply his awareness of himself as a locus for decision-making; and this consciousness of the self as a rational agent will often imply a readiness to accept some sort of 'responsibility' for those decisions, and a normal obligation to bear their consequences. Or we may simply be concerned with describing accurately the characters of oneself or others. That process may be purely normative, finding true adjectives to use of people and their

---

[1] C. Morris, *The Discovery of the Individual 1050-1200* (London, 1972).

[2] J. Burckhardt, *The Civilization of the Renaissance in Italy* (1860; Eng. trans. S. G. C. Middleton, London, 1955): the second part of the work is entitled 'The Development of the Individual'. Cf. esp. pp. 80-4, 279.

[3] L. Trilling, *Sincerity and Authenticity* (Oxford, 1972), 24 (16th or 17th cents.); L. Woolf, *After the Deluge: A Study in Communal Psychology*, i (London, 1931), 244 (more the 18th).

[4] However exactly that position is defined—a question which Taplin addresses in this volume.

actions, true classes to which they belong; or it may be concerned to mark out how a figure belies normal expectations—a process of 'individuation', if the inelegant word may be allowed. Once described, that individual may also inspire an effort to explain or to understand: that explanation may be given in terms of personal development, and it may be related to particular influences or circumstances—and those influences or circumstances may again be defined in ways which are more or less particular. Finally, we may be concerned with the consequences we draw from a discriminating self-awareness, one's duty or licence to be true to oneself, to follow and realize the implications of one's character rather than acquiesce in society's fixed norms of conduct—a form of 'individual*ism*', in fact. That concept is already visible in the supermen figures idealized in some fifth- and fourth-century thought, men who followed their own nature (*phusis*) and despised artificial human conventions (*nomoi*); and the idea became more sophisticated in later antiquity, with much more scope for individual variations of values and aims.[5] Self-consciousness, introspection, awareness of decision-making and responsibility, description, individuation, understanding, and individualism—all these aspects interrelate, and are explored in this volume.

Not, of course, that it is a critical history of individuality, still less of characterization: the task would be absurd, and the gaps are anyway obvious (nothing, for instance, on the Greek historians; nothing on the lyric poets; nothing on Hellenistic philosophy; nothing on visual art). But it is prompted by a feeling that discussions of principle and practice are, by the nature of the essay form, rather genre-dependent, and have indeed on the whole been limited to specific *poetic* genres: questions of self-consciousness and identity have for instance tended to be asked more of epic, and in a different sense of the lyric poets; while issues of psychological depth have tended to focus on tragedy, as has that of the relation between art and life—for example the question whether our construction of characters in an art-form differs significantly from the way we form a view of people in

<hr/>

[5] Cf. esp. Cic. *de Off.* 1. 107–14, drawing on Panaetius; Hor. *Epist.* 1. 7. 98; Sen. *Tranq.* 6. 2, 7. 2; Quint. 2. 8; Plut. *Mor.* 472c ff., etc. See further M. J. McGann, *Studies in Horace's First Book of* Epistles (Coll. Latomus, 100; Brussels, 1969), 10–14; N. Rudd, *Lines of Enquiry* (Cambridge, 1976), 155–6.

everyday existence. Yet the genres affected one another: several recent discussions of tragedy, for instance, refer in general terms to rhetoric or dialectic, but without the space to develop a more subtle comparison with Plato, Isocrates, or Demosthenes. And anyway we are often dealing with assumptions about character which go beyond literature: most fundamentally, the modern expectation of idiosyncrasy contrasts with the Greek taste for the normative, and that is a matter of our and their unreflective popular assumptions, not just of generic expectations. A collection of articles on different genres may be thought-provoking, and many of the issues raised have implications which transcend the authors or texts discussed.

The volume had its origins in an Oxford colloquium held on 20 March 1987. Five of the papers (those of Gill, Taplin, Easterling, Griffin, and Silk) were given there, and most of the other contributors were present. Our thanks to all who helped in the organization and participated in the discussion, especially to Martha Nussbaum, Judith Mossman, Nicholas Richardson, Richard Rutherford, Mary Lefkowitz, and Angus Bowie; and to Oxford University's Craven Committee for supporting the colloquium.

C.B.R.P.

Contents

I

The Character–Personality Distinction

CHRISTOPHER GILL

THE DISTINCTION

In this chapter, I want to explore further a distinction which I have used elsewhere in connection with characterization in ancient literature. In one discussion, I used the distinction to discriminate between what I saw as the prevailing approaches of ancient and modern biographers to their subjects, associating the ancient approach with 'character' and the modern one rather with 'personality'.[1] In a subsequent discussion, I used a related distinction (between a 'character-viewpoint' and a 'personality-viewpoint') to identify different types of audience-response to the presentation of figures in Greek tragedy. I suggested that Greek tragedies are typically designed to invite a mixture of these types of response; and that, at certain key moments, the audience is invited to shift from a character-viewpoint to a personality-viewpoint.[2] In another context, I examined the use of the distinction between *ēthos* and *pathos* (and between 'ethical' and 'pathetic' styles) in ancient rhetorical and poetic criticism from Aristotle to Longinus, and especially the ancient contrast between the *Iliad* as a poem of *pathos* and the *Odyssey* as one of *ēthos*. One of my reasons for doing so, though an implicit one, was the desire to see whether there were points of analogy between the *ēthos–pathos* distinction,

I am grateful to Martha Nussbaum and other participants in the Oxford Colloquium on 'Characterization and Individuality in Greek Literature' for comments on an oral version of this chapter, and to Pat Easterling and Stephen Halliwell for helpful criticisms of a written version. I am also grateful to Christopher Pelling for stimulating the writing of the chapter by organizing the conference and this volume.

[1] 'The Question of Character-Development: Plutarch and Tacitus', *CQ*, NS 33 (1983), 469–87, esp. 470–3; on the sense being given to 'character' and 'personality', see below.

[2] 'The Question of Character and Personality in Greek Tragedy', *Poetics Today*, 7/2 (1986) [Special Issue on 'Theory of Character'], 251–73.

as used by ancient critics, and the character–personality distinction, as I had been using this.[3] My aim here is closest to that
in my article on Greek tragedy: I want to consider the utility of
the character–personality distinction as a means of identifying
different perspectives in figures within Greek epic and tragic
poems. I also want to reflect further on the distinction, to consider some possible criticisms of it, and to outline a reformu-
lated version in which I try to take account of those criticisms.
Later in this chapter I shall apply this revised framework to
certain passages in Homer and tragedy, in an attempt to establish, in a provisional way, whether this framework is genuinely
useful for interpretative purposes.

Let me begin by summarizing the meaning I have given to this
distinction in earlier accounts. I have associated the term 'character' with the process of making moral judgements; and I
have taken this process to involve (i) placing people in a determinate ethical framework and (ii) treating them as psychological and moral 'agents', that is, as the originators of
intentional actions for which they are normally held responsible and which are treated as indexes of goodness or badness of
character. The term 'personality', on the other hand, I have
associated with responses of a different type. I have connected
it with a response to people that is empathetic rather than
moral: that is, with the desire to identify oneself with another
person, to 'get inside her skin', rather than to appraise her
'from the outside'.[4] I have also connected it with a concern with
the person as a unique individual (or as the possessor of a 'real'
or 'authentic' self) rather than as the bearer of character-traits
which are assessed by reference to general moral norms. I have
also associated it with a perspective in which the person is seen
as psychologically passive; that is, as someone whose nature
and behaviour are determined by forces which fall outside her
control as an agent and perhaps outside her consciousness as
well. In defining the distinction in this way, I have drawn on

---

[3] 'The *Ethos/Pathos* Distinction in Rhetorical and Literary Criticism', *CQ*, NS 34
(1984), 149–66, esp. 165–6, in which I indicate the larger critical implications of the
distinction.
[4] In this chapter I use 'he/him' and 'she/her' indifferently as indefinite personal pronouns.

some commonplace connotations of the terms 'character' and 'personality', especially the association of 'character' with moral appraisal, and that of 'personality' both with unique individuality or identity and with 'scientific' approaches to the person. I am well aware that the meanings of the two terms, in so far as they are distinguished at all, are not always distinguished in quite this way.[5] My main aim has not been simply to reproduce ordinary usage but to regiment or simplify it, so as to define more clearly two different ways of viewing persons, both in real life and in literature.[6]

However, there are grounds for questioning whether the distinction, as I have formulated it so far, is wholly clear and coherent at the theoretical level. The side of the distinction associated with 'character' may perhaps seem cohesive (although some would dispute the idea that the moral viewpoint necessarily involves regarding people as psychological agents).[7] But the side of the distinction associated with 'personality' may well seem to combine two or three different, and even incompatible, strands. Is there any prima-facie reason, for instance, to connect (*a*) sharing another person's individual viewpoint with (*b*) seeing him as subject to psychological forces which fall outside his agency?[8] This question may help to focus a sense of general unease about the theoretical grounding of the distinction. Arguably, my previous formulations of this distinction run together (at least) three different types of distinction, which should be separately identified. These distinctions relate to different aspects of our understanding of other people (and of ourselves), namely (i) the explanation of actions, (ii) evaluation, and (iii) the adoption of a perspective.

---

[5] Contrast e.g. A. Quinton's use of the distinction in *Thoughts and Thinkers* (London, 1982), 21–2.

[6] Cf. e.g. A. Morton's use of the distinction to demarcate agent-centred and psychoanalytic conceptions of the person, in R. Wollheim and J. Hopkins (edd.), *Philosophical Essays on Freud* (Cambridge, 1982), 60–74. For the distinction between an intentional 'action' (performed by a psychological 'agent') and an 'event', see D. Davidson, *Essays on Actions and Events* (Oxford, 1980), ch. 3.

[7] See e.g. B. A. O. Williams's critique of this assumption (esp. as articulated by Kant) in *Moral Luck* (Cambridge, 1981), ch. 2, and *Ethics and the Limits of Philosophy* (London, 1985), chs. 4 and 10; M. C. Nussbaum, *The Fragility of Goodness: Luck and Ethics in Greek Tragedy and Philosophy* (Cambridge, 1986), ch. 1.

[8] This question was raised, in a clear and forceful way, by Julia Annas, commenting on an earlier account of the distinction.

Let me take these three aspects in turn, indicating their connection with the interpretation of character or personality in each case.

(i) One can explain a person's actions by reference to her beliefs and desires, or more generally her *reasons* for acting in a given way, and this line of explanation might be extended to take account of her character as an agent (that is, as a source of intentional actions). Alternatively, one might try to explain her behaviour as determined by psychological *causes* which are distinct in kind from her conscious motives, for instance by reference to the unconscious desires which are typical of a narcissistic personality.[9]

(ii) One can identify an evaluative framework in which people are judged by their capacity to conform to certain norms of conduct and character which apply uniformly to all members of the society, or to all bearers of specific social roles. Alternatively, one can identify a framework in which evaluative status is given to the expression of personal individuality or distinctiveness (the possession of a powerful 'personality', as one might say) even in cases where this expression runs counter to the demands of normal social standards. (Or, to mark a different shade of this distinction, in this alternative framework, taking up a distinctively individual stance on ethical questions and formulating an ethic *for oneself* are regarded as inherently admirable.)

(iii) Relatedly, one can isolate a standpoint which takes no special account of the particular point of view or perspective of the individuals concerned (or of any one individual concerned), but which aspires to be impartial or even impersonal (let me call this an 'objective' standpoint). Alternatively, one can take up a standpoint which is strongly expressive of one's own subjective viewpoint, or in which one identifies oneself with another's subjective viewpoint.[10] In the latter case (though not the former), it may be regarded as important to isolate a 'first-personal' viewpoint, which is distinctively *one's own* (or at least distinctively *someone's*), as regards perceptions, memories, and emotional responses, for instance, and which is

---

[9] On the reason–cause distinction, see e.g. Wollheim and Hopkins (edd.), *Philosophical Essays on Freud*, x–xii.

[10] On this type of distinction, cf. T. Nagel, *The View from Nowhere* (Oxford, 1986).

distinct from another person's ('third-personal') view of oneself
and one's experiences. (The 'first-personal' viewpoint is sometimes taken as constitutive of a person's unique identity or individuality.)[11]

It is arguably the case that my previous formulations of the
character–personality distinction run together these, and perhaps other, distinctions. To do so is not unjustifiable if the
features thus associated are compatible and are in fact connected in our customary understanding of persons. Thus, I
think that the process of moral appraisal does often involve (i)
treating the person as a psychological agent, (ii) judging him
by general social norms, and (iii) viewing him objectively, that
is, in a way that gives no special status to his subjective view of
the situation.[12] Furthermore, I think one can plausibly connect
the validation of personal distinctiveness or uniqueness and that
of an individual's subjective point of view (the 'alternative'
items in distinctions (ii) and (iii) above). Indeed, in partial
qualification of a point made earlier, I think that giving attention to an individual's subjective viewpoint may sometimes be
associated with seeing the person's behaviour as determined by
forces external to her agency;[13] this is so when *the person concerned*
sees herself as being in the grip of external forces.[14] Thus, in the
following discussion, I shall sometimes continue to make such
connections, and to associate the relevant items with the terms
'character' or 'personality', respectively. For analytic clarity,
and for clarity of literary interpretation (which is the purpose
for which I am using these distinctions here), I shall make these
associations explicitly, and also explicate the sense I am giving
to 'character' and 'personality' in each case.[15]

---

[11] On the 'first-personal' viewpoint, cf. e.g. A. Rorty (ed.), *The Identities of Persons*
(Berkeley, 1976), 10–15; G. Madell, *The Identity of the Self* (Edinburgh, 1981), ch. 2;
R. Wollheim, *The Thread of Life* (Cambridge, 1984), 64 ff.

[12] To say this is not to say that moral appraisal ought to take this form (cf. the criticisms referred to in n. 7 above), only that it often does so.

[13] i.e. the 'alternative' items in distinctions (i) and (ii) above.

[14] Cf. the cases of Eteocles and Medea, discussed below. This is not the kind of case
envisaged in Julia Annas's objection (n. 8 above); she envisaged the two types of explanation as being both different in kind and mutually exclusive, as is normally the
case.

[15] It may be helpful at this point to tabulate these distinctions, marking the association with either 'character' or 'personality'. (The fact that I am presenting the distinc-

Spelling out these distinctions in this way may have additional advantages for my purposes here. For one thing, doing so underlines the point that our understanding of the notions of character and personality presupposes a complex set of related distinctions; and we cannot assume without argument that those notions or the related distinctions hold good in other cultures or historical periods. In attempting to deploy these notions and distinctions in connection with Greek literary texts (as I shall do later), I am not using them as transcultural absolutes but rather—as Steven Lukes puts it in another context—as 'floating bridgeheads' in our attempt to communicate with the concerns and concepts of Greek culture.[16] Secondly, unpacking these distinctions enables me to reconceive what I have been calling the 'character-' and 'personality-viewpoints' in ways that may be more perspicuous and more helpful for the interpretation of literary texts. For instance, one might suggest that the various features I have been associating with 'character', when embodied in literary form,[17] combine to make the literary work concerned one that is ethically affirmative, in so far as it confirms ethical attitudes and assumptions that are prevalent in the culture. (At least, this is true when those features correspond to the attitudes which *are* prevalent in the culture.) On the other hand, the features I have been associating with 'personality', when these predominate in a literary work (or when they are conjoined, unexpectedly, with 'character' features) will tend, I think, to make the work ethically

tions in this formulaic way should not be taken as an indication that I intend to apply them mechanically when discussing Greek texts.)

  (i) Explanation of action in terms of an agent's beliefs and desires ('character'). Explanation of action in terms of causes falling outside personal agency ('personality').

  (ii) Evaluation by reference to general social norms ('character'). Evaluation by reference to personal distinctiveness or individuality, or by reference to a distinctively individual ethic ('personality').

  (iii) 'Objective' standpoint, which aims at impartiality (even impersonality) as regards individuals ('character'). 'Subjective' standpoint, which gives special status to a person's individual (esp. 'first-personal') perspective ('personality').

I should also note that I shall present the terms 'character' and 'personality' in quotes when I am using them with reference to the distinctions outlined above.

[16] M. Carrithers, S. Collins, and S. Lukes (edd.), *The Category of the Person: Anthropology, Philosophy, History* (Cambridge, 1985), 298; Lukes is referring to the use of the notions of person and self in the exploration of the conceptual framework of other cultures.

[17] On the question of what is involved in such literary embodiment, see below.

non-standard or interrogatory in its impact, questioning rather than validating existing cultural assumptions.[18]

In what way do I suppose that drawing these distinctions can help us to understand characterization in Greek literature? It is important, first of all, to be clear about which aspects of the study of characterization we have in view. I make this point because the study of characterization in literature should not be regarded either as unitary and homogeneous (since it constitutes a nexus of related enquiries) or as surgically detachable from the study of other aspects of the literary work. The most obvious aspect of the subject is the study of what might be called 'character-markers', including character-indicating speeches and actions by the relevant figures and significant statements about them by the narrator or other figures. But clearly, in identifying what are to count as significant character-markers, we bring to bear a whole complex of psychological and social assumptions, in the light of which we 'read' the significance of these markers.[19] These assumptions also, of course, inform our 'reading' of persons in real life.[20] In applying these assumptions to literature (and other artistic forms) we also deploy a set of presuppositions about the way in which features such as motivation and status are 'encoded' in a given work and genre. The question of what is significant for characterization is closely related to the question of what is significant for plot or theme;[21] and it is understandable, therefore, that the semiotic study of character has developed out of structuralist attempts to analyse character as a function of plot-types or as part of the 'grammar' of narrative.[22] Literary theorists have

---

[18] For the distinction between affirmative and interrogatory uses of characterization, cf. e.g. J. Bayley, 'Character and Consciousness', *New Literary History*, 5/2 (1974), 225–35, esp. 226.

[19] Cf. J. Frow, 'Spectacle Binding: On Character', *Poetics Today*, 7/2 (1986), 227–50, esp. 227–8 and 232–5.

[20] This point is well brought out by P. E. Easterling, in her criticism of J. P. Gould (ch. 4 below, text to nn. 34–8). To this extent, Barthes's distinction between the (literary) *figure* and the (real) *person* (noted by S. Goldhill, ch. 5 below, text to n. 34) needs some qualification.

[21] O. Taplin notes this point (ch. 3 below, first paragraph) and illustrates it in his discussion of Homer's Agamemnon.

[22] Cf. Frow, 'Spectacle Binding', 230–2; U. Margolin, 'The Doer and the Deed: Action as a Basis for Characterization in Narrative', *Poetics Today*, 7/2 (1986), 205–25; and more generally, J. Culler, *Structuralist Poetics* (London, 1975); id., *The Pursuit of Signs* (London, 1981).

also explored the use of character as a means of identifying the centre of interest in a narrative, and as a way of defining a dominant point of view or consciousness.[23] A related topic is the analysis of audience- or reader-response to the presentation of figures, whether in the form of an ideal or implied response signalled by the work itself, or in the form of the history of the actual reception of a given literary work.[24]

To which of these aspects of the study of characterization is the 'character–personality' distinction designed to contribute? Principally, I have in view the related topics of the audience's assumptions (deployed in the reading of 'character-markers'), and the audience's responses to the figures thus characterized. To be more exact, I am concerned with trying to define the kinds of assumptions and responses which the works themselves seem to expect, rather than with the assumptions and responses which we, as contemporary readers, tend to provide, or with the history of such responses in classical scholarship.[25] It may seem to be a difficulty for this project that I am attempting to use modern notions and distinctions to define the expectations implied in ancient texts. I do not underestimate this difficulty (which is, of course, a difficulty which affects a great deal of 'historicist' interpretation of ancient texts). But I shall try to alleviate it by using the concepts I have discussed as (to reuse this term) 'floating bridgeheads' in the attempt to make contact with the ideas and assumptions of Greek culture rather than as normative or absolute categories.[26] Furthermore, while my primary focus is on the assumptions and responses to figures which the work seems to presuppose, that subject is not wholly

[23] Cf. S. Chatman, 'Charactors and Narrators', *Poetics Today*, 7/2 (1986), 189–204, who discusses Genette's use of the notion of the character as 'focus' or 'focalizer'.

[24] Cf. *Arethusa*, 19/2 (1986) [Special Issue on 'Audience-Oriented Criticism and the Classics'], esp. the contribution of P. J. Rabinowitz, 'Shifting Stands, Shifting Standards: Reading, Interpretation, and Literary Judgement', 115–34; and R. C. Holub, *Reception Theory: A Critical Introduction* (London, 1984), esp. 78–81, on H. Jauss, 'Levels of Identification of Hero and Audience', *New Literary History*, 5/2 (1974), 283–317.

[25] Thus, I am presupposing that one can intelligibly discuss the question of what 'the works themselves seem to expect', a presupposition some would dispute (cf. Rabinowitz, 'Shifting Stands', esp. p. 126), although in doing so I accept the fact that one's views on this question are inevitably informed, to some extent, by contemporary concerns and by the reception of the works in classical scholarship.

[26] See n. 16 above; also S. Collins, 'Categories, Concepts or Predicaments?', in Carrithers *et al.* (edd.), *The Category of the Person*, 46 ff.

detachable from (or fully intelligible without) the study of the way in which 'character', in the senses noted above, is embedded in the form and structure of the literary work as a whole.[27] While I shall not go very far in this chapter towards exploring the interconnections between these various aspects of the study of character, I am deeply aware of the need to take account of them in working out the implications of the distinctions I am using.

It is because of this latter consideration (the need to study character as embedded in the form and structure of particular texts) that I want to focus, for most of the remainder of this chapter, on a number of specific, and often rather famous, passages in Homer and Greek tragedy. I want to discuss these passages in terms of the twofold approaches or frameworks I have associated with 'character' on the one hand and 'personality' on the other.[28] In using these passages in this illustrative way, I shall have to presuppose certain interpretations rather than arguing fully for them. But I hope it will seem acceptable to take the interpretations presupposed on trust, as it were, so as to enable the exploration of the interpretative utility of the distinction.

HOMER

In ancient criticism, as I noted earlier, the *Odyssey* was sometimes contrasted with the *Iliad* as being an epic of *ēthos* rather than *pathos*;[29] and, while I would not want to make quite so sharp a contrast in the terms I am using, I think that the frameworks I am associating with 'character' are more consistently appropriate to the *Odyssey* than they are to the *Iliad*. The *Odyssey* typically presents its figures as agents who show their (ethical) character by their considered responses to certain key situations, in which a clear choice of action is demanded of them. This presentation is exemplified above all in Odysseus'

---

[27] Cf. the cautionary advice, for those wanting to study the history of moral and psychological ideas in Greek poetry, of K. J. Dover, *Greek Popular Morality in the Time of Plato and Aristotle* (Oxford, 1974), ch. 1, esp. 14–18; id., 'The Portrayal of Moral Evaluation in Greek Poetry', *JHS* 103 (1983), 35–48; also Nussbaum, *Fragility*, 424–5 n. 20.

[28] See n. 15 above.

[29] Arist. *Poet.* 24, 1459[b]13–15; Longin. 9. 15; cf. Gill. '*Ēthos/Pathos* Distinction', 149–50.

recurrent, and often noted, role as 'testing' those he encounters,
so as to judge, by their responses, whether they are 'violent,
savage, and unjust, or hospitable and godly in their mind
(νοῦς).'[30] The placing of figures in an ethical framework is pro-
moted by the use of approbatory stock epithets on the one
hand, such as 'sensible' and 'restrained' (περίφρων, ἐχέφρων,
and πεπνυμένος), and disapprobatory adjectives on the other,
such as 'arrogant' (ὑπερφίαλοι) and 'outrageous' (ἀτάσθαλοι).[31]
The poem promotes confidence in the application of these
terms by the consistency with which they are applied (it is not
only Odysseus and his human supporters who describe the
suitors as 'engaging in lawless violence, (ὑβρίζοντες), but also
Athena and sometimes the narrator),[32] and also by a clear correlation between the application of the terms and the kinds of
action to which they refer.[33] As regards the characteristic perspective of the poem, it is obvious that certain figures—
Odysseus, Telemachus, and Penelope—have a special claim on
our attention and concern, and that the story is told (sometimes
literally) from their standpoint. But this does not mean that
these figures are 'privileged' in the sense of being exempted
from the norms of ethical judgement applied elsewhere in the
poem. As Richard Rutherford has brought out, Odysseus'
retrospective judgements of his own past actions are in line with
those which others would make on him, and which he would
make on others. For instance, in the course of his narrative, he
underlines his own folly in insisting, against his men's advice,
on staying in the cave of the Cyclops and on taunting him when
blinded; and his account enables us to see why Eurylochus subsequently refers to these acts as ones in which Odysseus destroyed his men by his 'reckless acts' (ἀτασθαλίῃσιν).[34] To use
two of the distinctions I have discussed earlier, Odysseus

---

[30] See e.g. *Od.* 6. 120–1, 9. 175–6, 13. 201–2.

[31] Cf. S. Saïd, 'Les Crimes des Prétendants', in Saïd *et al.*, *Études de litterature ancienne* (Paris, 1979), esp. 9. The stock epithets of the *Iliad* (on which see W. Whallon, *Formula, Character and Context* (Cambridge, Mass., 1969), ch. 1) are not ethically value-laden in the same way.

[32] See e.g. *Od.* 1. 227 (cf. 32–4), 17. 481–2, 21. 285.

[33] Cf. R. B. Rutherford, 'The Philosophy of the *Odyssey*', *JHS* 106 (1986), 145–62, esp. 145–7; E. A. Havelock, *The Greek Concept of Justice* (Cambridge, Mass., 1978); A. Thornton, *People and Themes in Homer's Odyssey* (London, 1970), esp. chs. 4 and 7.

[34] *Od.* 9. 224–30, 492 ff., esp. 500–1, 10. 437 (for the phrasing of 10. 437, cf. 1. 7, 34); cf. Rutherford, 'The Philosophy of the *Odyssey*', 150–1.

accepts that his actions are open to assessment by general social norms; he does not claim that they should be judged by the standards of a private, individual ethic, or by a vision of the common ethic which only he really understands.[35] Although these actions are presented 'subjectively', in the sense that Odysseus' narrative draws on his own reported memories, there is no suggestion that his version of the relevant events is (simply by virtue of being *his* version) radically different from anyone else's version and distinctively 'first-personal'.[36]

The features I have underlined in Odysseus' narrative of the Cyclops episode, and in the *Odyssey* as a whole—the focus on agency, the framework of general social norms, the 'objective' perspective—are the ones I am associating with 'character' rather than 'personality'. These features might be illustrated by any number of passages in the poem, but I shall note just two. The first comes at the start of *Odyssey* 20 (9 ff.), when Odysseus holds back his initial impulse to take a premature revenge on his promiscuous serving-women. The passage presents Odysseus very much as a psychological 'agent' (a source of intentional or deliberated actions), who is here exerting agency with respect to his own plans and feelings. He does so, in part, by reminding himself of his own past agency in this respect: "τέτλαθι δή, κραδίη · καὶ κύντερον ἄλλο ποτ' ἔτλης . . . σὺ δ' ἐτόλμας . . ." τῷ δὲ μάλ' ἐν πείσῃ κραδίη μένε τετληυῖα | νωλεμέως ['"Endure, heart, once you endured something still worse . . . but you bore this" . . . and the heart in great obedience endured and remained firm . . .'] (18–24). This passage is often seen as unusual, in the context of Homeric vocabulary, for its psychological complexity and 'innerness', a quality which is produced by such features as the exceptional concentration of decision-making formulae and by the couching of the address to the heart (κραδίη) in highly personal terms.[37] But the overall effect of these features is not to make the speech of Odysseus subjective or 'first-personal', in the sense that he articulates a view of

---

[35] See distinction (ii) in n. 15 above, and contrast Achilles in *Il.* 9 (at least in some interpretations), discussed below.

[36] See distinction (iii) in n. 15 above.

[37] Cf. J. Böhme, *Die Seele und das Ich im homerischen Epos* (Leipzig, 1929), 66–9; Chr. Voigt, *Überlegung und Entscheidung* (Meisenheim am Glan, 1934), 87 ff.; J. Russo, 'Homer Against his Tradition', *Arion*, 7 (1968), 275–95, esp. 289–94.

himself (and of his present and past experience) which is radically different from that which other people might give.
Odysseus in this speech identifies, and reaffirms, the characteristics that make other people call him 'much-enduring'
(πολύτλας or ταλασίφρων). Similarly, the judgements he makes
on other people in the course of this 'inward' passage (on the
'overbearing suitors' or the 'violent and uncontrolled Cyclops')
are not uniquely personal ones but are based on common moral
norms; and they are judgements which the poem as a whole
invites its audience to endorse.[38]

The impact of the second passage I want to note in the
Odyssey also depends on our accepting that the stand Odysseus
makes is not a purely personal one but one that relies on
common moral standards and that we are inclined to endorse.
This is the speech in *Odyssey* 22 (61–4) in which Odysseus
rejects Eurymachus' offer of material compensation for in-
justices done by the suitors.

> Εὐρύμαχ', οὐδ' εἴ μοι πατρώϊα πάντ' ἀποδοῖτε,
> ὅσσα τε νῦν ὔμμ' ἐστὶ καὶ εἴ ποθεν ἄλλ' ἐπιθεῖτε,
> οὐδέ κεν ὣς ἔτι χεῖρας ἐμὰς λήξαιμι φόνοιο
> πρὶν πᾶσαν μνηστῆρας ὑπερβασίην ἀποτῖσαι.

Eurymachus, not if you gave me all your family estate, whatever you
have now and might add from elsewhere, not even so would I hold my
hands from killing, until I had made the suitors pay for all their criminal acts.

The overall pattern of phrasing, and some of the specific word-
ing, recalls the speeches in the *Iliad* in which Achilles rejects
first Agamemnon's offer of compensatory gifts and then
Hector's offer of ransom for his own burial.[39] But the differences are also marked, consisting not only in Odysseus' more
restricted and less passionate language, but also in the fact that
Odysseus presents his act in more 'objective' terms, as a
response to the transgression of shared moral standards
(ὑπερβασίην) rather than to a deeply felt ('heart-grieving') personal insult (θυμαλγέα λώβην, *Il.* 9. 387).[40] This presentation of

---

[38] *Od.* 20. 12, 19; cf. refs. in nn. 31 and 33 above.
[39] *Il.* 9. 378–87, esp. 380 and 386–7, 22. 349–54.
[40] Cf. Odysseus' self-presentation in *Od.* 22. 287–91, 312 ff., and esp. 411–18. On
Il. 9. 378–87, see below. The phrase 'heart-grieving insult' *is* used in connection with
Odysseus (*Od.* 20. 284–6), but not by him or in this context.

his act is one which we are disposed to accept (despite the problematic violence and scale of Odysseus' reprisal) because the suitors have been consistently presented as 'arrogant' and as 'engaging in lawless violence' (ὑπερφίαλοι and ὑβρίζοντες), and as committing the kind of criminal acts (ὑπερβασίην) that merit punishment.[41]

The same considerations do not apply to the parallel speech in *Iliad* 9 (378–87) in which Achilles rejects Agamemnon's offer of compensation:

> ἐχθρὰ δέ μοι τοῦ δῶρα, τίω δέ μιν ἐν καρὸς αἴσῃ.
> οὐδ' εἴ μοι δεκάκις τε καὶ εἰκοσάκις τόσα δοίη
> ὅσσα τέ οἱ νῦν ἔστι, καὶ εἴ ποθεν ἄλλα γένοιτο,
> οὐδ' ὅσ' ἐς 'Ορχομενὸν ποτινίσσεται, οὐδ' ὅσα Θήβας
> Αἰγυπτίας ...
>
> .   .   .   .
>
> οὐδ' εἴ μοι τόσα δοίη ὅσα ψάμαθός τε κόνις τε,
> οὐδέ κεν ὣς ἔτι θυμὸν ἐμὸν πείσει' 'Αγαμέμνων,
> πρίν γ' ἀπὸ πᾶσαν ἐμοὶ δόμεναι θυμαλγέα λώβην.

His gifts are hateful to me, and I have no respect for him. Not if he gave me ten and twenty times as much as he has now, and more besides from some other source, not if he gave me as much as comes into Orchomenus, as much as comes into Egyptian Thebes ... not if he gave me as many gifts as there are grains of sand and dust, not even so would Agamemnon win over my heart until he had paid me back all his heart-grieving insult.

I think one can see in a passage of this kind what makes it difficult to place Achilles in a determinate ethical framework, and hence to evaluate him as a 'character', in my sense. The passage also indicates why one might be inclined to say rather that we respond to Achilles both as 'character' and 'personality'. On the one hand, we can see in these lines the kinds of attitude and tone that lead Achilles' fellow chieftains (speaking from a standpoint of 'reactive' involvement with him,[42] and judging him by the norms governing relationships between men of their

---

[41] Cf. refs. in nn. 30–3 above. In *Od* 22. 45 ff. Eurymachus himself concedes that the suitors have performed many 'outrageous acts' (ἀτάσθαλα, 47), but claims that Antinous was wholly responsible for them.

[42] For the idea that judgements of moral character reflect the 'reactive attitudes' we adopt towards those with whom we are involved in interpersonal relationships, cf. P. F. Strawson (ed.), *Studies in the Philosophy of Thought and Action* (Oxford, 1968), 71–96, esp. 76 ff.

class) to characterize him elsewhere as 'terrible', 'pitiless', and 'harsh'.[43] We can see all too clearly why Diomedes later sums up the result of the embassy in these terms: 'He is a proud man anyway (ἀγήνωρ), and now you have driven him further into his pride' (9. 699–700). On the other hand, from a position less 'reactively' engaged in the situation, we can recognize in these lines the qualities which (as Friedrich and Redfield point out) make Achilles' speeches so distinctive in the context of Homeric discourse. These lines exhibit the verbal extravagance (in the accumulation of items in a hyperbolic list), the vivid 'lyrical' quality, the 'passionate and highly personal' tone that they describe as characteristic of Achilles' language.[44] In so far as we also respond, in a more aesthetic way, to the special quality of Achilles' 'voice', we are responding to him as a 'personality' in one of the senses in which I am using this term (that of a distinctive and unique individual) at the same time, though not with the same attitude, that we share his fellow chieftains' misgivings about his 'character' as a partner in war.

But there is more to the ambivalence of our response to Achilles' lines than this; another and deeper ambivalence arises from the difficulty I have mentioned of placing his speech in a determinate ethical framework. That such a difficulty exists comes out in the radical disagreements between Homeric scholars about how to understand, and to appraise, Achilles' rejection of the gifts. Some hold that, by his rejection, Achilles 'puts himself in the wrong' by refusing an offer that is consistent with the standards of co-operative behaviour endorsed elsewhere in the epic.[45] Others hold that it is rather Agamemnon who has put himself in the wrong, by the nature and style of his attempt to 'buy Achilles back', and that Achilles' rejection constitutes a proper reproof of Agamemnon.[46] There is dispute about whether Achilles' assertion that Agamemnon would not

[43] *Il.* 11. 653–4 (δεινός), 16. 33–5, 203–4; cf. 1. 177, 24. 40–5.
[44] P. Friedrich and J. Redfield, 'Speech as a Personality Symbol: The Case of Achilles', *Language*, 54 (1978), 263–88; cf. J. Griffin, 'Words and Speakers in Homer', *JHS* 106 (1986), 50–6.
[45] See e.g. H. Lloyd-Jones, *The Justice of Zeus* (Berkeley, 1971), 18; C. M. Bowra, *Tradition and Design in the Iliad* (Oxford, 1930), 19; M. I. Finley, *The World of Odysseus*² (London, 1977), 117–18. Achilles is sometimes taken to concede this point himself in *Il.* 9. 644–5; but see further on these lines n. 56 below.
[46] See esp. D. Claus, '*Aidōs* in the Language of Achilles', *TAPA* 105 (1975), 13–28.

win over his heart (*thumos*) until he had paid back all his 'heart-grieving insult' (θυμαλγέα λώβην, 386–7) is an impossible demand, or one which Agamemnon could meet by further suffering or self-abasement.[47] Indeed, there is no general agreement about the precise ethical basis of the quarrel between the two men. Should it be seen as a dispute conducted within a specific code of values (whether we call them 'competitive', 'co-operative', or 'heroic')?[48] Or does Achilles' rejection of the gifts constitute a rejection of that code; and if so, is his stance purely negative, or positive at least in the sense that it asserts the right of an individual hero to determine *his own* response to a given situation?[49] I do not propose to try to adjudicate between these competing positions here. But I cite them because I think they reflect not only differences in critical assumptions—though they do reflect such differences—but also a real complexity in the speech itself. To put the position much too simply, Achilles' speech cannot be appraised properly either in terms of a purely social or a purely 'individualistic' ethic, because it probes the relationship between these, and to that extent explores their basis. In the way he discusses the question, 'Why should I fight for Agamemnon (given the way Agamemnon treats me)?', he raises further, more fundamental questions, about the reasons why any individual should risk his life in co-operative warfare.[50] The difficulty, then, in placing Achilles as a 'character' turns partly on the fact that Achilles himself questions the nature of the kind of ethical framework in terms of which we might be inclined to judge him.

Furthermore, in so far as we follow, and respond to, Achilles'

---

[47] See, on the one side, M. D. Reeve, 'The Language of Achilles', *CQ*, NS 33 (1973), 193–6; and on the other, O. Tsagarakis, 'The Achaean Embassy and the Wrath of Achilles', *Hermes*, 99 (1971), 257–77.

[48] M. Schofield, '*Euboulia* in the *Iliad*', *CQ*, NS 36 (1986), 6–31 brings out the point that the values of the *Iliad* are sufficiently complex to allow for disputes to take place within them. For J. Redfield, in *Nature and Culture in the Iliad* (Chicago, 1975), 104 ff., Achilles' stance is an expression of tensions that are already inherent in the heroic ethic.

[49] Cf. A. Parry, 'The Language of Achilles', *TAPA* 87 (1956), 1–7 (= G. S. Kirk (ed.), *The Language and Background of Homer* (Cambridge, 1964), 48–54); C. Whitman, *Homer and the Heroic Tradition* (Cambridge, Mass., and London, 1958), ch. 9, esp. 213.

[50] Cf. esp. *Il.* 9. 315 ff., 367 ff.; to put it differently, Achilles here makes a distinctive (individual) contribution to a shared (common) dialogue about the grounds and objectives of the expedition, a dialogue which pervades the whole poem: I hope to elaborate elsewhere this way of reading the speech.

ethical probing, he acquires a special kind of claim on our attention and concern (in addition to any claim that accrues from the fact that we can recognize his 'point of view' in the dispute).[51] He becomes the vehicle through which we, so to speak, think through these issues (just as, elsewhere, he serves to articulate the sense of pathos we feel at the tragic waste of life, as the course of the epic unfolds).[52] To use John Bayley's distinction, he takes on the role of acting as a certain kind of 'consciousness' (and one which we, partly, share) rather than of being a certain kind of 'character', whom we view and 'place' within the world of the poem.[53] To use one of the distinctions I drew earlier, we view Achilles 'subjectively', in so far as we merge our point of view with his, rather than situating him 'objectively' in his context.[54] I hope this example will clarify why I suggested earlier that the combination of viewpoints I am associating with 'personality' rather than 'character' (and especially the shift from the latter to the former viewpoint) serves as an index of an exploratory or interrogative mode of writing, rather than a confirmatory or affirmative one.[55]

Before going on to consider some illustrative passages in tragedy, I should like to make it plain that I am not suggesting that the figures of the *Iliad* are uniformly presented from the same kind of viewpoint (and with the same subtle combination of viewpoints) as Achilles is presented in his great speech in book 9. For instance, in book 19 Agamemnon makes his celebrated claim (86–7) that: ἐγὼ δ' οὐκ αἴτιος εἰμι, | ἀλλὰ Ζεὺς καὶ Μοῖρα καὶ ἠεοφοῖτις Ἐρινύς ['I am not responsible, but Zeus and Fate and the Fury that walks in mist']. I should not want to suggest in this case (what I shall suggest in some cases in tragedy) that Agamemnon's presentation of himself as psycho-

---

[51] In the case of Ajax and Eteocles, discussed below, I suggest that seeing their point of view (when the other stage figures do not) gives us a sense of privileged access to their thoughts. I would not want to make quite this claim here, although I think that our relative detachment from the situation enables us to engage with Achilles' probing in a way that would be impossible for his fellow chieftains, whose concerns are more immediate and pressing.

[52] Cf. e.g. *Il*. 21. 106–13, 24. 525–48.

[53] See n. 18 above.

[54] See n. 15 above. Contrast the case of Odysseus, discussed above, in which the question of tension between 'subjective' and 'objective' views, as of 'social' and 'individualistic' ethics, does not arise in the same way.

[55] Cf. discussion above, and n. 18.

logically passive is designed to produce in the audience a sense of empathy with Agamemnon's subjective ('first-personal') view of himself.[56] I am persuaded by Oliver Taplin's claim, outlined elsewhere in this volume, that we are intended to take Agamemnon's statement as an attempt at unjustified self-exculpation, an attempt which carries implications for our reading of his character and its inadequacies.[57] The large and dubious inferences about Homeric ethics and psychology often based on this passage (which Taplin notes) derive not so much from reading the passage, wrongly, in moral terms, as from doing so in a way that fails to situate the passage within the complex ethical and psychological framework of the poem. This example should serve to make it plain that I do not regard the distinction between 'character' and 'personality' (and between the frameworks I am associating with this distinction) as providing a formula to be applied mechanically to a given poem, or as a substitute for critical discrimination between the different perspectives or registers within a given poem; rather, I regard the distinction as a reminder that such perspectives exist, and as a starting-point towards identifying them.

TRAGEDY

In the case of tragedy, as of Homer, I shall focus on specific passages as a way of indicating how these distinctions may promote such critical discrimination. In the corpus of surviving tragedies, there is variety of perspective both between different

---

[56] I think such a claim might more plausibly be made in connection with e.g. *Il.* 9. 645–8 and 16. 52–5, where Achilles ascribes his perpetuation of the quarrel with Agamemnon to the fact that his 'heart swells with bile', and that 'a terrible pain comes on [his] heart and spirit', when he thinks of Agamemnon's ill-treatment of him. The former passage is more often read (in terms of 'character') as one in which he criticizes his 'passionate nature' (so e.g. J. Griffin, *Homer on Life and Death* (Oxford, 1980), 74); but a reading of the words (in terms of 'personality') as vouchsafing access to his 'subjective' sense of being the victim of his own emotions is at least as plausible. However, more plausible again is a reading which takes the comment about the 'swelling heart' to be Achilles' statement of his grounds for perpetuating the quarrel; i.e. Achilles regards his emotional response not as a personal defect or misfortune but as itself constituting *a reason* (though a problematic one) for maintaining his anger. On this reading (which I shall defend more fully elsewhere), Achilles' comment (like his great speech) evades neat categorization in terms of 'character' or 'personality' alone.

[57] Cf. ch. 3 below, text to nn. 14–16; the case is argued more fully in an unpublished paper, 'Explanation and Self-Justification in the *Iliad*'.

plays and within particular plays. But I think that the *Iliad* is,
in general, a better guide than the *Odyssey* towards understanding the perspectives that are characteristic of tragedy; and that
the complexity of Achilles' great speech in *Iliad* 9 gives us a
model of the kind of complexity with which the main figures of
tragedy are typically presented at key moments. As Bernard
Knox above all has shown, a recurrent tragic pattern is one in
which the main figure, like Achilles in book 9, appears to his
companions extreme and unreasonable, by the normal standards of social co-operation, but in which we are made aware
that his stance depends on a deeper and more probing response
to his situation than that of the companions who judge him by
those standards.[58] The division in our responses which such a
presentation invites (in so far as we engage sympathetically
both with the main figures and his companions) is sometimes
underlined in the plays by having the main figure's real
thoughts or feelings misinterpreted, or ignored, by his companions, thus accentuating our sense of privileged access to
them.[59] Furthermore, we find in tragedy, to a greater extent
than in epic, I think, a special complexity in the presentation of
the main figure as regards psychological agency and passivity,
and an emphasis on the paradoxes which arise out of a combination of these psychological modes.[60] This complexity takes
various forms; for instance, in one type of case, the figure is
judged by his companions as a psychological agent (and a bad
one), while he presents himself as wholly or partly passive.[61] In
another type of case, to which I shall give special attention, the
figure presents himself as one who plays an active role in bringing about his own psychological subjection. This complexity as
regards psychological agency and passivity is itself sometimes
linked to a complexity as regards the ethical framework and
perspective in which we are invited to view the figure concerned; and these forms of complexity cumulatively militate
against a straightforward 'placing' of the figure within a single,

---

[58] B. M. W. Knox, *The Heroic Temper* (Berkeley, 1966), chs. 1 and 2.

[59] See n. 51 above.

[60] Of course, 'double motivation' in epic involves such a combination (cf. A. Lesky, *Göttliche und menschliche Motivation im homerischen Epos*, (*Sitzungsber. Heid. AK. Wiss.* 1961/4), esp. 22–32); but the paradoxes entailed seem to be underlined more clearly in tragedy.

[61] e.g. Clytemnestra in A. *Ag.* 1497 ff., discussed below.

normative framework of reference. The net result, as I have already suggested in the case of the *Iliad*, is to make the plays ethically, and sometimes psychologically, exploratory or interrogatory rather than affirmative.[62]

I think that the kind of complexity of presentation I have in mind comes out clearly in the case of the so-called 'Deception Speech' in Sophocles' *Ajax* (646–92). Like some other critics, I take it that this speech is intended to be 'heard', or interpreted, by the audience in two different ways: as Tecmessa and the chorus hear it (a way in which Ajax allows them to deceive themselves about his meaning), and as Ajax himself intends it.[63] This double 'hearing' sets up one of the types of duality I am interested in (that of perspective): the audience, detecting the ironies in Ajax's apparent change of heart, has a sense of privileged access to him, and of sharing his subjective view of himself and his situation, even while it also hears, and understands, the reactions of the other figures to him. This ambivalence of perspective relates closely to the ethical duality articulated in the speech itself. On the surface, Ajax embraces the kind of ethic which (as he sees it) he needs to adopt if he is to respond to Tecmessa's appeal for pity, namely the ethic of common sense and pragmatic compromise (as Ajax puts it, 'being sensible', σωφρονεῖν), which is often associated with Odysseus, from the *Iliad* onwards.[64] But the speech also implies, through the extravagance with which that ethic is articulated, Ajax's ironic distance from it and his 'Achillean' adherence to the interpretation of 'nobility' (εὐγένεια) that requires him to act on his earlier decision to die 'finely' (καλῶς).[65] In these ways, the speech invites us to maintain a dual perspective on

[62] S. Goldhill, *Reading Greek Tragedy* (Cambridge, 1986), esp. 55–6, 285–6, also emphasizes the interrogatory and 'open-ended' quality of Greek tragedy, though some of his reasons for doing so are different from those given here.

[63] B. M. W. Knox, *Word and Action* (Baltimore, 1979), 135 ff.; R. P. Winnington-Ingram, *Sophocles: An Interpretation* (Cambridge, 1980), 46–56. This is not to say, of course, that Ajax's own intended meaning is unequivocally clear even to us, as the continuing controversy about the speech shows (cf. most recently P. T. Stevens, 'Ajax in the *Trugrede*', *CQ*, NS 36 (1986), 327–36), but it seems clear that a second meaning of some sort is intended to be audible.

[64] S. *Ai.* 650–3, 666–77, 485 ff. On Odysseus as the paradigm of σωφρονεῖν in this sense, in contrast to Achilles' 'heroic' obduracy, cf. H. North, *Sophrosune* (Ithaca, 1966), 1–2 and (on Ajax) 58–61.

[65] Cf. *Ai.* 479–80 (and 522–4); also Knox, *Word and Action,* 135 ff.; Winnington-Ingram, *Sophocles,* 46–56.

20 — Christopher Gill

Ajax, seeing him both as his immediate society sees him, with the ethical standards this implies, and as he sees, and judges, himself. Thus we see him from the perspectives of both 'character' and 'personality' (in two of the senses I have distinguished).[66]

What is also interesting about the *Ajax*, for my concerns here, is that the issue raised by the speech, that of the perspective and ethical framework in which Ajax should be viewed, becomes a dominant one in the latter part of the play, and pervades the debate about Ajax's right to burial. What is also striking in this debate is not just the variety of perspectives employed, but the variety of *types* of perspective. The Atreidae are the most ready to cast judgement on Ajax and to do so in assertively evaluative terms. His attempted attack on them is taken as an act of lawless violence (ὕβρις) which constitutes a breach of 'discipline' (which is what they understand by σωφρονεῖν), and one which Teucer perpetuates by his defence of Ajax's claims.[67] Their comments constitute a judgement, of a kind, on Ajax's character (in an ethical sense), but one which makes no attempt to situate the action they have in view (his recent attack on them) in the context of his life as a whole, and thus to make a fair estimate of his character. Odysseus, on the other hand, does attempt to make that kind of estimate, weighing against his recent attack (by which Ajax made himself Odysseus' greatest enemy (ἔχθιστος)) the earlier achievements that made Ajax ἄριστον Ἀργείων ... πλὴν Ἀχιλλέως and ἐσθλόν ['the best of the Greeks ... except for Achilles' and 'noble'].[68] This defence of Ajax's right to burial is based (as is appropriate for the judicial context) on an appraisal of Ajax's 'character', that is, of the merits and demerits of Ajax's actions, as judged by the normal standards of behaviour in his social group.[69] But it seems also to be informed by a different, and less evaluative, response: that of pity for, and to an extent 'identification' with, Ajax. In the

[66] For these senses, see distinctions (ii) and (iii) in n. 15 above; here as often elsewhere, the two senses are closely associated.
[67] See *Ai.* 1061, 1071 ff., 1236 ff., esp. 1258–9; cf. Goldhill, *Reading Greek Tragedy*, 193 ff.
[68] *Ai.* 1336, 1340–1, 1345 (cf. Winnington-Ingram, *Sophocles*, 58–9), 441–4 (Ajax's own judgement on himself).
[69] On 'character', in this sense, as relevant to a judicial context, cf. e.g. Arist. *Rh.* 1. 2. 3 and 1. 9; G. Kennedy, *The Art of Persuasion in Greece* (London, 1963), s.v. *ēthos*.

opening scene of the play, Odysseus, through Athena's contrivance, is given special insight into Ajax's state of mind and situation. He responds with a speech of remarkable generosity of spirit, placing himself imaginatively in the position of his humiliated enemy, a response which is sharply counterpointed by Athena's crude moralizing about Ajax's lack of 'self-control' (σωφροσύνη, 121–33). That response seems to be echoed in the way in which, in the final scene, he places himself in imagination in Ajax's position (a response palpably misinterpreted by Agamemnon at 1365–7).

This strand in Odysseus' responses is distinct from his fair-minded appraisal of Ajax's 'character', and is not dependent on that.[70] But I should not be inclined to describe it as a response to Ajax's 'personality' (even in the extended sense in which I am using this term). Odysseus' response is rather a sense of fellow-feeling with *anyone* (even an enemy) who finds himself 'yoked to disaster (ἄτη)' or who is in need of burial; it is thus a response to Ajax's situation rather than to the person himself. But in the lamentation at Ajax's death by Tecmessa and the chorus there are moments when it seems right to say they are responding to Ajax as a person, and indeed as a distinctive personality. Thus, for instance, when the chorus trace back Ajax's κακὰν μοῖραν ['evil fate'] to his bitter sorrow at the award of the arms to Odysseus, they seem to be stressing not just their sense of the logic of events but also the relentless way in which Ajax's own nature, 'tough-minded' and 'raw-minded' as it is (στερεόφρων and ὠμόφρων), has worked towards his own destruction (925–36). The tone, I think, is not so much of condemnation of Ajax's response (although it has worked to their disadvantage) as of sorrowful recognition of the way in which Ajax's own distinctive, extreme nature has made its own destiny. A speech by Tecmessa in the same context has a similar tone (961–73). She is, more directly than the chorus, disadvantaged by the suicide she tried to prevent, as she herself indicates. But her mood now is not that of criticism but of sorrowful recognition that he has won the death *he* wanted.

---

[70] In *Ai* 121–6 Ajax's character is not mentioned, only his status as Odysseus' enemy, *in spite of which* Odysseus pities him; even in the later scene, Odysseus' imaginative self-association with Ajax (1365–7) is not explicitly linked to the appraisal of his character (1338–45).

And in her dismissal of the expected exultation of his enemies, she seems to be, as it were, 'protecting' the private and special quality of his death *for Ajax*.[71] In her remarks, and those of the chorus, there is more than simply a response to Ajax's individuality; her remarks, in particular, need to be understood in terms of the ethics of friendship and enmity. But the reactions include an unjudging acceptance that Ajax's death was, distinctively, *his* chosen end, and, in this respect, their response is to his 'personality', in two of the senses I have attached to that term.[72]

So far, in talking about the interplay between 'character' and 'personality' in tragedy, I have focused on the aspects of the distinction that relate to values on the one hand and perspectives on the other, rather than the aspect of psychological agency and passivity. The relationship between psychological agency and passivity can clearly serve as a theme on its own in tragedy; but it is sometimes brought into connection with at least one other aspect of the distinction, and in a way that produces the characteristically tragic combination of 'character' and 'personality'. As an example of this, I want to consider especially a famous dialogue in Aeschylus' *Seven Against Thebes* (653–719); but I shall approach this by noting two other famous Aeschylean passages which help to bring out what is most striking in that dialogue. In all three passages, the feature I want to focus on is the relationship between psychological explanation and point of view. I suggested earlier that there was a clear prima-facie distinction between explaining acts by reference to the beliefs and desires of the person as agent, and doing so by reference to causes which are seen as determining behaviour in ways other than through the person's conscious agency.[73] Either type of explanation can, in principle, be

---

[71] ἐμοὶ πικρὸς τέθνηκεν ἢ κείνοις γλυκύς · | αὐτῷ δὲ τερπνός. ὧν γὰρ ἠράσθη τυχεῖν | ἐκτήσαθ' αὑτῷ, θάνατον ὅνπερ ἤθελεν. | τί δῆτα τοῦδ' ἐπεγγελῷεν ἂν κάτα; | θεοῖς τέθνηκεν οὗτος, οὐ κείνοισιν, οὔ. ['His death was bitter to me rather than being sweet for them; and it gave pleasure to the man himself. For he obtained what he desired for himself, the death he wanted. So why should they jeer at him; he died for the gods, not for them, no.'] (966–70.)

[72] They respond to him *qua* unique individual not *qua* 'character' (assessed by common moral standards), and to his distinctively personal, 'subjective' wish, though a wish for something that is 'objectively' bad; see n. 15 above.

[73] See discussion above and n. 9.

employed by the person concerned, or by an outside observer; but there is an obvious way in which it is more natural to expect the person concerned to explain her acts by reference to her beliefs and desires, and to expect the mode of explanation by external causes to be used by an outside observer.

In the chorus's recreation of Agamemnon's decision to sacrifice his own daughter (*Ag.* 205–27), though there is much that is curious and paradoxical, this (more natural) distribution of types of explanation is, for the most part, maintained. The antistrophe articulates Agamemnon's response, as a deliberating agent, to his dilemma, culminating in his appalling conclusion that 'it is right to desire with exceedingly impassioned passion the sacrifice of the maiden's blood, to stop the winds'.[74] The following strophe sustains this understanding of Agamemnon's act, namely as an intentional 'action'[75] ('he dared (ἔτλα) to become the sacrificer of his daughter', 224–5), and one that Agamemnon, in some sense, deliberates and 'owns' as his ('blowing his thought in an impious change of direction . . . he changed his mind and turned to thinking the all-daring', 219–21).[76] It is true that the language in which the chorus describe this motivation gives us the impression that Agamemnon is, and perhaps sees himself as, bowing to overwhelming pressure;[77] but the description, like the preceding utterance of Agamemnon, is that of someone carrying out an action that is, in some sense, deliberate, and 'owned' as his. However, the chorus add their own explanatory comment on the act and its motivation: 'For (γάρ, marking their remark as explanatory) men are made bold by wretched madness (παρακοπά) that gives men bad

---

[74] As Nussbaum emphasizes, *Fragility*, 35–6, the curious phrase ὀργᾷ περιόργως ἐπιθυμεῖν (216–17) underlines Agamemnon's emotional involvement with the act of sacrifice. The speech the chorus attribute to Agamemnon has a strongly 'narrative' feel, esp. in 214–17, and it seems to serve as a prelude for their analysis of his motivation in 218 ff.; but their quasi-narrative recreation of his speech is still that of someone functioning *as an agent*.

[75] On the distinction between an 'action' and an 'event', see n. 6 above.

[76] Trans. Nussbaum, *Fragility*, 36.

[77] Esp. 'he put on himself (ἔδυ) the harness of necessity' (218); and the image of 'blowing his thought' (219) seems to evoke the earlier description of Agamemnon 'blowing with the pressure of circumstances' (ἐμπαίοις τύχαισι συμπνέων, 187), a connection R. D. Dawe would like to underline by rearranging the text to bring the two passages close together: 'Some Reflections on Ate and Hamartia', *HSCP* 72 (1968), 89–123, esp. 110–11.

advice (αἰσχρόμητις) and is the beginning of sorrows (πρωτοπήμων)' (222–3). As Dawe points out, the use of παρακοπά instead of the more familiar ἄτη (delusion) suggests that Agamemnon's 'mental processes are . . . *knocked sideways*';[78] and this underlines the fact that the explanatory comments presents Agamemnon as psychologically passive, subject to a madness that 'forces' his mind in the wrong direction.[79] In this respect, the passage maintains the distinction I described earlier: the participant is envisaged as understanding his act in terms of personal agency; the observers, while confirming that way of understanding the act, also explain the motivation for Agamemnon's act in terms of a cause external to his agency ('madness'), of which he is presumably unaware. Later in the same play, the two modes of explanation are deployed in a different but related way. Clytemnestra, having initially presented her murder of Agamemnon, in iambics, and in emphatic terms, as a deliberated personal action (especially 1377 ff.), now, in lyric exchange with the chorus, explains—and in a way justifies—her act as the work of the τριπάχυντον | δαίμονα γέννης ['thrice-fattened spirit of the family'] (1476–7) and of the παλαιὸς δριμὺς ἀλάστωρ | Ἀτρέως ['ancient harsh avenger of Atreus'] (1501–2). Her explanation of her action is retrospective; she now looks at it from outside, participating in the chorus's attempt to find deeper levels of explanation for the appalling act (see especially 1468 ff.). In another way she is using the explanation itself as a subsidiary source of justification for her act, as being a way of taking vengeance for past wrongs in the house.

What is strikingly different about Eteocles' stance in the dialogue with the chorus before going to battle is that, before taking action, while he is still (in some sense) 'deciding' what to do, he presents the causal type of explanation as a kind of motive (or, perhaps, as taking the place of motivation) for killing his brother. The dialogue has been much discussed recently; but only A. A. Long's account brings out fully its par-

---

[78] Ibid.

[79] However (nothing is simple in this stanza), the 'madness' involved seems to allow *some* role for personal agency in so far as it operates by 'advising' men to perform bad acts (αἰσχρόμητις) and 'emboldens' them to do so (θρασύνει); i.e. men know what they are doing, and (perhaps) know that it is bad (or 'base'), but not that they are driven by 'madness' to do so.

adoxical quality in this respect.[80] This centres on the fact that Eteocles only presents himself as a psychological agent (acting on motives which he 'owns' and justifies) as regards the soldierly aspect of his act, namely going to meet his brother *as the enemy leader*, avoiding the 'cowardice' of not doing so, and thus winning glory.[81] But his justification of the act glosses over the obviously 'miasmic' character of the killing of his brother. The chorus repeatedly accuse him of being activated by a positive, hideous desire for fratricide, a desire they urge him to resist;[82] and at one point Eteocles seems to concede the truth of this accusation.[83] But, both at this point and elsewhere, Eteocles' own account of his attitude to the fratricide does not bear out their accusations. He presents the killing of his brother (which he sees as involving his own death) as being something that is inherently bad ($\kappa\alpha\kappa\acute{o}\nu$).[84] What drives him to this act is his father's curse (which he earlier saw as the mark of a family 'driven mad by the gods') which 'besets' him 'with its dry, unlamenting eyes'. This curse, as he sees it, makes useless any lamentation of his own at what he must do, maintaining (what he accepts) that the only 'profitable' course of action is an honourable, though appalling, death.[85]

Eteocles' tone, as he utters these sentiments, does not seem to be that of a person suppressing a covert passion for fratricide, but rather of someone experiencing a nightmarish loss of will (in the ordinary sense) and surrendering to (what he sees as) irrational forces at work within himself.[86] It is true that his

---

[80] A. A. Long, '*Pro* and *contra* Fratricide: Aeschylus' *Septem* 653–719', in J. Betts (ed.), *Studies in Honour of T. B. L. Webster*, i (Bristol, 1986), 179–89.

[81] See *Th.* 658–75 (esp. 674–5, in which the unemphatic inclusion of 'brother to brother' between 'leader to leader' and 'enemy to enemy' elides its significance (cf. Nussbaum, *Fragility*, 38)), 683–5, 697, 716–17; on the connotations of 'shame' and 'profit' in these lines, cf. R. P. Winnington-Ingram, *Studies in Aeschylus* (Cambridge, 1983), 35 ff.

[82] *Th.* 677–8, 686–8, 692–4, 698, 718. Some critics accept that the chorus's description of Eteocles' motivation is a correct one, though they allow that Eteocles' alleged 'madness' is not fully reflected in his own words: see e.g. Nussbaum, *Fragility*, 432–3 n. 46; Aeschylus, *Septem contra Thebes*, ed. G. O. Hutchinson (Oxford, 1985), 148.

[83] 695 (taking the $\gamma\acute{\alpha}\rho$ as concessive: 'Yes, for . . .').

[84] 683, 685, 719; contrast the attitude of Polyneices, who, as reported in 636, seems positively to want mutual fratricide, or at least to accept it readily as the price of vengeance.

[85] 695–7; cf. 653–7, 683–5.

[86] Cf. Long's comment in 'Fratricide', 186: 'He is a Kafka-like figure, who sees all and is totally trapped by his own vision.'

words, as the dialogue continues, admit some degree of agency; he rejects the chorus's urging not to give way to these forces, and in that sense he persists in giving way to them.[87] But he still sees himself as psychologically passive with regard to the fratricide, even if this very passivity is one he himself accepts. As I noted earlier, what is unusual—even bizarre and surd—in the dialogue is the way in which what would more naturally figure as an outsider's *explanation* for his act is presented by the participant as a *motive*, though one which functions by subduing or replacing the participant's own desire rather than constituting it.

So far, the complexity, or duality, I have examined in this scene relates wholly to the curious interplay between agency and passivity in Eteocles' motivation. But this is related to other kinds of duality, of a sort we have considered elsewhere. Within the dialogue, we find a version of the dispute about values we have seen in other contexts. The chorus, taking the desire for fratricide to be in some sense his, advocate a kind of pragmatic self-control, if only in the form of not giving way to the irrational forces that threaten to master him. But Eteocles, like Achilles or Ajax, insists that 'nobility' (as he understands this) involves rejecting this advice; although his acceptance of the 'badness' entailed in achieving the 'profit' of nobility rather undercuts this insistence.[88] Furthermore, the fact that the chorus partly misread Eteocles' state of mind, first in failing to recognize its passivity, and then in underestimating his adherence to his passive state, serves to create a sense of privileged access or complicity that is not unlike our response to Ajax, in his Deception Speech, or, in a different way, to Achilles.[89] Thus, in these respects too, the exchange provides a combination of the responses I am associating with 'character' and 'personality'; although the sense of special access to Eteocles is, I think, qualified by the peculiar, surd quality of his state of mind. That a fratricidal desire can be explained by reference to

---

[87] See 698, 705–8; and cf. refs. in n. 82 above.

[88] Cf. nn. 81–4 above; the undercutting is stronger and more overt than in Ajax's (ironic) disowning of 'manly' obduracy in S. *Ai.* 650 ff. Achilles' only concession (if it is one) on the rightness of his stand comes in *Il.* 9. 645–8 (on which see n. 56 above).

[89] For the two stages of chorus's reaction, see A. *Th.* 677–94, 698 ff.; on this complicity elsewhere, see discussion above, incl. n. 51.

a 'family curse' makes some kind of sense; but that such an explanation can count as a motive is deeply puzzling.

In these respects, the case of Euripides' Medea is instructive both as a parallel and a contrast with Eteocles, especially in her great monologue (1021–80).[90] For instance, in Medea's dialogue with the chorus in 811–19, and still more in her debate with herself in 1021 ff., we find the familiar contrast between the voice of common sense and shared humanity (expressed by Medea when she speaks as a sorrowing mother), and that of the extreme, 'individualistic' heroism that demands infanticide as a means of avenging dishonour.[91] We also find, as in the case of Eteocles, a striking combination of psychological agency and passivity, and one with several points of similarity. Like Eteocles, she sees the killing of kin as being, in itself, bad (κακόν) and not the object of her desire; like him, she presents the act as justifiable (and herself as an agent) only with regard to the goal of the killing, namely redeeming her honour through vengeance.[92] Like him, she sometimes presents the kin-killing as something that will occur by its own momentum and against her will; like him, she sometimes presents herself as psychologically subject to the force within her that activates this killing.[93] Her monologue ends with these famous lines: καὶ μανθάνω μὲν οἷα δρᾶν μέλλω κακά, | θυμὸς δὲ κρείσσων τῶν ἐμῶν βουλευμάτων, | ὅσπερ μεγίστων αἴτιος κακῶν βροτοῖς ['I know that what I am going to do is bad, but anger, the source of mankind's greatest miseries' (or 'bad things') 'is master of my plans']. These lines convey a similar sense of conscious, but helpless, self-surrender to that conveyed by Eteocles' declaration that he is beset by his father's curse, 'with its dry,

---

[90] On the question of the authenticity of this speech, I find the position of D. Kovacs in 'On Euripides' Great Monologue (E. *Med.* 1021–80)', *CQ*, ns 36 (1986), 343–52, in which he argues for the excision of 1056–64, more credible than that of those who argue for a larger excision; but for present purposes, I treat the speech as wholly Euripidean.

[91] See esp. E. *Med.* 791–7, 807–10, 816–19, 1046–55, 1059–61; cf. Knox, *Word and Action*, 297 ff.; (on Medea's two 'voices') C. Gill, 'Two Monologues of Self-Division: Euripides, *Medea* 1021–80 and Seneca, *Medea* 893–977', in M. Whitby, P. Hardie, and M. Whitby (edd.), Homo Viator: *Classical Essays for John Bramble* (Bristol, 1987), 25–37, esp. 26 ff.

[92] See E. *Med.* 1078–80; also 1021–39, 1067 (in which the κακά for herself and the children are fully realized); also refs. in n. 91 and nn. 81–4 above.

[93] E. *Med.* 1240–1 (= 1062–3), and *Med.* refs. in preceding note (see further Gill, 'Two Monologues', 26–8); cf. A. *Th.* 653–7, 683–4, 689–91, 695–7, 702–4, 709–11, 719.

unlamenting eyes', urging him to the fratricidal act he sees as
bad (κακόν).[94] As with Eteocles, it is in so far as we share
Medea's view of herself as trapped in her situation, and as a
psychological victim, that we feel most keenly a sense of special
access to her, and sympathy with her, and thus respond to her
as, in my terms, a 'personality'.[95]

However, there are also important differences between the
two cases. For one thing, Medea, as well as playing a more
active role than Eteocles seems to do in engineering the situation by which she eventually feels trapped, also plays a more
active role in promoting the 'heroic', vengeful side of herself, to
which she finally feels subject.[96] And although Eteocles' state of
mind is not unambiguously clear (the chorus, as we saw, view it
rather differently from Eteocles himself), it is less obvious than
it is in the case of Medea that he is experiencing inner conflict.
Furthermore, although she too (in 1079–80) talks about her
act, as a quasi-observer, in causal terms, her 'subjection' to
thumos (anger) does not have the same psychologically opaque
or surd quality as we found in Eteocles' case. The preceding
monologue, and especially the dialogue between her alternative 'selves', in 1040 ff., articulates much more fully the way in
which she persuades herself into the state of mind to which she
eventually feels 'subject'. Both the 'mastering' *thumos*, and the
motherly feelings which are mastered, are given voice by
Medea, and thus 'owned' by her;[97] the *thumos* forms an integral
part of her motivation, and is not introduced, like Eteocles'
curse, *in place of* a normal pattern of motivation. In this respect,
and others too (if we think of the nurse's earlier comments on

---

[94] E. *Med.* 1078–80 (on the psychology of which cf. C. Gill, 'Did Chrysippus Understand Medea?', *Phronesis*, 28 (1983), 136–49); A. *Th.* 695-7, 683-5.

[95] This sense is accentuated, as in Ajax's Deception Speech, by the fact that we hear
her speaking *across* the children, first to the chorus, her confidantes (1043), and then,
for the most part, to herself. The degree of sympathy also varies according to the 'self'
who speaks, being strongest in 1021–39 and 1065 ff.; cf. Gill, 'Two Monologues', 26 ff.
On the sense of 'personality' involved, see n. 15 above, distinction (iii).

[96] See refs. in nn. 91–2 above. Eteocles 'chooses', in the ordinary sense of the word, to
go to meet his brother, but he does so in a situation that has more obvious external and
internal 'constraints' (esp. the curse) than in Medea's case. See further (on Medea's
manipulation of her situation) P. E. Easterling, 'The Infanticide in Euripides' *Medea*',
YCS 35 (1977), 177–92; (on Eteocles) *Septem*, ed. Hutchinson, 142–3, 148–9, 160–1,
xxiii–xxx.

[97] See E. *Med.* 1040–8 (the motherly voice), 1049–55 (the avenging voice)—a
sequence replayed (if the lines are authentic; see n. 90 above) in 1056–8 and 1059–64.

her 'wild character and the hateful nature of her harsh mind'⁹⁸), we feel that we know Media, both as 'character' and 'personality', and that her tragedy originates from this, in a way that is not so true of Eteocles and many other tragic figures. Indeed, if we press this point, we might be inclined to reserve the use of the terms 'character' and 'personality' for a case of this kind, and to analyse the other cases in rather different terms (such as those of 'agency and passivity' and 'conflicts of value'). However, my practice here, presenting all these as aspects of a single, if complex, distinction (between 'character' and 'personality') has the merit of underlining the connections between these different aspects, and of emphasizing that our understanding of dramatic character (or personality), is typically made up of these, and related, strands.

CONCLUSION

I shall end this chapter by indicating certain ways in which this discussion of the 'character–personality' distinction might be brought into connection with certain other, and more familiar, approaches to characterization in Greek literature. Many of the passages I have noted are often used as material in the attempt to construct a process of development in Greek moral thinking, that of the 'evolution of the will', for instance, or of an alleged shift from a 'competitive' to a 'co-operative' ethic.⁹⁹ If the suggestions made here have any validity, it would seem important that any developmental model of this kind should not 'flatten out', as it were, the types of duality or complexity which seem to be an integral part of the presentation of figures in many Greek tragedies, as in the *Iliad*; and that, at the same time, it should not eliminate their distinctively interrogatory or exploratory impact. The use of Athenian tragic material for the

⁹⁸ ἄγριον ἦθος στυγερáν τε φύσιν | φρενòς αὐθάδους (103–4); cf. μεγαλóσπλαγχνος δυσκατáπαυστος ψυχή ['her splenetic temperament, hard to keep in check'] (109–10). The nurse's comments imply that the children are endangered by a kind of instinctive, 'animal' irascibility (cf. 90 ff.) in Medea; but the later scenes disclose 'character' (and 'personality') in a deeper and more complex sense. Attempts to 'read' Eteocles' character (e.g. *Septem*, ed. Hutchinson, xxxv ff.; Nussbaum, *Fragility*, 39–40) need to draw on less obviously relevant material.

⁹⁹ See e.g. A. W. H. Adkins, *Merit and Responsibility* (Oxford, 1960), chs. 6–9; J.-P. Vernant and P. Vidal-Naquet, *Tragedy and Myth in Ancient Greece*, trans. J. Lloyd (Brighton, 1981), ch. 3; S. Saïd, *La Faute tragique* (Paris, 1978), pt. 2.

construction of these models of moral development constitutes, to some extent, an assimilation of the tragic theatre to an adjacent area of discourse, that of the lawcourts; and the tragic genre is sometimes treated for this purpose as being, in effect, an application of Greek judicial thinking to the 'hard cases' of the mythological tradition. Whatever the general merits of this procedure, it is important to underline that the tragic theatre constitutes a meeting-place of several types of discourse and concern, including the religious as well as the judicial. And it seems clear that some at least of the dualities I have discussed derive, in ways too complex to pursue here, from this composite character of the tragic genre.[100]

The aspect of my distinction which is perhaps least familiar is that of types of perspective; and the idea of a perspective which gives a special importance to an individual's subjective view may seem distinctively modern and not obviously relevant to Greek literature. However, I think there are features of the *Iliad* and of many Greek tragedies which promote such a perspective, including the fact that certain figures in these works enjoy a special (sometimes semi-divine) status in their society or world, as well as having a privileged claim on our attention because of their role as narrative focuses;[101] and that this special status invites a sympathetic concern which is at odds with the response these figures also arouse by the morally worrying or unacceptable character of their actions, if these are viewed in a more impartial or objective way.[102] I also think that this perspective should be connected (to a greater extent than I have attempted here) with the way in which certain poetic forms, such as the passionate monologue, or the lament, invite a

---

[100] This is most obvious in the case of the duality of psychological agency and passivity (on which cf. Vernant and Vidal-Naquet, *Tragedy and Myth*, 11–14), and, perhaps, in the case of the duality of social and 'individualistic' (or 'heroic') ethics (on which cf. Knox, *Heroic Temper*, 53 ff.); on the tragic theatre as a festal arena for the questioning of civic values, cf. Goldhill, *Reading Greek Tragedy*, 75–8.

[101] On this aspect of characterization, see n. 23 above.

[102] These features are sometimes seen as derivative from the status of the figures as 'heroic' (e.g. by Knox) or, in structuralist terms, as 'marginal', and on the borders of humanity and divinity or bestiality (e.g. by C. P. Segal, *Tragedy and Civilization: An Interpretation of Sophocles* (Cambridge, Mass., 1981), 8 ff.). But this does not invalidate the description of these features in the terms used here; indeed, all three types of critical framework seem to be defining a rather similar type of tension in our responses to 'problematic' figures, though one which is rather differently conceived.

heightened degree of audience involvement with the expression of deeply felt personal sentiments of a kind which are often morally non-standard and problematic in their implications.[103] I realise that my remarks here are sketchy and promissory in the extreme;[104] but I hope that, taken in conjunction with my discussion of specific passages, they will be sufficient to suggest that the deployment of the distinction between 'character' and 'personality' in this connection need not be as anachronistic or aridly theoretical as it might seem.

[103] See e.g. Achilles' great speech in *Il.* 9, and the laments for Ajax (S. *Ai.* 925–32, 966–70) discussed above. Such forms serve as vehicles for what the ancient critics sometimes called *pathos*; cf. n. 3 above.

[104] I hope to redeem some of the promises made or implied in this chapter in a forthcoming book, *Character and Personality in Greek Literature and Philosophy.*

2

Traditional Greek Conceptions of Character

STEPHEN HALLIWELL

I

In Prodicus' parable 'The Choice of Heracles', epitomized in
Xenophon's *Memorabilia* (2. 1. 21–33), the figure of Virtue tells
the adolescent hero, as he sits contemplating the ethical divergence of 'roads' which defines the possibilities of his adult life: 'I
approach you, Heracles, with knowledge of who your parents
were, and having learnt your own nature (*phusis*) in the course
of your education. As a result, I hope that if you take the road
which leads to me, you will certainly become an excellent agent
of fine and proud deeds' (2. 1. 27). The words of Virtue intimate, in the first place, a typical Greek admiration of, and faith
in, εὐγένεια, the 'breeding' which marks a man's familial status,
links him with his ancestors, and forms the matrix of his own
identity. The import of the allegory perhaps allows us to interpret Heracles' good birth as indicative not just of this strictly
aristocratic factor, but also of that part of any man's make-up
which is 'given', innate, or inherited, rather than acquired. But
εὐγένεια, as is apparent, is not a static possession, and certainly
not enough to shape all the qualities of a person's active life. It
is a component of identity which needs to be recreated, realized, and fulfilled in the positive development of the individual's own 'nature'.[1] This 'nature' is itself a dynamic
potential, requiring to be tended and brought to fruition, like
Pindar's 'vine-plant of *aretē*' (*Nem.* 8. 40), through careful processes of nurture and education.

Heracles' capabilities of choice, then, as he experiences the
competing appeals of Virtue and Vice, have already been

[1] That Heracles' 'nature' is distinguishable from, yet related to, his parentage is
clear from Virtue's words at 2. 1. 27. Cf. n. 22 below.

partly engendered and formed by his lineage, his natural endowments, and his upbringing. These influences give Virtue reason for confidence in the young hero, but they do not wholly predetermine the outcome of his choice of life. There remains, as the allegory indicates, an irreducibly personal element of responsibility: Heracles, now in control of his own life (αὐτοκράτωρ), goes out to a secluded spot, to ponder alone (21). Without this element—whose locus is the individual conscious-ness of, and deliberation on, matters of pleasure and pain, honour and shame, good and evil—the story would lose its essential significance for the understanding and evaluation of human living. Prodicus' parable allegorizes the process of ethi-cal commitment emergent from the mind's reactions to the world which confronts it. But this process is not an exercise of 'pure' will (even supposing we believe in such a thing). Prodi-cus portrays his female personifications of Virtue and Vice with expressive details of style and deportment, in order to suggest the complex of factors involved in the choice of lives before Heracles, and the way in which they engage his emotions, his perception, and his rational cognition. The voices of Virtue and Vice are pressures and allurements in the world in which Heracles must move, but also internal voices in the 'dialogue of the soul' which represents his conscious responses to that world.

So the parable can be read as the condensed story of the formation and exercise of character in the growing person's active experience of the world. I have begun with this quasi-dramatic example because character is not a subject which we can afford to explore from the starting-point of a fixed defini-tion or a set of terminology. We can, however, provisionally mark out its sphere of importance for Greek culture by describ-ing it, in the terms dramatized by Prodicus, as a matter of the shaping of a human life by an ethical motivation and agency ascribed, at its core, to the individual himself, and for which he may be held responsible, albeit in a context of forces (inherited status, natural capacities, nurture and education, and, not least, the larger order (27–8) of a world controlled by the gods) which help to create, and to limit, the conditions within which such agency and its attendant responsibility can operate.

The factors and issues broached by these remarks on 'The Choice of Heracles' will all be taken up again in the second part of this chapter, where I shall explore some of the assumptions, themes, and preoccupations which repeatedly recur in the presentation and evaluation of character in Greek texts of the archaic and classical periods (and, indeed, beyond). The continuing availability of certain beliefs and standards is the phenomenon covered by the word 'traditional' in my title, though I shall inevitably have to offer representative rather than extensive evidence for the continuity of this tradition. Much of my case will later be structured around consideration of a single document, Isocrates' *Evagoras*, but I shall use this as a framework within which to adduce relevant material from a variety of other sources. My hope is to keep the argument close to the particularity of individual texts, while allowing at the same time for an engagement with some strands in the Greek conceptualization of character.

I wish to proceed first, however, by laying down some principles of interpretation of a kind which will involve the rejection of an influential modern view of the development of Greek culture and thought. It is my initial contention that we could hardly begin to enquire into any culture's conceptions of character unless we could recognize and assume certain basic constituents in the understanding and evaluation of human behaviour. If it were possible, for example, to sustain the remarkable proposition that 'our own *basic antithesis* between self and not-self does not yet exist in Homeric consciousness' (my italics), we would not even, I submit, be in a position to affirm that there *was* any humanly intelligible 'Homeric consciousness' open to our inspection, still less to entertain simultaneously the idea that 'Homeric man . . . felt himself as a unitary being'.[2] Since my two quotations come from the same source, the first can surely only prompt us to ask of the second: Without any notion of 'self' (for one cannot have a notion of that which is indistinguishable from its contradictory), how could 'Homeric man' regard 'himself' as anything at all?

It will be an axiom of my argument that the assessment of psychological and ethical conceptions operative in another culture requires at least a limited postulate of what one might call anthropological 'realism': unless we can presuppose certain

---

[2] H. Fränkel, *Early Greek Poetry and Philosophy* (Oxford, 1975), 80, 76.

fundamental factors in human experience, there will be no basis on which to identify and comprehend significant cultural traits and distinctions in the interpretation of character. The nature of these factors must here be indicated summarily, but without, I think, begging or underestimating any questions about the more specific categories of self-understanding to be found in different cultures (or indeed shifts in these categories within the same culture).[3] The chief elements I have in mind are as follows: first, a basic recognition of the psychological identity of individuals, which is not to be equated with a theory of individualism and which does not override social or status-based components of identity; second, the ascription to individuals of at least some powers of choice and self-directed agency; third, the existence of criteria, however rudimentary, of rationality (in particular, criteria bearing on the *reasons* which can be given for choices of action); fourth, some conception of human responsibility, involving a sense of standards of applicability of praise and blame to agents and their actions.

Two important qualifications must be made at once; one has been already touched on. First, the above set of principles is not meant to exclude or prejudge the significant kinds of variation which may exist between cultures, or within a culture, in the emphasis and ordering of beliefs about human behaviour and character. The extent of interest shown in the life of the mind, the precise ways in which it is deemed to contribute to the understanding of persons, the degree to which individual identity and agency are conceived as discrete forces or, alternatively, as subordinate to larger forces—these and many other matters involve culturally variable phenomena which I do not underestimate. Secondly, these baldly stated prerequisite conditions for the existence of notions of character represent assumptions which may in some cases operate below the level of fully explicit or articulated formulation, as well as below the level of conscious consistency. The term 'conceptions' in my title should be understood to allow for this qualification, which expresses a rejection of the idea that conceptions can be identified primarily

---

[3] Many issues pertinent to this question are discussed in M. Carrithers, S. Collins, and S. Lukes (edd.), *The Category of the Person: Anthropology, Philosophy, History* (Cambridge, 1985). I should emphasize that my own basic postulates do not purport to address particular *theories* of the person (behaviourist, Buddhist, etc.).

by reference to particular lexical items in a language. The importance of this last point will emerge clearly enough in what follows.

From the great texts of Homeric and Hesiodic poetry onwards, Greek literature has its means, both descriptive and dramatic, of conveying conceptions and judgements of character. These conceptions rest on, without being cleanly restricted to, versions of the fundamental premises of agency, rationality, and responsibility indicated above. Even where countervailing ideas of human passivity or irrationality, environmental influences, divine impingement, etc. enter the picture, it is to be stressed that these ideas themselves, by negative implication, often entail the possibility of precisely the conceptions in question: when Priam excuses Helen at *Iliad* 3. 164, or Agamemnon excuses himself at 19. 86–7, we can observe that, particular issues of interpretation aside, the very terms of the exculpations imply the thinkable alternatives that these humans (who are identified, we notice, with their personal histories) *were* actively responsible and blameworthy. Agency, rationality, and responsibility, however imperfectly realized in practice, cannot be understood without some sense of psychological integrity, that is, of the mind as a coherent locus of consciousness and motivation within the person. But integrity does not mean indivisible homogeneity, and we can trace from the beginnings of the Greek literary tradition a strong awareness of the ways in which the mind can contain disparate, even contradictory, forces, variable in the degree to which they can be subjected to conscious control. It is plausible, in fact, that at a deep level these two ideas—psychic integrity and psychic conflict— are complementary (a Platonic insight, incidentally). A unitary notion of mind which did not allow for the practical reality of psychic complexity would be descriptively inadequate, while the recognition of the diverse energies that can be at work in consciousness requires the supposition of a basic mental coherence within which to perceive and define the nature of psychic discord.

The complementary nature of these two psychological principles, and their coexistence as active principles from the beginnings of Greek literature, have been strongly denied by a number of influential modern scholars who have seen a pro-

gressive evolution in archaic and classical Greece from the
'primitive' and 'fragmented' psychology of the Homeric poems,
in which there is allegedly no sense at all of psychic unity,
towards much more cohesive views of the nature of mind and
personality. Such contentions, particularly associated with
Bruno Snell's *The Discovery of the Mind*, carry an initial plausibility from the undoubted development of new *theories* of mind
and soul in the course of the archaic and classical periods. But
in their attempts to deny to the Homeric epics, and, by doubt-
ful extrapolation from them, to the world in which they were
produced,[4] a recognition of the basic unity of human consciousness, Snell and others have applied a faulty method and drawn
unwarranted conclusions from it. I shall try briefly to make
good these criticisms, and shall pass from them to some demonstration of the two psychological principles I have mentioned at
work in Homer. In addition to the intrinsic importance of this
issue for the interpretation of the Homeric epics, it has a substantial bearing on the continuity of the subsequent Greek tradition of characterization.

The claim that Homer lacks a unitary concept of mind or
soul depends on considerations of two kinds, one negative and
one positive: first, the absence of any particular term in Homer
which we can translate unequivocally as 'mind'; secondly, the
Homeric manner of describing psychological processes and
events by reference to different 'organs' (νόος, θυμός, φρένες,
etc.) which, according to one formulation, 'are not felt as part
of the self' but show themselves as 'detached entities'.[5] Both
halves of this argument are impaired by what one might call a
lexical bias—an assumption, to which I have already referred,
that individual lexical items and locutions, or the lack of them,
are the most significant facts about the way in which a
language shapes the conceptions expressible within it. This
assumption is often hazardous, but particularly so in the

---

[4] A. W. H. Adkins, *From the Many to the One* (London, 1970) after reasonably identifying 'Homeric man' with 'the human beings ... portrayed in the Homeric poems'
(13), suggests that 'Homeric language ... would have *tended to encourage* the fragmentation of Homeric man's psychological experience' (23, my ital.), a proposition which
implies that Homeric man and his language existed outside the poems. Similarly with
the idea of Homeric speech as a 'direct record' of experience (22). Cf. A. A. Long,
'Moral Values in Homer', *JHS* 90 (1970), 122.

[5] E. R. Dodds, *The Greeks and the Irrational* (Berkeley, 1951), 16.

psychological sphere. It may be right to suppose that the language used to describe or analyse psychological experience is partly constitutive of the nature of that experience, but it is one-sided to translate this supposition into the principle that individual lexical items in themselves carry a greater weight than the total discourse of which they form a part. In Homer's case, it should not be one particular area of vocabulary, but the entire narrative and dramatic style of the poet, and the images created by this style, which give expression to a view of men and the workings of their minds.

The kind of lexical analysis which ignores this principle can readily produce the conclusion that in Homeric psychology 'the parts are more in evidence than the whole',[6] for such analysis is *itself* only an account of the parts. In fact, close and sensitive scrutiny of the functions of νόος, θυμός, etc. in Homer will actually confirm that the sense of mental and emotional complexity which they sometimes convey has to be interpreted within the underlying wholeness of psychological identity and self-awareness. How else, at the most elementary level, can (say) a man's *thumos* be called 'his' at all, unless it is conceived as constitutive of his conscious 'self'? How, similarly, can passages in which someone addresses his *thumos* be adduced as evidence for the independence of the latter, when these same passages are permeated by the language of an 'I' to which the *thumos* is entirely ascribed? What, moreover, are we to make of those four Iliadic passages in which a character addresses his *thumos* only to pull himself up with the question 'Why does my *thumos say this to me?*',[7] if not that they dramatize, through a stylized presentation, a mentally integral process or experience? It is difficult from these considerations, which could be multiplied, to see how the medium of such experiences can consist of 'detached entities'.

The argument can best be taken further by looking at a particular passage; I choose one which demonstrates well the compelling psychological characterization of which the Homeric epics are capable—the night scene at the start of *Odyssey* 20, where Odysseus holds back from premature vengeance against

---

[6] Adkins, *From the Many*, 26–7.
[7] 11. 403, 407; 17. 90, 97; 21. 552, 562; 22. 98, 122.

the suitors' mistresses, before being assuaged and granted sleep by Athena (5–55). The passage illustrates the combination of descriptive and dramatic means of characterization; the narrative of Odysseus' state of mind is enlarged by the direct voicing of his dilemma through soliloquy or self-address (18–21). This latter technique, showing us how Odysseus 'scolded his heart', is not a symptom of mental fragmentation, but a paradigm of the dramatic demonstration of a complex psychological process, the internal anguish of a mind faced by alternatives which evoke from it competing impulses. There is no reason to treat the technique as essentially different from later literary uses of self-address, such as, say, that of the distraught Demeas at Menander, *Samia* 325–56 (though there the element of audience address imports an additional factor).

Of course the scene in *Od.* 20 suggests a strong sense of psychological tension and convulsion, but the conflict of impulses *within* Odysseus is exactly that; and far from being an impediment to a coherent conception of the person, it would be unintelligible, I submit, without one. It is only because we know what it is for an individual mind to be caught in an agitated dilemma of contending impulses, and yet for the experience to be played out within an integral state of consciousness, that we can understand this remarkable scene and implicitly relate it to other possible experiences of psychic tension (such as that of Plato's Leontius, *Rep.* 439e–440a). The presentation of Odysseus' condition is not an aggregate of discrete and self-sufficient statements about his *thumos* and other 'organs': we interpret the psychological force of the particular components from the dramatic nature of the whole, not vice versa.

But this passage shows, in any case, how the range of psychological language employed by Homer is handled with a dynamic or expressive flexibility, not with an analytic sense of 'detached entities' operating somehow independently of, or in contradiction to, the mind's sense of itself. To try to attach a specific function to *thumos*, for example, will produce a confusion which is not present in the scene itself.[8] Far from having a specific function, *thumos* can represent any strong impulse or

---

[8] Fränkel, *Early Greek Poetry*, 78, talks of a 'specific function' for each Homeric organ: he then attributes some sixteen different 'emotions', 'intimations', 'deliberations', and other states of mind to *thumos*.

motivation, and its urgings straddle analytical distinctions between the cognitive and the emotional; its particular significance must always be taken from the circumstances of the scene. When we are told how Odysseus' *thumos* swelled or roused up (9) after he heard the laughter of the maids, we do not need to consult the usage of *thumos* elsewhere to interpret this psychological moment; if we did, we would find, for example, that the other two occurrences of precisely the same phrase in the work (18. 75, 24. 318), and a further instance in the *Iliad* (9. 595), all represent subtly different states of feeling from the present passage—a point which can be established and elucidated only by dramatic, not by purely lexical, judgement.

Far from fragmenting the effect, in fact, some details of the references to *thumos* and other actuating springs of behaviour will serve only to show how they contribute to a complex but unitary sense of the mind and character of Odysseus. As regards the *thumos*, the point is conveyed in part by the variation between Odysseus himself (10, 28, 41) and his *thumos* (38) as the subject of the same crucial verb, μερμηρίζειν: the direct equation between 28–30 (with the poet's 'he') and 38–40 (with Odysseus' 'my *thumos*'), and the same shift within Odysseus' own speech at 38–41, are both incomprehensible without the presumption of an essential 'self'. Moreover, *thumos* functions variously as the medium of Odysseus' plans for retribution (5), as a passionate impulsion towards immediate revenge (9, 38), and as an element in the counter-impulse to wait for the opportunity for a fuller and more perfect vengeance (10-12). With the κραδίη, 'heart', we observe how a drive of (here) a strong animal character, as expressed by the dog simile, can yet be closely associated with the belief, recalled from a previous occasion, 'that you would die' (21); so the κραδίη too, if one wishes to press the analysis, has a cognitive aspect, and is more than 'pure' emotion.[9] If, indeed, we were consistently analytical here, we should have to say that the κραδίη as such possesses memory, since 'Odysseus' reminds it of its previous experiences. This point is critical. It would evidently be absurd to apportion memory to one segment of Odysseus' mind at this moment, and

---

[9] The address to the κραδίη not only employs a way of addressing a *person*, it turns into just that: the gender of the participle in 21 shows that Odysseus is addressing *himself*, yet within the address to his heart.

that is because we are compelled, by fundamental psychological postulates as well as by the clear import of the Greek, to take Odysseus' words as precisely *self*-address, a dramatization of the acute experience of conflict within a single mind, whose memory—the bonding of the sense of self—interpenetrates and integrates emotion and rationality.

The purpose of these remarks is to show that if the psychology of this scene is interpreted with due sense of its dramatic nuances and its full effect, we do not find in it evidence for a Homeric view of the fissionable nature of consciousness, but rather a manifestation of the way in which the mental experience of the character precisely *embraces* and holds together a complexity of drives and motivations. The scene gives us, in fact, a fine dramatic equivalent to the theories of psychological faculties later elaborated by the philosophers, in that for them too the existence of psychological 'parts' or components is predicated on the basic unity of the mind.[10] Moreover, the impact of the scene serves a function of ethical characterization. The μῆτις, 'cunning', of which Odysseus reminds himself, as his previous salvation (20), and the controlled endurance which it entails (18–23), are salient marks of the character which he shows and develops in the course of the entire poem. The present passage is itself a revelation of that μῆτις and endurance at work, and of the way in which they have to be exercised so as to achieve a hard-won control over other psychological forces which might impede their success. It is also, of course, important that we see Odysseus' character in operation unaided, *before* Athena's reassurance is given.

Emergent from a fraught experience of mental turmoil, Odysseus' difficult preservation of μῆτις is all the more rational for that; it depends on his sense that there are strong prudential reasons (30, 40–3), tied up with the nature of his preparations for revenge, why he should restrain himself from intervening at this point. Odysseus' heart may bark like a dog, but his animal drives are subject to the control (a control of heroic dimensions, in this case) of his larger awareness of the possibilities of his situation. Odysseus is not only conscious of his own mind, he is also

---

[10] Arist. *EN* 1102ᵃ28–32, on the different senses of 'parts', is especially pertinent. Cf. *De An.* 432ᵃ15 ff.; *EE* 1219ᵇ32–4.

responsible for the final promptings to which it moves him. Psychology and characterization are therefore functionally at one in this episode. If Prodicus' parable, with which I started, might seem to delineate, in its allegorical schematism, too tranquil a model of ethical choice, the poet of the *Odyssey* offers us a wonderful image of the torments of such choice for one entrammelled in immediate complexities of action.

I suggested earlier that part of the importance of grasping the existence in Homer of a sense—an active, dramatic sense— of the unity-in-complexity of the mind, is that it establishes in the most influential texts of Greek literature an outlook which was capable of surviving or transcending later developments in the language and attitudes of Greek psychological thinking, and of remaining vitally intelligible to subsequent Greek culture. Without this continuity, it would be difficult to explain the lasting significance to the Greeks of Homer's images of man, still less to understand how even philosophers such as Plato and Aristotle could cite examples of Homeric psychology without any recognition of the 'gulf' which has been discerned between Homer's and classical Greek views of the mind.[11] Rather than positing such a gulf, it is more economical to accept that the shifts and changes in Greek psychology between the time of Homer and that of Aristotle, important though they were especially on the level of philosophical theory, did not obliterate an underlying continuity in assumptions about the workings of the mind, as well as about their relevance to human character. Various further aspects of this tradition of enduring, shared assumptions will emerge in the course of the examination of a particular exercise in characterization, Isocrates' *Evagoras*, to which I now turn.

II

The *Evagoras*, an encomiastic biography (or biographically structured encomium) of the King of Cypriot Salamis, was

---

[11] 'Gulf': B. Snell, *The Discovery of the Mind* (Eng. trans., Oxford, 1953), 1. Given Snell's view, it is curious that he should allow that Plato 'deliberately echoes Homeric ideas' (312 n. 20). For Platonic references to Homeric psychology, see esp. *Phaedo* 94d–e; *Rep.* 390d, 441b, where precisely the passage I have considered from *Od.* 20 is assimilated (tendentiously) to Plato's own psychological ideas. For Aristotle, see e.g. *EN* 1116^{b}26–30.

written towards the mid-360s, some years after the death of its
subject in 374/3, and was addressed, by way of dedication, to
Evagoras' son, Nicocles. Its historical motivation and credibility, which are intricately related to the work's rhetorical
nature, and about whose implications Isocrates shows a degree
of delicacy (5, 9–11, 21, 39, 48), are not of direct interest here.
The undoubted excesses consequent upon the eulogistic function, as well as what some might see as its author's mediocrity of
ideas, do not impair its value as a document which can usefully
exemplify a number of conventional Greek attitudes towards
human character. In fact, its high degree of reliance on stereo-
types and clichés (something for which the ageing writer seems
to apologize at 73) actually gives it just the kind of representa-
tiveness, at least at the level of ethical outlook, which suits my
illustrative purposes. I shall begin by examining a number of
points which emerge from the final chapters of the work
(73–81), where Isocrates summarizes its purport and possible
effect. I shall then move back to the details of the treatment of
Evagoras' life and character, and to consideration of the types
of attitude in which it is grounded.

There is an obvious temptation to describe the *Evagoras* as a
biographical 'portrait'. It is interesting that Isocrates himself,
in the work's epilogue, develops an analogy and a contrast with
sculptured and painted portraiture (73–5). He does so in part
in order to challenge comparison with the power of visual
memorials to preserve a man's reputation after his death and to
endow him with 'immortality', which is one dimension of Isocrates' own encomiastic function in regard to Evagoras (3–4).[12]
But the comparison, or rather the contrast, with visual memorials serves a further and more emphatic purpose, by giving
Isocrates a means of asserting his concern with his subject's
mind and character. To do so, it is true, he has to ignore the
possibility that visual portraits too can express something of a
man's particular nature and qualities.[13] Even so, his contrast

---

[12] Cf. 67, 70–1. It is relevant that the Athenians had erected a memorial statue of
Evagoras in memory of his military help against Sparta (57). Note also that Isocrates'
'immortalizing' function is throughout conceived in competition with the ability of
poetry to perpetuate a man's memory (a Greek cliché): see esp. 6, 8–11, 40, 65, 72.

[13] The earliest references to character (*ēthos*) and related topics in the visual arts
occur at Xen. *Mem.* 3. 10. 1–8; Arist. *Pol.* 1340ª38; *Poet.* 1450ª26–9; but none of these

has some justification; there are necessary limitations on what
can be learnt about character from appearance alone, and
hence from a portrait: 'there is no mark of a man's mind in his
face' (Hyperides fr. 196 Kenyon).[14] A sculptured portrait
might communicate a striking sense of some aspects of a personality, but it could hardly be expected, unaided, to offer extensive insight into the nature of an individual's mind or life as a
whole. Isocrates' verbal 'portrait', by contrast, with its narrative, expository, and analytical means, can claim to be able to
exhibit the 'actions and mind' of the man, his true character, as
revealed in the ethical shape of his entire career.

Evagoras' 'actions and mind' (73)—here we have Isocrates'
central subject, the theme which justifies the application of the
term 'biography' to his work, though of course with due qualifications.[15] In contrast to the historian, who might place some of
Evagoras' actions within the larger framework of, say, a war, a
period, or the events of a region, Isocrates' purpose is to show
and explain the unity of an individual life in its own right and
for its own sake. More than this, it is his aim to demonstrate
how such unity is at root a matter precisely of character—a
matter of the shaping of a life by its own agency, an agency
which consistently reflects and embodies the dispositions,
choices, and virtues predicable of the person himself. This biographical task claims to match, by its encomiastic design, one of
the main *internal* dynamics of the kind of life in question:
Evagoras shares with all καλοὶ κἀγαθοί, all who have ambition
to excel (φιλοτιμία), a pride in active achievements and the
force of mind which is manifested in them (τοῖς ἔργοις καὶ τῇ
γνώμῃ, 74). The underlying ideas here, which Isocrates had
stressed at the start of his work too (2–5), are old and well-tried.
One will not need to dwell on the pervasive importance in
many areas of Greek culture of an ambitious, striving ethic,
feeding on values of success, honour, and lasting fame. Iso-

passages refers directly to portraiture. R. P. Hinks, *Greek and Roman Portrait Sculpture*
(London, 1935; 2nd edn. 1976), ch. 1, takes the development of portraiture as reflecting beliefs in the integrity of the self.

[14] One is irresistibly reminded of Duncan's 'There's no art | To find the mind's con-
struction in the face' (*Macbeth* I. iv. 11–12). Hes. *Op.* 714 implies the possibility of an
appearance which disguises one's mind. Cf. n. 32 below.
[15] A. Momigliano, *The Development of Greek Biography* (Cambridge, Mass., 1971),
ch. 3.

crates' work identifies such values in operation in Evagoras' life, just as it validates and perpetuates them itself by its own panegyric function. The whole process is self-renewing: the *Evagoras* has been written in part so as to encourage others, especially Evagoras' own son, to emulation (74–81)—a well-recognized capability of encomium.[16]

There are, it can already be discerned, certain notions about character implicit in, and associated with, such an ethical outlook. Though Isocrates may advert to the novelty and difficulty of prose encomium (8–11), the new form (if it is that) grows naturally out of the soil of an old, varied, Greek tradition of praise and blame. Praise and blame are ethical exercises and forces; they are, in fact, paradigmatic forms of ethical judgement, as Aristotle emphasized.[17] They entail not only the existence but also the *sharing* of values, since effective praise and blame must be addressed to audiences which will recognize and endorse their function: their function and effect are constituted precisely by people's responses to them. And this function is in turn predicated on the assumption that, in certain respects at least, men have some personal, conscious control over the determination of their actions and lives. Isocrates makes this point explicitly. Nicocles, Evagoras' son, the addressee of the work, is urged to continue with his quest for virtuous pre-eminence and recognition: 'it is in your power', he is told, 'not to miss these goals' (81). That which is 'in one's power' depends on character for its realization. Character, as Isocrates' epilogue makes clear, centres on a man's actions and on the personal direction which motivates and shapes them: his mind and thought (διάνοια, γνώμη), his choice and will (75), his practical intelligence (φρόνησις), and the habits, practices, and way of life (τρόποι, ἐπιτηδεύματα, διατριβαί) which the exercise of thought and choice generates.[18] This cluster of terms and motifs occurs in the work's protreptic epilogue to Nicocles, supporting Isocrates' contention that it is now *his* turn to follow his father's example and perpetuate the reputation of his ancestors. But

---

[16] See e.g. Isoc. 4. 159, with Aristoph. *Ran.* 1026–7, 1039–42; Pl. *Prt.* 326a; *Phdr.* 245a.

[17] *EN* 1101ᵇ31–2, 1103ᵃ8–10, 1109ᵇ30f.; *EE* 1223ᵃ9–15.

[18] διάνοια/-αι: 42, 73, 75; γνώμη: 27, 29, 41, 61, 71, 74; φρόνησις: 65, 80; τρόπος/-οι: 24, 51,75; ἐπιτηδεύματα: 2, 77; διατριβαί 78. Note also the use of ψυχή in this connection (80, matching 41).

these same ideas had also occurred insistently in the main body of the work, helping to substantiate the account of Evagoras' own character. Some features of this account will allow us to see more fully the conceptions of character which Isocrates employs and presupposes.

The encomium proper starts by situating Evagoras in the perspective of his ancestral γένος, the Teucridae (12–18). This is noteworthy not just as an opportunity to rival (by borrowing) some of the 'ornaments' (9–11) and mythology (36) supposedly reserved for poetry, but also as a way of suggesting an inherited potential which gives Evagoras' character one strand of its significance: the family or clan, stretching back into mythical time, is the matrix of Evagoras' *phusis* (12), which will later be shown to have grown and materialized in his own life (29, 49, 72). This is a clear case, then, of εὐγένεια, inherited nobility and 'breeding', a factor which we saw in 'The Choice of Heracles'. Such a pedigree seems to operate in a double manner, both as a model or standard for Evagoras' emulation (the παραδείγματα of 12; cf. 77), and as a natural element internal to his make-up, though requiring active realization. The first of these points is indicated by the specific theme of 'dangers' (κίνδυνοι), which the mythical figures Peleus (16) and Achilles (18) are cited for having faced, and which run as a leitmotiv through the treatment of Evagoras' own life (2, 27, 29, 35–6, 38, 46, 65). But that Evagoras was capable of living up to such exalted standards (12–13) was possible in part only because of his natural endowment (19, 41). His life manifests a character which validates, by sustaining, the norms of his γένος (32); his 'nature' belongs to him, but it can be fully appreciated only in the light of his ancestry.

Although Evagoras' Teucrid pedigree is a special, quasi-heroic factor, Isocrates' treatment of the king's 'nature' reflects a Greek attitude of much wider applicability—a tendency to see one dimension of character as something natural. The term *phusis*, as in this work, is often used to present a person's character as a matter of that which is most intrinsic and integral to him; where appropriate, the superiority of the natural over the acquired is an additional implication. Yet this poses a paradox, for character is also commonly conceived, as the etymology of *ēthos* suggests, in terms of dispositions induced by habit, practice, and training: 'all character (*ēthos*) grows through habit (*ethos*)'.[19] This duality of categories runs through much Greek thinking about character, sometimes resolved by the assertion of the priority of one force over the other, but often handled in such a way as to allow the interfusion of the two factors. It seems likely, in fact, that the two basic conceptions—of a natural, innate temperament, and of a habitual way of life— effectively cross-fertilized one another, so that to call a man's character his 'nature' became the most emphatic means of por- traying (for good or bad) the pervasive qualities of his exist- ence, while the primary evidence for a person's 'nature' would inevitably be the consistent attributes of his behaviour.[20] This issue is therefore implicated in the relation between mind and action which will shortly be considered.

One original context of the idea of character as natural was probably aristocratic; the conception could derive an obvious impetus from societies (both real and mythological) in which there was a dominant presumption of the inherited superiority of members of political and social élites. Hence, for one thing, the frequency of such notions in Pindaric epinician, proclaim- ing and celebrating the quality of ancestral merit in those fami- lies which could lay claim to it.[21] Yet even Pindar can praise only those who have *displayed* and thereby proved the capabil- ity of their 'natural' character. Eugenic nature is only an acceptable warrant of character where the evidence of deeds provides confirmation of it. The tensions which might arise in such a scheme of values are dramatically explored in Sophocles' *Philoctetes*, where the issue of Neoptolemus' 'nature' is sus- pended ambiguously between two factors: his inherited identity as son of Achilles, and his active attempts to emulate and re- create the heroic implications of that paternity in his own life.[22]

[19] Pl. *Leg.* 792e2 (though the verb 'grows' seems to admit a natural basis to the pro- cess: cf. *Rep.* 395d2 and n. 24 below); cf. Arist. *EN* 1103ᵃ17 ff.

[20] There is much relevant material in K. J. Dover, *Greek Popular Morality* (Oxford, 1974), 88–95. For the superiority of the natural, see e.g. Thuc. 1. 138. 3, on Themis- tocles; E. *Hipp.* 79–80.

[21] e.g. *Ol.* 9. 100–2, 11. 19–20 (NB ἐμφυές ... ἦθος), 13. 13 (συγγενὲς ἦθος). The imagery of *Nem.* 8. 40 f. suggests that *aretē* is like a plant: natural, but in need of careful tending.

[22] *Phil.* 88–9, 874–5 clearly indicate that Neoptolemus' *phusis* is distinguishable from his parentage (cf. n. 1 above), even though, as the whole play suggests, the former aspires towards the standards of the latter.

In Evagoras' case too, as in Prodicus' allegorical treatment of Heracles', a man's natural inheritance, however historically illustrious, calls for practical, visible realization in his personal achievements. Otherwise, nature becomes degenerate, disappointing; εὐγένεια alone is seen to be insufficient for an excellence which men can discern and to which they can respond.[23] If the fragile identification of character with inherited claims to 'breeding' is something which could be perceived with impunity in a democratic society, we should not attribute entirely to this cause the acuteness of the debates over the rival claims of nature and education attested so clearly for the age of the sophists and reflected in the thinking of Plato.[24] It had always been possible to think the thoughts of a Thersites, by observing discrepancies between the expectations attaching to socially transmitted status and the realities of an individual's behaviour.

By the later fifth century 'nature' had become a term applicable to anyone's character of life, regardless of pedigree. It would perhaps be a mistake to see this as entirely a matter of extension from an originally aristocratic frame of reference, a kind of democratization of the language of inherited merit, though certainly a process of that kind can be interestingly seen at work in the 'moralization' of the specific terminology of εὐγένεια.[25] But more generally, a view of character which, as commonly in a traditional Greek outlook, aligns expectations of individual behaviour with position within the structures of family and society, and therefore with such determinants as sex, age, and political status, might well find it persuasively convenient to translate such conventional expectations into the terms of natural roles.[26] If so, this is a further element tending

---

[23] Degenerate εὐγένεια: Theogn. 183–92, 436; Phocylides fr. 3 Diehl; S. *El.* 287, 341 ff.; E. *El.* 368–72, 550–1; Arist. *Rh.* 1390ᵇ22–4.

[24] The 5th-cent. debate over natural versus learnt character is reflected at e.g. E. *Hec.* 592 ff.; *Suppl.* 911–17; Pl. *Meno passim; Prt.* 318–28; but, as Pl. *Meno* 95d–96a observes, the issue is older (see Theogn. 31–8, 429–38). Arist. *EN* 1103ᵃ17 ff., 1114ᵃ31–ᵇ25, denies altogether that character is a matter of nature (though see e.g. *Rh.* 1390ᵇ16–31 for some allowance); Plato's position is much more equivocal and complex: see e.g. *Rep.* 374c ff., 424a, 431c7, and cf. the remarkable physiological explanation of mental diseases at *Tim.* 86d–87b.

[25] e.g. E. *Hipp.* 1390; *El.* 253, 262; fr. 336 N²; Men. *Dysc.* 281, 321, 723, 835; *Sam.* 356. Cf. the kindred idea of the aristocracy of merit at Pl. *Menex.* 238c–239a.

[26] For some formal acknowledgement of the link between character and status see

towards complication of the conceptual relationship between nature and 'practice' (including nurture, education, and habitual behaviour), for the latter influences are themselves to be regarded, where status-defined standards are prevalent, as enabling the processes of nature to be socially realized and embodied. A person who fulfils his or her normative role within the family or society can be held to possess a character which is the completion of nature. Nature here functions as an ultimate sanction and justification for the (hierarchical) structuring of human relations, and the individual is not praised or blamed for an existentially independent choice of life, but for successfully complying with the determining forces of his natural place in the world. Similar assumptions can of course be translated onto an even larger scale, contributing to chauvinistic conceptions of the natural 'character' of a whole society, or even to a sense of the racial superiority of Greeks over barbarians.[27]

In the acclaimed case of Evagoras, to return to Isocrates, nature and character, the 'given' and the actualized, are synonymous, or at any rate in perfect harmony. The portrayal of active character is marked by the emphasis on the presence of virtues in Evagoras' life from his childhood onwards (22 ff.). The virtues are clustered in such a way as to suggest a complete array: self-control or discipline ($\sigma\omega\phi\rho\sigma\sigma\acute{\nu}\eta$, 22), courage ($\dot{\alpha}\nu\delta\rho\acute{\iota}\alpha$, 23), practical intelligence ($\sigma\sigma\phi\acute{\iota}\alpha$, 23), justice ($\delta\iota\kappa\alpha\iota\sigma\sigma\acute{\nu}\eta$, 23), piety ($\acute{\sigma}\sigma\iota\acute{\sigma}\tau\eta\varsigma$, $\epsilon\dot{\nu}\sigma\acute{\epsilon}\beta\epsilon\iota\alpha$, 25–6). Each of these qualities reappears and is confirmed later: $\sigma\omega\phi\rho\sigma\sigma\acute{\nu}\eta$ is exemplified by Evagoras' mastery over the force of pleasure (45), courage is central to the subsequent narrative of the recovery of power (esp. 27–32; cf. 65), the force of intelligence is accentuated at 41–6, while justice and piety receive regular reference (26, 38–9, 43, 51). This range of excellences covers many major dimensions of ethical activity—appropriate treatment of others, both friends and enemies; regulation of one's own conduct, and

e.g. Pl. *Meno* 71c–72a (where Meno voices traditional sentiments); Arist. *Rh.* 1388[b]31–1391[b]7. The relevance of the point to literary characterization is apparent at Pl. *Ion* 540b; Arist. *Poet.* 1454[a]19–31.

[27] Athenian national character: Aristoph. *Pax* 607; Thuc. 2. 36 ff., 7. 14. 2–4, 48. 4; Pl. *Menex.* 237–8; cf. the spurious prologue to Theophr. *Char.* on differences of character between Greek states. Greek character *vis-à-vis* barbarian: e.g. A. *Pers.* 231–44; Arist. *Pol.* 1285[a]19–22; Hippoc. *Aër. passim*. On these two points, cf. also Dover, *Greek Popular Morality*, 83–7.

control over internal forces capable of impeding prudence; the pursuit of honourable goals even at the risk of one's life; behaviour of a kind likely to find favour with the gods.[28]

It would be difficult to exaggerate the Greek tendency to evaluate character in overtly ethical terms—that is to say, to judge people primarily by reference to their possession or lack of *aretai*, excellences or virtues, which are active exemplifications of standards sustained by the currency of wide social approval, and embodiable in particular forms of life. This is, arguably, the most important fact about Greek conceptions of character—a cultural fact deeply embedded in the vocabulary of evaluation used at all levels and in all types of context (which does not imply, it should be stressed, universal subscription to an identical set of values). This ethical culture incorporates the traditions of praise and blame which I mentioned earlier, and its nature well suits Isocrates' purpose in the *Evagoras*: the encomiastic form exactly satisfies one aspect of the preoccupation of traditional Greek ethics with honour and shame, with success and failure, with publicly sanctioned criteria of good and evil. It may be worth adding to this, though without directly addressing the problematic history of changes in ethical values in Greece, that Isocrates' portrayal of Evagoras illustrates the difficulty of applying in this sphere a neat distinction between 'competitive' and 'co-operative' standards. Evagoras is esteemed and commended for a life which in various ways fuses the pursuit of personal glory with the display of virtues from which others—his family, his city and people, his foreign allies—benefit.

Rather as in the Aristotelian systematization of ethics, Isocrates regards Evagoras' individual virtues as crowned by a certain greatness of mind (μεγαλοψυχία, μεγαλοφροσύνη: 3, 45, 59), thus stamping his portrait of the man with a sense of a special potency of character. It must be reiterated that the credibility of the portrait is not our concern, only its characterizing terms and assumptions. These are perhaps seen at their clearest in chs. 41–6, where Isocrates gives a kind of epitome of the character which Evagoras displayed throughout his rule in

---

[28] Isocrates perhaps exploits a certain tendency, not unique to Socrates, to believe in the unitary nature of *aretē*: for some earlier evidence of this see Theogn. 145–7 (cited as proverbial at Arist. *EN* 1129ᵇ29–30), 378–80.

Salamis. Complementing the earlier emphasis on bold, quasi-heroic courage, exhibited in his recovery of Teucrid power, we are now given an image of Evagoras' prudence and intelligence as a king and leader.[29] This is, in essence, an account of practical wisdom (φρόνησις, 41) and good judgement (εὐβουλία, 46). But these are not abstract virtues; like everything else attributed to Evagoras by Isocrates, they are manifested in action and behaviour: 'that Evagoras possessed all these qualities, and more besides, can easily be learnt from his deeds themselves' (46).

So the virtues of Evagoras were the result of a certain cast of mind; but all the evidence cited to support this belief is derived from active policy and way of life. Character is exhibited by action, and action allows Isocrates to deduce and establish the nature of character. The same correlation between qualities of mind and action was already present in the earlier account of the winning of the kingship (27–40), and the correlation resembles a pattern of attitudes which we have met in the conception of a man's 'nature'. With the mind as with nature, the crucial test is that of observable behaviour; we can adduce here the semantic stress of many Greek terms relating to character (ἦθος, τρόπος, διατριβή, ἐπιτήδευμα, δίαιτα) on the orientation or regularity of behaviour. But the Greeks were not behaviourists, and the persistent assumption is that actions express or reflect the ethical and intentional qualities of mind which lie behind and prompt them—a fact which explains the frequency of cognitive terms (νοεῖν, φρονεῖν, γιγνώσκειν, with various cognates) in Greek descriptions of personal dispositions. In this sense, character can be spoken of as 'in the mind',[30] but this point of view is typically counterbalanced, and made inimical to any preoccupation with introspective psychology, by the equal tendency to diagnose character from action: 'one cannot know the mind of man or woman, until you put them to the test like a beast of burden' (Theogn. 125–6). This is a generalization of an attitude whose validity for political life acquired the status of proverbial wisdom.[31]

---

[29] This exemplifies the old ideal of combining excellence in deeds and words (see specifically chs. 44 and 77): e.g. Hom. *Il.* 9. 443; Pind. *Nem.* 8. 8; Thuc. 1. 139. 4. On εὐβουλία, cf. M. Schofield, '*Euboulia* in the *Iliad*', *CQ*, NS 36 (1986), 6–31.

[30] ἐν φρεσὶν ἦθος Theogn. 1261; cf. e.g. Hes. *Op.* 67, νόον καὶ ... ἦθος.

[31] Arist. *EN* 1130ᵃ1–2, quoting Bias' wisdom, echoed at S. *Ant.* 175–7.

The mutually explanatory correspondence between character and action may be a necessary working presupposition of human self-understanding. But it acquires a distinctive Greek complexion through association with an ethical outlook which locates the finest human excellences in overt, publicly recognizable activities. This is something which can be discerned in various forms. Its place in the mythological society dramatized by heroic poetry is patent, but it also appears prominently, for example, in the attitudes underlying Pindaric epinician, where observable success and failure are strong clues (though the gods may spoil the process) to the nature of those who experience them: 'the test of experience shows definitively who is superior—boy among boys, man among men, and likewise, finally, among elders' (*Nem.* 3. 70–3). This same criterion, the test of experience, operates on a different level as a premiss implicit in much of the forensic rhetoric of classical Athenian courts. One justifies oneself in such an arena, and impugns one's opponent, by exploiting in every available way the principle that the nature of a man is manifest in his deeds and his way of life. With the inevitable exception of the dissembler (truly, the exception that proves the rule),[32] there is little room here for the possibility that the quality of a life, or a particular cast of character, may be just of the sort which is *not* open to easy or direct inspection. The bond between character and activity is carried to the point of great philosophical sophistication in the ethics of Aristotle, who can thus be seen, in this as in other respects, to be refining assumptions widely and traditionally held about human nature.[33]

A number of the points made above can be illustrated by the elegiac prayer of complaint at lines 373–400 of the Theognid corpus. This brief meditation on the lack of alignment between a man's character and the conditions of material life which the world (or Zeus) allots him offers us some typical reflections of Greek folk moralizing. We find here the primary postulate of an essential link between the mind of a man and his ethical

---

[32] Dissimulation is a recurrent theme of moralizing, betokening the anti-behavourist streak in Greek psychology: see e.g. Hom. *Il.* 9. 312–13; Hes. *Op.* 67, 78; Theogn. 117–18, 213–18, 363–4, 963–7; E. *Med.* 516–19; *Hipp.* 925–31; and the Attic σκόλιον PMG 889 (which Plato may have had in mind at *Rep.* 577a).

[33] Compare Arist. *EN* 1103ᵇ1–25 with Dem. 13. 25; and cf. *EN* 1114ᵃ9–10 for the currency of the principle.

actions. The idea of 'the mind and spirit of every man' (375) is explained by the division of the world into the just and the unjust (377–8), who are further described as those whose 'mind is turned' either to restraint or to violence (379). This thread continues with the reference to those who 'hold back their impulses (*thumos*) from base deeds' (383–4). Thus action is held to manifest mind or character, while the latter is itself predicated on the basis of the virtues or vices embodied in action. Against the background of this correlation, however, it is then possible for the poet to suggest that the pressure of circumstances—the 'harsh necessity' of poverty—may lead even the good astray into involuntary, because *uncharacteristic*, wrongdoing (386–92). This picture presupposes that we can observe the degradation of a person's good character, and judge it as precisely that, because of our previous experience of their worth. At the same time, the faith in action as the demonstration of character is maintained: even in poverty, one will tell the good and the base apart (393–4), and the behaviour of the just man in these circumstances will give one proof of the straightness of his mind (395–6).

The poem is interesting partly for its acknowledgement of the kind of external forces which may undermine a person's stable behaviour,[34] but also for the way in which, in the face of these facts, it manages to reaffirm the correlation of 'mind' and action, and to suggest that this correlation is the medium in which the excellences and defects of character are constituted. The elegy additionally allows, though hardly with much force, for an element of psychological inwardness in character: 'You, Zeus, know well the mind and spirit of every man', says the poet (375), with a hint of the possible human limitations on seeing into each man's heart. The deployment of the familiar Homeric terms νόος and θυμός implies the dynamics of a rudimentary psychology: the motive forces in each person are focused in an individual agency, and yet not reducible to a single kind of motivation. It is part of the linguistic inheritance of the words from Homeric poetry, as sketched earlier in this chapter, that the components of this psychological picture have

---

[34] For the force of ἀνάγκη, 'necessity', undermining character, cf. e.g. S. *El.* 307–9, 616–21; E. *El.* 375–6; Dover, *Greek Popular Morality*, 109–10.

a flexible capacity: they do not stand as self-contained mental 'faculties', but depend on a descriptive, narrative, or dramatic context for their full significance. In the present passage, we might notice that νόος and θυμός seem close to being inter-changeable (379, 384, 386, 395), and between them cover both the emotional drives and the deliberative functioning of the mind.

If we now return to Isocrates, we can pick out two further and necessary factors in the traditional understanding of char-acter, which reinforce the posited relation between mind and action that I have been outlining. These factors, responsibility and consistency, are made explicit in chs. 41–6 of the *Evagoras*. The nature of Evagoras' leadership, we are told, depended on his personal and active knowledge of his subjects, allowing for first-hand rather then delegated judgements of them (42). 'Nor was he disorganized or capricious in any respect; he maintained consistency in deed and in word alike. His pride [μέγα φρονεῖν; cf. on μεγαλοφροσύνη above] was grounded not in the results of fortune, but in the things for which he himself was responsible' (44–5). This last phrase echoes a contrast which Isocrates had previously drawn between Evagoras' fearless quest for the re-covery of power, and the element of fortune or guile in many traditional myths of heroic home-comings (36). In so far as success is due to fortune, it cannot be wholly due to character; and apart from an oblique acknowledgement of the possible coexistence of the two causes (59), Isocrates' encomiastic pur-pose inhibits him from limiting his subject's personal respons-ibility for his achievements.

Even so, it remains for anyone working within the spirit of a traditional Greek outlook to observe that Evagoras' remark-able life must have been blessed and favoured by the gods. And so indeed, Isocrates helpfully confirms, it was. If Evagoras is comparable in excellence to heroic figures of myth, he has sur-passed them in the happiness of a life lived without tragedy or lesser impairments, a life which almost merits for him the hyperbole of the poetic appellation 'a god among men' (70–2; cf. 29). But this recognition of the divine background poses a possible question about the factor of responsibility mentioned above. The suppleness of traditional religious beliefs allows for fluctuation, according to context and the frame of mind of the

observer, in the degree to which gods can be held causally engaged within or behind ostensibly human actions. If the power
of gods is real, then it can even invade the mind and pervert the
channels of human agency.[35] Yet this supposition, which may
provide a compelling explanation of some events in the world,
is inimical to the general conceptions of choice, intention, and
responsibility, and consequently to the judgements of merit and
blame which depend on them. The belief that the gods are responsible for *everything* may be theoretically tenable, but its implications are hardly sustainable in practical terms through all
the circumstances of a life; the assumption of a mysterious interweaving of divine and human agency is more flexible.[36] These
stresses in Greek thinking are particularly reflected in the complex ways in which the idea of a personal δαίμων, an idea found
on different levels of belief, could be conceived as relating to the
notion of human character.[37]

Even Isocrates' affirmation of Evagoras' supreme happiness
lightly acknowledges, in the midst of its fulsome felicitations,
the existence of these traditional Greek concerns with forces
capable of overriding human character and of causing tragedy.
Yet his encomiastic design and function require him to avoid
the more pessimistic thoughts of conventional wisdom, and to
assert that he is describing a case in which character and divine
support matched one another, or were interwoven, with perfect
accord. It is rhetorically understandable that Isocrates should
stress that Evagoras' claimed success, blessed though it was
with the avoidance of tragedy, was not a matter of purely contingent help from the gods: it was the consummation, the perfect endorsement, of Evagoras' own nature and character (71).
At one point Isocrates posits a provident δαίμων active in protecting Evagoras, but the δαίμων arranges that Evagoras

---

[35] 'Psychic intervention' from the gods is an old idea: e.g. Hom. *Il.* 6. 234; Archil. fr.
96 West. S. *Ant.* 683 exemplifies the related 'folk' notion that the gods are responsible
for men's wits.

[36] The gods are responsible for everything: Hom. *Od.* 1. 347–9; *Il.* 3. 164–5; Theogn.
133–42, 169–72; the denial of this: Hom. *Od.* 1. 32–4; Solon frs. 4. 1–8, 11. 1–2 West;
Theogn. 833–6.

[37] Hes. *Op.* 122–3; Theogn. 149–50, 161–3; Lys. 2. 78; Men. *Dysc.* 282; fr. 714 Körte,
all exemplify the view of the δαίμων as independent of the person's own character;
Heraclit. fr. 119 DK; Theogn. 165–6; Epicharm. fr. 258; Democr. fr. 171 DK; Pl. *Rep.*
617c; Xenocrates *apud* Arist. *Top.* 112ª36–8, all variously translate the belief into an
equation between δαίμων and character.

should shun impious circumstances and grasp the opportunity
for pious, just kingship (25-6): providence is channelled into
the virtues of the man's own character, in a way which simultaneously looks back to a traditional duality of Greek religious
thought and anticipates an important feature of Stoicism.
When Evagoras' life is subsequently called 'dear to the gods'
(43, 70), it is hard to disentangle the active from the passive
aspect of this predication. The force of human nature and
character has been asserted, but not its complete independence
from a larger scheme of things.

III

My remarks on the *Evagoras* have tried to accentuate those
features which exhibit fundamental themes in traditional
Greek conceptions of character. What the work does not display, and what I have therefore not been concerned with, is
any great range of *means* of characterization, and I should like
to finish by offering some brief thoughts on this point. Isocrates
is working here in a descriptive and narrative mode of rhetoric;
despite the fact that his piece is an early example of the growing
Greek interest in biography, it almost entirely lacks a sense of
closeness to, or inwardness with, its subject. Interest in the individual, without which we would have no biographical form at
all, is qualified and coloured by the tendency to see him as an
exemplar of general, ethical qualities—qualities, that is, which
are not uniquely his. While this is symptomatic of much Greek
thinking about character, it must still be said that two particular kinds of material are largely absent from Isocrates' picture:
psychological immediacy, and 'circumstantial' or specifically
personal detail.

This negative dimension of the work is due to various factors,
some doubtless peculiar to it (such as the relation between
writer, subject, and audience), but others evincing the conventions of characterization with which Isocrates operates. The
paucity of personal detail (there are the merest hints in chs.
42-5) belongs to a stylized elevation of tone which suits the
immediate pupose of the work while also ensuring conformity
to certain canons of literary tradition. A wealth of circumstantial detail would detract from the grand, quasi-heroic status
which Isocrates seeks to establish for Evagoras, as well as from

the purity of the 'immortalizing' function of the work. In this connection it is worth recalling the epilogue's comparison of verbal encomium with the sculptured portrait (p. 43 above): Isocrates' work is equivalent to an idealized portrait in striving to give us a powerful sense of the great individual, but without being drawn into an exact realism of detail. The exclusion of the mundane and the commonplace is a broad stylistic feature of most serious forms of Greek literature from Homer onwards; when 'low' elements do intrude, it is usually for pointed effect. By contrast, the literary 'line' which embraces iambus, parody, and comedy, and which helps to generate Theophrastus' *Characters*,[38] gives scope for precisely the everyday, even the sordid, detail which higher genres consciously exclude.

I mention these large, familiar phenomena only to stress their implications for characterization—implications which, as we can see from the debate in Aristophanes' *Frogs*, were of conscious interest in classical Athens.[39] If character is thought of as a matter of the distinctively individual and particular, then conventions of stylized elevation will place restrictions on its presentation in serious literature, while it will be left to the earthier genres of comic and satirical writing to bring us close to the texture of individual lives. But it is precisely the premiss here—the alignment of character with the distinctively, even uniquely, individual—which cannot be automatically assumed for Greek culture. The strong tradition of literary stylization which I have adduced marks a significant divergence from the kinds of individualism familiar to us in our own dominant literary forms, and involves a countervailing tendency towards the understanding and evaluation of people by reference to wider, ethical categories and standards; and it is just these standards or *aretai* which, as was earlier stressed, form the foundation for Greek judgements of character.

While it might at first sight be thought related to this ethical tendency, Isocrates' lack of psychological inwardness with his subject requires a different explanation, though one which

---

[38] But the *Characters* well shows how a detailed texture of characterization (personal mannerisms, quirks of speech, etc.) does not eliminate ethical evaluation, and need not have an individualistic focus either.

[39] See esp. *Ran.* 1043–62 for the criticism of Euripidean 'realism' as destructive of the (ethically and stylistically) elevated tone of tragedy.

again reflects the nature of literary tradition. Large areas of
Greek literature—represented by much elegy and iambus, by
epinician lyric, and by much history, oratory, and
philosophy—depend primarily on descriptive and narrative
means of characterization. Standing in a broad, though not
unequivocal, contrast to this material are those genres—
principally epic, tragedy, and comedy—which make extensive
use of *dramatic* modes. These two broad categories are meant to
be indicative of major modes of presenting character, but they
are not, of course, exclusively separate: direct speech, the dramatic mode, has its limited place in the first of them (influencing historiography, for example), just as descriptive means do
in the second. Even so, the contrast between the modes as such
is real and important.

   The first mode, the descriptive or narrative, tends to give us
more 'distanced', sometimes moralistic, images of individuals,
set firmly in the terms of general ethical categories. The second,
while not eschewing material of this same kind, has in addition
the means to bring characters close to its audiences: to put them
dramatically before our eyes, to let them speak for themselves,
even, at the extreme, to give us privileged access to the workings of their minds in the kind of scene of which I earlier considered an example from *Odyssey* 20. Both major modes of
representation and characterization develop distinctively literary techniques, but they are also derived from non-literary
ways of looking at people in the world.[40] That Isocrates'
Evagoras employs exclusively the first of these two modes largely
explains the work's lack of psychological closeness to its subject.
The intrinsic strength of the dramatic mode, on the other hand,
lies in its capacity to convey immediacy, vividness, and intensity of personal life, and to allow us to observe at close range, so
to speak, the processes of thought, feeling, and motivation.

   But this closeness of focus does not entail a view of people that
is radically different from or more individualistic than the kind
conveyed by narrative and descriptive means. The dramatic
mode does not commit one to seeing persons as irreducibly private individuals, since the psychological workings of the mind

   [40] See D. W. Harding, 'Psychological Processes in the Reading of Fiction', *Brit.
Journ. of Aesthetics*, 2 (1962), 133–47 (repr. in H. Osborne (ed.), *Aesthetics in the Modern
World* (London, 1968), 300–17).

are rarely conceived in the Greek tradition as an enclosed world of their own (though they may sometimes *conceal* or dissemble their contents), but rather as the source and springs of ethically significant action. Much of the traditional Greek understanding of character lies in the attempt to find ways of affirming the authentic force and integrity of human agency and responsibility, the components of character, at the point where many different potencies—internal and external; psychological, social, natural, and divine—intersect and become entangled. Against this background, the conception of character, the sense of a person as potentially the source of his own motivation and ethical agency, has to be won and maintained in the face of the competing possibility that people are at the mercy of powers and causes larger than themselves.

3

Agamemnon's Role in the *Iliad*

OLIVER TAPLIN

I

We have a good idea of what a succinct characterization of Agamemnon in the *Iliad* should look like: phrases such as 'physically courageous, morally weak' or more fully 'A good fighter, he is arrogant and brusque when confident of success ... easily deceived and prone to misunderstand ... combines the self-confident and defeatist sides ...'.[1] For myself I like 'cloaked in unscrupulousness' or 'wrapped in lack of moral sense', which is of course what Achilles calls him at 1. 149: ἀναιδείην ἐπιειμένε. This is, however, the view of a far from scholarly or impartial party and I shall not be calling on Achilles' words again. None the less, the citation makes the point that characterization is not a strand or a code which subsists in its own right; it is distilled from an interpretation or a complex of interpretations.

This chapter is, in effect, a plate of *crudités* picked out of a book on the poetic architecture of the *Iliad* which I hope to complete in the near future. I am most grateful for constructive criticism from the audiences at the Oxford Colloquium on 'Characterization and Individuality in Greek Literature' and at the University of California at Los Angeles. I have not attempted any thoroughgoing bibliography and should like to acknowledge at the start that I have been helped by many writings that do not appear in the footnotes, which I have tried to keep few. At the time of first drafting, I had not looked at two substantial studies of Agamemnon in the *Iliad*, namely E. Kalinka, '*Agamemnon in der Ilias* (*Sitzungsber. Ak. Wiss. Wien*, 221/4; 1943) (60 pages), and A. M. van Erp Taalman Kip, *Agamemnon in epos en tragedie* (Assen, 1971), 8–69 (Eng. summary on pp. 257–63). I was glad to find, therefore, that the gist of both was similar to mine without too much duplication (though Kalinka's initial thesis, that the portrait of Agamemnon is that of a real and nasty Mycenaean king which the poet has not managed to expurgate, is incredible!). I can do no more than register L. Collins, *Studies in Characterisation in the* Iliad (Frankfurt, 1988). All substantial passages of translation of the *Iliad* are taken, occasionally with minor changes, from the new Penguin trans. by Martin Hammond (Harmondsworth, 1988). I am most grateful for permission to use this version which is at once close and yet in good English.

[1] Drawn, purely for illustration, from two contributors to this volume, respectively M. Silk, *The Iliad* (Cambridge, 1987), 85, and J. Griffin, *Homer on Life and Death* (Oxford, 1980), 70–3.

I shall bring to bear two particular subjects of interpretation which have, I think, been far from exhausted, and which both point to an even less favourable picture of Agamemnon than is usual.[2] One is the construction of the poem as a whole, once one applies a unitarian working hypothesis. The other, which I shall consider first, is the political and social relationships among the Achaeans.

Most readers tend naturally to adapt the *Iliad* to the political and military hierarchies most familiar to them. Thus, for example, Pope's translation calls to mind the British monarchy, when in the first pages we find Chalcas saying:

> Bold is the task, when subjects, grown too wise,
> Instruct a monarch where his error lies

and Agamemnon himself (to Achilles):

> Hence shalt thou prove my might, and curse the hour
> Thou stood'st a rival of imperial power.

This kind of thing was no less prevalent in the ancient world than in the modern. The scholia, written in the times of Hellenistic monarchy or of Roman empire, betray political assumptions in their treatment of Agamemnon. N. Richardson has to concede: 'scholia reflect attempts to defend him from criticism, as he is the Greek leader and so ought to be a model of kingship, but', he adds, 'they cannot whitewash him entirely'.[3] Even the 'neutrality' of Erbse's Index to his great edition of the scholia hides Roman presuppositions: Ἀγαμέμνων is glossed as 'dux Graecorum' while Ἀχιλλεύς is glossed 'Achilles'!

An even more authoritarian social structure is presupposed by a reader of yet earlier times than the scholia. Plato in *Republic* book 3 (389e–390a) excludes from his polity the kind of abusive language which Achilles addresses to Agamemnon

---

[2] I have no wish to conceal that there have been accounts of Agamemnon of a similar tenor and approach to mine. I have in mind, above all, W. Schadewaldt, *Iliasstudien* (Leipzig, 1943; repr. Darmstadt, 1966), 37–9, esp. 38 n. 1; also Kalinka, 'Agamemnon'; van Erp Taalman Kip, *Agamemnon*; S. E. Bassett, 'The ἁμαρτία of Achilles', *TAPA* 65 (1934), 48–58; D. Lohmann, *Die Komposition der Reden in der Ilias* (Berlin, 1970), 35, 76, 221. W. Donlan, 'Homer's Agamemnon', *CW* 65 (1971–2), 109–15, does his best to be sympathetic towards Agamemnon, while recognizing his failings.

[3] 'Literary Criticism in the Exegetical Scholia to the *Iliad*: A Sketch', *CQ* NS 30 (1980), 272.

(quoting 1. 225 ff.), and condemns καὶ ὅσα ἄλλα τις ἐν λόγῳ ἢ ἐν ποιήσει εἴρηκε νεανιεύματα ἰδιωτῶν εἰς ἄρχοντας ['all such impertinences, in prose or verse, spoken by commoners against their lords']. Were Plato justified in regarding Achilles as an ἰδιώτης and Agamemnon as his ἄρχων, then clearly this would be of fundamental importance for the characterization of the two men and for the whole interpretation of the poem.

So if our assessment of Agamemnon's character is closely bound up with his roles and relationships, then we have to give some thought to those roles and relationships. I suggest that the political world of the *Iliad* has been generally over-simplified, and that, as a combination of the cause and effect of this, Agamemnon's faults have been over-indulgently excused. One of the main simplifications has been the instinctive use of the definite article with Agamemnon's role. He is '*the* king' or '*the* general', etc. In his recent book R. Drews denies, rightly in my view, that Agamemnon is 'the *basileus*', but does no better by substituting that he is 'the commander-in-chief'.[4] I shall argue, first, that there is no such clear hierarchy, and no absolute authority for Agamemnon. It is time to get down to the words of the poem.

The passage that most people think of first in this connection is the last part of Nestor's attempt at reconciliation in book 1.

> μήτε σὺ τόνδ' ἀγαθός περ ἐὼν ἀποαίρεο κούρην,
> ἀλλ' ἔα, ὡς οἱ πρῶτα δόσαν γέρας υἷες Ἀχαιῶν.
> μήτε σύ, Πηλείδη, ἔθελ' ἐριζέμεναι βασιλῆϊ
> ἀντιβίην, ἐπεὶ οὔ ποθ' ὁμοίης ἔμμορε τιμῆς
> σκηπτοῦχος βασιλεύς, ᾧ τε Ζεὺς κῦδος ἔδωκεν.
> εἰ δὲ σὺ καρτερός ἐσσι, θεὰ δέ σε γείνατο μήτηρ,
> ἀλλ' ὅ γε φέρτερός ἐστιν, ἐπεὶ πλεόνεσσιν ἀνάσσει.

You, great man though you are, do not take the girl from him, but let her be, as the sons of the Achaeans gave to her to him in the beginning as his prize. And you, son of Peleus, do not seek open quarrel with the king (βασιλῆϊ), since there is no equality with the honour granted to a sceptred king (βασιλεύς), whom Zeus has glorified. You may be a man of strength, with a goddess for your mother, but he is the more powerful, because his role is wider. (1. 275–81).

4 *Basileus: The Evidence for Kingship in Geometric Greece* (New Haven, 1983), 100–4.

But it would surely be a mistake to infer from 277–9 that Agamemnon is *the* king, *the* βασιλεύς, since it is clear from many passages that there is a multiplicity of βασιλῆες. Is there any passage which confines the title βασιλεύς to Agamemnon? I shall examine what seem to be the three best candidates.

First, at 1. 410 Achilles wants Zeus to harm the Achaeans ἵνα πάντες ἐπαύρωνται βασιλῆος ['so that they all may have enjoyment of their king (βασιλῆος)']. I suggest that the phrasing there conveys the contemptuous implication that by their subservient acquiescence in Agamemnon's behaviour the other leading Achaeans have behaved as if they were below the status of βασιλεύς. The second passage, often cited in this connection in ancient and modern times, is Odysseus' words when he is rallying the scattered troops:

> οὐ μέν πως πάντες βασιλεύσομεν ἐνθάδ᾽ Ἀχαιοί.
> οὐκ ἀγαθὸν πολυκοιρανίη · εἷς κοίρανος ἔστω,
> εἷς βασιλεύς, ᾧ δῶκε Κρόνου πάϊς ἀγκυλομήτεω.

We cannot all be kings (βασιλεύομεν) here, every one of the Achaeans. To have each man his own master is ruin: there must be one master, one king (βασιλεύς), the man endowed by the son of devious-minded Kronos. (2. 203–5).

But this one chief is not Agamemnon. This is what Odysseus says to any δήμου ἄνδρα ['common man'] that he encounters (198), as opposed to any βασιλῆα καὶ ἔξοχον ἄνδρα ['king or man of importance'] (188)—there is a different speech for them. In other words, he is not saying that the whole army should have one single βασιλεύς, but only that every common man should have one. Thirdly, Nestor gives in book 9 an interesting reason why Agamemnon should provide a feast for the leaders:

> Ἀτρεΐδη, σὺ μὲν ἄρχε · σὺ γὰρ βασιλεύτατός ἐσσι.
> δαίνυ δαῖτα γέρουσιν · ἔοικέ τοι, οὔ τοι ἀεικές.

But then you, son of Atreus, should take the lead, as you are the greatest king [lit. 'the most βασιλεύς'] among us. Give a feast for the elders: it is right for you to do this, and quite what is proper. (9. 69–70).

But this curious superlative suggests precisely that his standing as βασιλεύς is not absolute but is a matter of comparative degree. This is confirmed by Agamemnon's own use of the comparative βασιλεύτερος at 9. 160.[5]

Returning to Nestor in book 1, it might be claimed that Agamemnon is the only σκηπτοῦχος βασιλεύς ['sceptred king'] recalling the emphasis on the Zeus-given ancestral sceptre of the Pelopids (2. 100–9).[6] But most if not all βασιλῆες have sceptres: thus, for example, the one on the shield of Achilles stands watching the harvest σκῆπτρον ἔχων ['holding his sceptre'] (18. 557), and at 2. 86 there is a multiplicity of σκηπτοῦχοι βασιλῆες (so too, by the way, διοτρεφέες βασιλῆες are plural, at e.g. 1. 176, 2. 445). So far as I can see, Nestor is only saying, in a rather overblown way, that not every σκηπτοῦχος βασιλεύς has equal honour, and that Zeus has not given them all glory. This wisdom turns out, I should add, to be true, but against Agamemnon and in favour of Achilles. Fooled by the Dream Agamemnon is νήπιος, οὐδὲ τὰ ἤδη ἅ ῥα Ζεὺς μήδετο ἔργα ['poor fool, he knew nothing of Zeus' design'] (2. 38); and when he prays for victory on that very day, Zeus not only does not grant it, but gives him 'joyless hardship' (2. 419–20). Yet Agamemnon believes, like Nestor, that Zeus grants him special τιμή (1. 175).

So Nestor cannot be treated as the last word. He is, after all, a character caught up in the action, who is attempting to take the steam out of the quarrel; he cannot give a god's-eye, or an audience's-eye, adjudication. He is saying, in effect, that they are both right and both wrong. Yet the points he makes are hardly equally balanced. The objection to Agamemnon—that he is taking away the γέρας, the special prize,[7] already bestowed by the Achaeans—is more 'respectable' than that against Achilles—that Agamemnon rules over more men. That is true enough, and confirmed by the Catalogue, where Achilles has forty ships of men while Agamemnon has brought a hundred, which is most of all (though Nestor with ninety and

---

[5] βασιλεύτερος also occurs in a less controversial context at *Od.* 15. 533. The question of the meaning of βασιλεύς has been usefully reopened not only by Drews, *Basileus*, but also by A. G. Geddes, 'Who's Who in Homeric Society?', *CQ*, NS 34 (1984), 28 ff.; and T. Rihll, 'Kings and Commoners in Homeric Society', *LCM* 11/6 (1986), 89–91.

[6] C. M. Bowra, *Tradition and Design in the Iliad* (Oxford, 1930), 173, even writes 'his divine right is symbolised by his sceptre'.

[7] The institution of the γέρας, and its difference from ordinary booty, has not been given sufficient attention in recent discussions of the rights and wrongs of the quarrel.

Diomedes with eighty are not far behind). But Nestor's point—that if it came to a punch-up Agamemnon's men would overwhelm Achilles'—does not amount to a justification of Agamemnon's behaviour. And Nestor does not know the one big thing Achilles knows; that Athena has given him personal assurance that he will be recompensed, and that she has described Agamemnon's behaviour as ὕβρις (214).

If it is granted that Agamemnon is not *the* βασιλεύς, might he still be uniquely the ἄναξ ἀνδρῶν ['lord of men']? It is true that this formula is used predominantly of him, but it is also applied to Anchises, Aeneas, Augeias, Euphetes, and Eumelus. Similarly, ποιμένα (and –ι) λαῶν ['shepherd of the people'] is used of many others besides Agamemnon. εὐρὺ κρείων ['broad-ruling'] occurs eleven times with Agamemnon, and otherwise just once of Poseidon; but that reflects the extent of his kingdom rather than any absolute status.

Agamemnon is presented as a powerful ruler, a considerable warrior, and a dominating presence. I am questioning whether Homer, by means of this power and status, encourages us to admire, defend, or like him; and I am suggesting, rather, that the early narrative leads us to feel that, despite all his power, he is a nasty piece of work. In the nutshell of the Homeric formula, ἀγαθός περ ἐών, though he has every advantage, he behaves like a rat.

Agamemnon's stature is mainly established in books 2 to 4, after the initial quarrel and before the actual battle (I shall finally return to book 1 after looking at the rest of the poem). The first time that he is unreservedly pre-eminent is at the summons for the parade at 2. 441 ff., where he is singled out by similes concluding:

> τοῖον ἄρ' Ἀτρείδην θῆκε Ζεὺς ἤματι κείνῳ,
> ἐκπρεπέ' ἐν πολλοῖσι καὶ ἔξοχον ἡρώεσσιν.

so Zeus made the son of Atreus on that day, outstanding in the mass and foremost among the heroes. (2. 482–3).

During the Catalogue he is similarly distinguished, especially by lines 579–80; but note that he takes his place in the order, and that the opportunity is not taken to mark him formally out as *the* king or commander-in-chief. In the *teichoscopia* Agamemnon is the first of only four leaders whom Priam picks out, and he comments:

> καλὸν δ' οὕτω ἐγὼν οὔ πω ἴδον ὀφθαλμοῖσιν,
> οὐδ' οὕτω γεραρόν · βασιλῆϊ γὰρ ἀνδρὶ ἔοικε.

but I have never yet set eyes on a man so fine-looking or so dignified: he has the look of a king. (3. 169–70).

He is indeed ἀμφότερον βασιλεύς τ' ἀγαθὸς κρατερός τ' αἰχμητής ['both a good king and a strong fighter with the spear'] (179), replies Helen, making the most of her self-reproach.

It confirms Agamemnon's importance that it is he who in book 4 goes round inspecting and exhorting the Achaeans in the *epipolēsis* (223–421); but the figure he cuts there is less handsome. After speaking favourably to several leaders, he is vehemently rude to Odysseus without any good cause (327 ff.). Odysseus contradicts him firmly, and while Agamemnon retracts fairly, his initial haste and discourtesy are patent. Finally he goes on to censure Diomedes with just as little cause (365 ff.). Sthenelus answers back, but Diomedes overrules him. He does not resent Agamemnon's taunts:

> τούτῳ μὲν γὰρ κῦδος ἅμ' ἕψεται, εἴ κεν Ἀχαιοὶ
> Τρῶας δῃώσωσιν ἑλωσί τε Ἴλιον ἱρήν,
> τούτῳ δ' αὖ μέγα πένθος Ἀχαιῶν δῃωθέντων.

because his will be the glory that follows if the Achaeans slaughter the Trojans and capture sacred Ilios, but his again the depth of grief if the Achaeans are slaughtered. (4. 415–17).

Diomedes' response is in striking contrast to Achilles' in book 1. But the fact that Agamemnon does not similarly alienate him does not make his ill-founded domineering any more well-advised or admirable.

In the fighting that follows (book 5 to 8) Agamemnon confirms his place as one of the leading Achaean warriors, though his prowess is less distinguished than that of Ajax and Odysseus, let alone Diomedes. He is not among the first to kill, but he heads a catalogue of Achaean hits at 5. 37 ff., and is eighth in a list of ten at 6. 5–36. He is one of the nine who eventually offer themselves for the ballot to fight against Hector (7. 161 ff.), and he is one of the nine who lead an Achaean rally at 8. 253 ff. In discussion and negotiation, on the other hand, such as the arrangement of the duels in 3 and 7 and the assemblies at the end of 7, he takes a leading role, and is usually a sort of 'spokesman' for the Achaeans. So, while he is not the king or supreme commander in any official sense, he undeniably has a special status. He is in some way *at the centre* of the Achaeans. How should this be so?

I suggest that, in so far as Agamemnon's centrality is explained in the poem, it is because he is Menelaus' elder brother. The war is undertaken on Menelaus' quarrel. When Agamemnon fears that Menelaus has been fatally wounded, he supposes that the whole expedition will have to be abandoned (4. 169 ff.). But, for all practical purposes, the more powerful brother has taken over. Had it been Idomeneus' quarrel then he would have been the leader in the way that Agamemnon is; had it been Teucer's then Ajax would have been. Not everyone could have raised a large allied expedition, of course: the greater the power and wealth of the βασιλεύς, the greater the force he might recruit. Only the Atreidae, perhaps, could have gathered such a huge pan-Achaean force. The warriors have come to Troy, then, to fight for the τιμή of the Atreidae, one or both. Thus, for example, Krethon and Orsilochus, killed by Aeneas, came to Troy τιμὴν Ἀτρεΐδῃς, Ἀγαμέμνονι καὶ Μενελάῳ, | ἀρνυμένω ['to win honour (τιμή) for the sons of Atreus, Agamemnon and Menelaus'] (5. 552–3). At 17. 92 Menelaus himself recognizes that Patroclus κεῖται ἐμῆς ἕνεκ' ἐνθάδε τιμῆς ['lies here killed for my honour (τιμή)']. At *Odyssey* 14. 70 and 117 Odysseus is said to have gone to Troy Ἀγαμέμνονος εἵνεκα τιμῆς ['for the sake of Agamemnon's honour (τιμή)']. (I have abjured any quotation of Achilles.)

It is possible to make a coherent quasi-reconstruction of this sort of offensive alliance by piecing together scattered circumstantial details. This is like the method used by Moses Finley for transforming Homer into history, but, unlike him, I do not wish to claim that the presuppositions of the poem necessarily reflect the historical reality of any particular time or place. It may well be that the gathering of the host was an established episode in other epics. We know that the *Cypria* covered the one for Troy, though not at what length; and more importantly, the *Iliad*'s catalogue of ships evidently derives originally from

some such poem. Agamemnon's anecdote about Tydeus levy-
ing troops (4. 376 ff.) also presupposes such stories.

Here, then, is the 'scenario' implied by the *Iliad*. First the
person for whose τιμή the war is to be fought, or his representatives, go around collecting allies. In *Odyssey* 24. 115–19 Agamemnon recalls how he himself came with Menelaus to Ithaca to
raise Odysseus' support, and how it took them a whole month.
In *Iliad* book 11 Nestor, working on Patroclus, reminds him
how he and Odysseus came to Peleus' palace λαὸν ἀγείροντες
κατ᾽ Ἀχαιΐδα πουλυβότειραν ['on our journey through fertile
Achaea, gathering troops'] (770). (The same occasion is
recalled by Odysseus at 9. 252 ff.) After due hospitality, ἦρχον
ἐγὼ μύθοιο, κελεύων ὔμμ᾽ ἅμ᾽ ἕπεσθαι · | σφὼ δὲ μάλ᾽ ἠθέλετον . . .
['I began the talking, and urged you both to come with us. You
two were fully willing . . .'] (11. 780–1). In the course of
'urging' such envoys would presumably bring to bear pre-
existent relations and past obligations, and would hold out the
promise of booty and of glory. Once one leader has agreed to go
at the call of another, his subjects have less choice. When
Hermes pretends to be a young Myrmidon, he tells how he and
his six brothers shook lots to decide which one would follow
Achilles (24. 398–400). There would be even more pressure on
those who lived in the kingdoms of the Atreidae themselves. At
13. 663 ff. we hear of Euchenor of Corinth who came to his
death at Troy to avoid the fine (θωήν) that would have been
imposed; and at 23. 296 ff. there is Echepolos of Sicyon who
gave Agamemnon a superb horse in return for staying at home.

Once the host is gathered, there will be much feasting and
other morale-boosting activities at the expense of the summoner. At 8. 228 ff. Agamemnon reminds the Achaeans how
confident they were *en route* at Lemnos when they were full
of meat and drink. At this stage oaths of loyalty presumably
might be taken. But in the *Iliad* there are only three glancing
references to anything like an oath of this sort. At 2. 286–8
Odysseus says that in wanting to go home the Achaeans
οὐδέ τοι ἐκτελέουσιν ὑπόσχεσιν ἥν περ ὑπέσταν ['will not make
good the promise they undertook'] when they set out from
Argos, to return after sacking Troy. This undertaking sounds
less formal and less binding than an oath. Next Nestor rebukes
them:

πῆ δὴ συνθεσίαι τε καὶ ὅρκια βήσεται ἥμιν;
ἐν πυρὶ δὴ βουλαί τε γενοίατο μήδεά τ᾽ ἀνδρῶν,
σπονδαί τ᾽ ἄκρητοι καὶ δεξιαί, ᾗς ἐπέπιθμεν.

Where will our agreements be gone, and the oaths we swore? Let the fire take our deliberations and the strategies that men devised, our solemn pledges poured in wine, and the giving of right hands, in which we had trusted! (2. 339-41).

This is certainly a reference to proper oaths, but Nestor does not specify who took them nor whether they included loyalty to Agamemnon. Finally, Idomeneus replies to Agamemnon in the *epipolēsis*:

Ἀτρεΐδη, μάλα μέν τοι ἐγὼν ἐρίηρος ἑταῖρος
ἔσσομαι, ὡς τὸ πρῶτον ὑπέστην καὶ κατένευσα.

Son of Atreus, for my part I shall be fully loyal in your support, as I promised and pledged at the beginning. (4. 266-7).

This may refer to the initial agreement to join the expedition, rather than to a proper oath. There is no direct allusion whatsoever to the oath to Tyndareus taken by the suitors for Helen.[8] This oath may have been in Troy-poems before Homer; but if so, he has suppressed any allusion to it for the good reason that it would close up the open rights and wrongs of the dispute between Achilles and Agamemnon.

During the course of the war the summoner should do his best to preserve his troops, to keep up morale, and to be materially generous, especially with feasts. It is a precondition of the presence there of other leaders that those who fight well will be properly rewarded. It is, of course, in this very matter that Achilles claims that Agamemnon has been so inadequate as to have cancelled his obligations.

If this 'scenario' is along the right lines, then Agamemnon in relation to the leading Achaeans, who come from kingdoms other than Menelaus' or his own, has an authority—or centrality—which is not absolute, but is based on mutual obligation. It is, when one comes to think of it, essential for the poem that there should not be a definitive hierarchy, and that

---

[8] The earliest source [Hes.] *Cat.* fr. 204. 87-9 M-W, points out that Achilles was too young for the oath to Tyndareus. G. S. Kirk, *The* Iliad: *A Commentary*, i (Cambridge, 1985), on 1. 175-6 and on 1. 276-81, puts unwarranted emphasis on an oath of allegiance which he presumes to have been taken.

there should be an element of assessable obligation about Agamemnon's position. If Achilles could be simply put in front of
the firing-squad, or convicted of oath-breaking, then there
would be no real conflict sufficient to carry the epic. Granted
the underlying obligations which I have sketched, it makes
sense, on the one hand, for Calchas to allude to Agamemnon as
the man ὃς μέγα πάντων | Ἀργείων κρατέει καὶ οἱ πείθονται
Ἀχαιοί ['who holds great power over all the Argives and command among the Achaeans'] (1. 78–9)—because it is all the
Atreidae's show—while, on the other hand, Achilles can claim
without absurdity that Agamemnon has forfeited his right to
obedience from others. But what I am going to say in the
second half of this chapter does not depend on taking Achilles'
part (nor even necessarily on accepting my account of Agamemnon's political standing).

II

Up till now we have been looking mainly at the early books of
the poem, as it is there that Agamemnon's social and political
roles are established. I shall now go on to consider his place
within the shaping of the poem as a whole from book 9
onwards, before returning at the end to the very opening
scenes.

While he fights well enough in books 5 to 8, he hardly
emerges with flying colours. The casualties inflicted on the
Achaeans, especially in book 8, have been the worst during
nine years, and for the first time Hector and the Trojans are
able to bivouac outside the walls. This is the setting of Agamemnon's despairing speech to the meeting at 9. 16 ff., when he
proposes an ignominious return home. It consists almost entirely of lines repeated from his miscalculated proposal after the
dream at 2. 110–41; but there his speech was supposed to be
false, whereas here it is in earnest. There it met with enthusi-
astic acceptance; here he seems to have once again miscalculated the mood of the men, in that their response is silence and
grief (9. 27–30). Eventually it is Diomedes who contradicts him
and advocates a fight to the last, reminding Agamemnon of his
unfair rebuke in the *epipolēsis* (see p. 66 above). The Achaeans

approve, and Nestor protects Agamemnon by proposing a more private meeting of the elders.

At this Nestor diplomatically points out that it was against his advice that Agamemnon took the γέρας of another man, a man moreover granted τιμή by Zeus, and then advises him to climb down and to placate Achilles, concluding:

ἀλλ' ἔτι καὶ νῦν
φραζώμεσθ' ὥς κέν μιν ἀρεσσάμενοι πεπίθωμεν
δώροισίν τ' ἀγανοῖσιν ἔπεσσί τε μειλιχίοισι.

But even at this late day let us consider how we may appease him and win him over with soothing gifts and kind persuasion. (9. 109–13).

Agamemnon accepts Nestor's assessment, admitting his ἄτη folly; and he proceeds to catalogue a huge inventory of gifts (indeed it perhaps includes *too many* women—note the change at 19. 242 ff.). But what about the *words*? In 47 lines Agamemnon cannot even bring himself to pronounce Achilles' name. His phrasing bristles with resentment, which emerges openly in the last four lines, 158–61 (lines that Odysseus is careful not to pass on).

Critics seem to have been so overwhelmed by the quantity of Agamemnon's gifts that they have not noticed his failure to say anything about how the offer is to be conveyed or by whom. Nestor is more alert:

δῶρα μὲν οὐκέτ' ὀνοστὰ διδοῖς Ἀχιλῆϊ ἄνακτι ·
ἀλλ' ἄγετε, κλητοὺς ὀτρύνομεν, οἵ κε τάχιστα
ἔλθωσ' ἐς κλισίην Πηληϊάδεω Ἀχιλῆος.

no one can now find fault with the gifts (δῶρα μὲν) you offer to lord Achilles. Come then, let us pick men and send them on their way to go quickly to the hut of Achilles son of Peleus. (9. 164–6)

Behind Nestor's μέν I detect disappointment that Agamemnon has made no proposal to go to Achilles in person;[9] at any rate, it surely implies that while Agamemnon has been strong with 'soothing gifts' he has not excelled with 'kind persuasion'. Of course it would not be *in character* for Agamemnon to go to Achilles personally and make things up with him. That is the whole point.

⁹ Similarly A. Thornton, *Homer's Iliad: Its Composition and the Motif of Supplication* (Hypomnemata, 81; Göttingen, 1984), 126–7.

So Agamemnon stays behind in his tent with the other leaders, and there Odysseus and Ajax find him when they return from Achilles (9. 669 ff.). Again, as at the meeting before the embassy, there is consternation, and again it is Diomedes who speaks with blunt practicality. He advises Agamemnon that at dawn he should draw up the army καὶ δ᾽ αὐτὸς ἐνὶ πρώτοισι μάχεσθαι ['and fight yourself among the leaders'] (9. 709). Agamemnon goes along with this, and next morning his arming scene is given special attention (11. 15–46). His alarming shield creates, as J. Armstrong puts it, 'an atmosphere of foreboding and uncertainty which is most appropriate to the context and the subsequent story'.[10]

The core of Agamemnon's *aristeia* lasts nearly 100 lines, from 11. 91 to 180. We must not be mesmerized by the label *aristeia*: this is a briefer and less distinguished spell in the spotlight than those enjoyed by Achilles, Diomedes, Patroclus, Ajax, and Hector. He drives the Trojans back to Troy, but there is no sense of substantial strategic gain; there is more signposting towards the ruthlessness of Agamemnon's killing. He kills two sons of Priam, whom Achilles had previously ransomed, like a lion crunching fawns (101–21). He then rejects the supplication of Peisandros and Hippolochos, the sons of Antimachos, in very much the same style as his intervention at 6. 53–65 when Menelaus had been inclined to spare the suppliant Adrestos.[11] Note how Agamemnon chops off both Hippolochos' arms at the shoulders ὅλμον δ᾽ ὣς ἔσσευε κυλίνδεσθαι δι᾽ ὁμίλου ['and sent the trunk rolling log-like through the mass of men'] (147). B. Fenik remarks that brutal butchery is the speciality of certain warriors, for instance Meriones and the lesser Ajax; and that 'grisly slayings are typical for Agamemnon'.[12]

[10] 'The Arming Motif in the *Iliad*', *AJP* 79 (1958), 345—a justly classic article, for its demonstration that Homer uses the repetition characteristic of oral poetry constructively.

[11] I should add that I take αἴσιμα παρειπών ['saying what seemed right'] at 6. 62 not as the poet's own moral corroboration, but as marking that the sentiments strike Menelaus as αἴσιμα. So also with the same formula at 7. 121, or indeed with ἀλλὰ κακῶς ἀφίει ['he dismissed him shamefully'] at 1. 25, where Homer is not explicitly condemning Agamemnon—it is for Chryses that the dismissal is κακόν. See, more generally, Griffin, *Homer on Life and Death*, 85 n. 9; id., 'Words and Speakers in Homer', *JHS* 106 (1986), 36 ff.

[12] *Typical Battle Scenes in the* Iliad, (Hermes Einzelschr., 21; Wiesbaden, 1968), 15, 84.

When Agamemnon is getting near the walls, Zeus sends Iris
with a message to Hector (181 ff.): that as long as Agamemnon
is active, he should hold back, but that once he is wounded and
leaves the field, it will be Hector's day. The narrative of Agamemnon's *aristeia* resumes with a grand invocation to the
Muses (218–20)—'tell me who was the first to stand against
Agamemnon'—but, with Iris' message fresh in mind, the invocation prepares for the wounding of Agamemnon rather
than his triumph. And we do not have to wait long: in fact he
kills only two more Trojans, Iphidamas and his eldest brother
Koon (their parents Antenor and Theano lose a fine dynasty of
sons during the *Iliad*). Koon has his head cut off over his
brother as he tries to avenge and rescue him, but he wins glory
first by stabbing Agamemnon in the arm. The wound is bad
enough to take him off the field, and it is recalled on the next
day at 19. 53. So Agamemnon leaves the battlefield for the last
time in the *Iliad*, before it is half over. He exhorts the Argives to
carry on defending the ships ἐπεὶ οὐκ ἐμὲ μητίετα Ζεὺς | εἴασε
Τρώεσσι πανημέριον πολεμίζειν ['since Zeus the counsellor has
not allowed me to fight the whole day long against the
Trojans'] (278–9). Immediately we have

> ἔνθα τίνα πρῶτον, τίνα δ' ὕστερον ἐξενάριξεν
> Ἕκτωρ Πριαμίδης, ὅτε οἱ Ζεὺς κῦδος ἔδωκεν;

Then who was the first, and who the last slaughtered by Hector,
Priam's son, when Zeus gave him the glory? (11. 299–300)

—less than 100 lines after the invocation of the Muses for Agamemnon. So much for his special τιμή from Zeus.

His next prominent appearance will be when he returns
Briseis in book 19, but there are two passages worth attention
before that. Nestor gathers the three disabled leaders to discuss
the battle. For a third time Agamemnon proposes ignominious
flight home (14. 65–81). But while his speeches in books 2 and 9
were almost identical, here he makes the proposal that the ships
nearest the sea should be launched at once and moored in
deep water, leaving the rest to be collected at night. Odysseus
immediately and bluntly rebukes Agamemnon, not only for
his cowardice but for the strategic lunacy of trying to launch
ships while the enemy hacks at you (presumably they would
also loot and burn the ships left behind). Agamemnon gives in

without demur, saying that he will go along with any better plan; and again it is the younger Diomedes who gives courageous counsel (110–32). It is true that the three other leaders, not the whole host, are the only witnesses, and that Poseidon gives Agamemnon some bluff encouragement soon after (135 ff.); even so, this is perhaps his lowest point of cowardice and incompetence.

Also relevant is a passage which does not involve Agamemnon directly, but gives a god's insight into Achaean morale. Soon after Hector and the Trojans have breached the wall and gates, Poseidon, in the form of Calchas, rallies the young second-rung Achaean leaders (13. 95–124). Pointing to the Trojans' unprecendented success he says:

> νῦν δὲ ἑκὰς πόλιος κοίλῃς ἐπὶ νηυσὶ μάχονται
> ἡγεμόνος κακότητι μεθημοσύνῃσί τε λαῶν,
> οἳ κείνῳ ἐρίσαντες ἀμυνέμεν οὐκ ἐθέλουσι
> νηῶν ὠκυπόρων, ἀλλὰ κτείνονται ἀν' αὐτάς.
> ἀλλ' εἰ δὴ καὶ πάμπαν ἐτήτυμον αἴτιός ἐστιν
> ἥρως Ἀτρεΐδης, εὐρὺ κρείων Ἀγαμέμνων,
> οὕνεκ' ἀπητίμησε ποδώκεα Πηλεΐωνα,
> ἡμέας γ' οὔ πως ἔστι μεθιέμεναι πολέμοιο.
> ἀλλ' ἀκεώμεθα θᾶσσον· ἀκεσταί τοι φρένες ἐσθλῶν.

But now they have brought the fight far from their city right to our hollow ships, through the fault of our leader and the reluctance of his people, who in their resentment of him are not willing to fight for the speedy ships, but allow themselves to be killed among them. But even if all the blame truly belongs to the hero son of Atreus, wide-ruling Agamemnon, for his slighting of the swift-footed son of Peleus, yet we cannot possibly hold back from fighting. No, we must be quick to set it right—brave men's hearts are easily righted. (13. 107–15)

Poseidon takes special care with line 111 not to commit himself on whether Agamemnon really is fully to blame. But the passage only makes sense if it carries the implications that it is widely felt among the Achaeans that Agamemnon is to blame (αἴτιος); but that the people (which includes these leaders) are inclined to attribute κακότης ['fault'] to him; and that this is one reason why they are not fighting at their best. So this suggests an element in their motivation and morale which could not have easily been brought to the fore in any other way: that Agamemnon's treatment of Achilles—whatever the rights and wrongs—has damaged the will of the Achaean λαός to fight against the Trojans.

The predisposition to make the best of Agamemnon has been nowhere more evident, perhaps, than in discussion of his so-called 'apology' in book 19.[13] Even that least authoritarian of scholars, E. R. Dodds, treated Agamemnon's words as though they were gospel and a clear source for early Greek ethics. According to Dodds and the orthodox view Agamemnon is not to blame and yet must still pay the price.[14] Certainly he says unequivocally:

> ἐγὼ δ' οὐκ αἴτιός εἰμι,
> ἀλλὰ Ζεὺς καὶ Μοῖρα καὶ ἠεροφοῖτις Ἐρινύς,
> οἵ τέ μοι ἐν ἀγορῇ φρεσὶν ἔμβαλον ἄγριον ἄτην,
> ἤματι τῷ ὅτ' Ἀχιλλῆος γέρας αὐτὸς ἀπηύρων.
> ἀλλὰ τί κεν ῥέξαιμι; θεὸς διὰ πάντα τελευτᾷ.

But I am not to blame, but rather Zeus and Fate and Erinys that walks in darkness: they put a cruel blindness in my mind at the assembly on that day when by my own act I took away his prize from Achilles. But what could I do? It is God who brings all things to their end. (19. 86–90)

And certainly he goes on to offer‚ Achilles reparation. But (unless I am miles off the track) the point of a claim of "οὐκ αἴτιος" ['not to blame'] is that this, if accepted, exempts you from retribution. To give only two examples out of many. In book 1 Achilles reassures the heralds who come to fetch Briseis: οὔ τί μοι ὔμμες ἐπαίτιοι, ἀλλ' Ἀγαμέμνων, | ὅ σφῶϊ προΐει ['It is not you I blame, but Agamemnon who has sent you'] (1. 335–6). They need not fear him, as he holds someone else to blame. In *Odyssey* 22. 350 ff. the bard Phemius pleads that he did not sing willingly and the suitors forced him to; and Telemachus confirms his plea—ἴσχεο μηδέ τι τοῦτον ἀναίτιον οὔταε χαλκῷ ['Hold back, do not strike this man with the sword as he is blame-free'] (356). Since he is blame-free, he does not have to

---

[13] I have selected the central argument from the fuller case in an unpublished lecture 'Explanation and Self-justification in the *Iliad*' which I gave in 1986 in London, Regensburg, and Tübingen.

[14] There is an unusual degree of agreement among scholars as various as E. R. Dodds, *The Greeks and the Irrational* (Berkeley, 1951), 3; A. W. H. Adkins, *Merit and Responsibility* (Oxford, 1960), 51–2; H. Lloyd-Jones, *The Justice of Zeus* (Berkeley, 1971), 23; and M. M. Willcock, *A Companion to the* Iliad (Chicago, 1976), 217.

suffer. Of course, it is not so simple when the third party who is held to blame is the gods: double motivation and hence human responsibility is the usual model in Homer.[15] So any claim to put *all* the blame on the gods is open to contradiction, just as Helen herself does not accept Priam's attempt to exculpate her (3. 164: οὔ τί μοι αἰτίη ἐσσί, θεοί νύ μοι αἴτιοί εἰσιν ['It is not you I blame: I blame the gods']), and as Zeus at the very start of the *Odyssey* rejects the way that mortals blame their troubles on the gods. Thus, to return to Agamemnon's 'apology', when he says that the gods are αἴτιοι, not he, and that *since* this is so he will give Achilles recompense—

> ἀλλ' ἐπεὶ ἀασάμην καί μευ φρένας ἐξέλετο Ζεύς,
> ἂψ ἐθέλω ἀρέσαι, δόμεναί τ' ἀπερείσι' ἄποινα.

But since I was blinded and Zeus took away my wits, I am ready to take it back and offer the appeasement of limitless reparation. (19. 137–8)

—he is, according to my argument, indulging in obvious special pleading. This fudging is only left unchallenged because no one wants to prolong the quarrel.

But this unorthodox interpretation of the 'apology' is not essential in order to see that Agamemnon emerges from the book 19 meeting in a less than golden light. As in book 1, it is Achilles who has to summon it in the first place. He then opens his brief and direct speech (56–73) with a vocative, Ἀτρεΐδη, and he uses conciliatory duals and first-person plurals. Agamemnon's reply, on the other hand, is long and uncomfortable (78–144). He sits throughout, or at least he does not stand in the proper place.[16] He begins with awkward parrying; he never uses any vocative to Achilles, whom he addresses only in the last five lines; and he does not use duals or first-person plurals either.[17] Once he has so gracelessly gone through this first stage,

---

[15] The classic exposition is A. Lesky, 'Göttliche und menschliche Motivation im homerischen Epos', *SHAW* 1961/4.

[16] l. 77, αὐτόθεν ἐξ ἕδρης, οὐδ' ἐν μέσσοισιν ἀναστάς ['from his place where he was, and not standing in the centre'], is ambiguous. H. Erbse, 'Bemerkungen zu Homer und zu seinen Interpreten', *Glotta*, 32 (1952), 243–7, favours standing. Thornton's suggestion (*Homer's Iliad: Its Composition*, 128–9) that Agamemnon's sitting would betoken 'the suppliant's self-abasement' is highly implausible.

[17] Cf. Lohmann, *Die Komposition der Reden*, 76 n. 133, which concludes 'selten jedoch zeigt sich sein sicheres Erfassen psychologischer Nuances so deutlich wie hier'.

he still has to hear Odysseus lecture him—'Ἀτρεΐδη, σὺ δ' ἔπειτα δικαιότερος καὶ ἐπ' ἄλλῳ | ἔσσεαι ['And you, son of Atreus, will be readier after this to give others their due'] (181-2)—and to hear Achilles agree (270-5) that he, Agamemnon, certainly was affected by ἄτη, 'folly' (note how Achilles restores double motivation and makes Agamemnon the subject of active verbs).

I have not seen the question asked, or answered: what are the last words of direct speech by Agamemnon in the entire *Iliad*? They are his public oath at 19. 258-66 that he has not sexually interfered with Briseis. Not exactly his finest hour.

Throughout books 20 to 22 Agamemnon is out of sight and out of mind. In 23 he plays a proper but unobtrusive part in the funeral of Patroclus (though without direct speech). In the funeral games, however, where Achilles is restored to heroic society through his admirable chivalry, Agamemnon does not participate in the chariot race, by far the most prestigious event, though he does lend his mares to Menelaus, who comes in a disputed third with them. In fact Agamemnon plays no part at all until the very last event, the spear-throwing. Achilles puts up as prizes a spear and a cauldron worth one ox. Agamemnon and the ever-willing Meriones step forward, but Achilles intervenes:

" Ἀτρεΐδη· ἴδμεν γὰρ ὅσον προβέβηκας ἁπάντων
ἠδ' ὅσσον δυνάμει τε καὶ ἤμασιν ἔπλευ ἄριστος·
ἀλλὰ σὺ μὲν τόδ' ἄεθλον ἔχων κοίλας ἐπὶ νῆας
ἔρχευ, ἀτὰρ δόρυ Μηριόνῃ ἥρωϊ πόρωμεν,
εἰ σύ γε σῷ θυμῷ ἐθέλοις· κέλομαι γὰρ ἔγωγε."
    Ὣς ἔφατ', οὐδ' ἀπίθησεν ἄναξ ἀνδρῶν Ἀγαμέμνων·
δῶκε δὲ Μηριόνῃ δόρυ χάλκεον· αὐτὰρ ὅ γ' ἥρως
Ταλθυβίῳ κήρυκι δίδου περικαλλὲς ἄεθλον.

'Son of Atreus, we know how superior you are to all others, and how much you are the best in strength for the spear-throw. So you take this prize with you on your way to the hollow ships, and let us give the spear to the hero Meriones, if that might be the wish of your own heart—that is what I suggest.'

So he spoke, and Agamemnon, lord of men, did not fail to agree. The hero gave the bronze spear to Meriones, and then handed his own beautiful prize to his herald Talthybios. (23. 890-7)

This can hardly be, as it is often claimed, the restoration of

Agamemnon to an honourable and admirable stature. The contest is minor; the prize is cheap (for the wrestling there was a tripod worth twelve oxen and a woman worth four). Above all, Agamemnon does not speak a word. By comparison, Diomedes, Odysseus, Menelaus, Antilochus, and even Nestor all go out in a blaze of attention. The truth is that the *Iliad* almost fades Agamemnon out, once he is no longer the object of Achilles' anger.

After this he is directly alluded to in the remaining 800 lines just twice, both in passing. At 24. 653–5 Achilles says that, if someone reports to Agamemnon that Priam is ransoming Hector, then there will be difficulties.[18] And Hermes says to Priam (686–8) that if Agamemnon catches him in the Achaean camp, there will have to be a huge ransom. So in both places Agamemnon's grasping meanness is contrasted with Achilles' magnanimity.

There may be one last indirect allusion. At 24. 697 ff. the first person to see Priam's return is Cassandra, who is looking out from the Pergamos. Why Cassandra? Some have suggested that through her prophecy she is associated with the fall of Troy. But there is nothing about her prophetic power in the *Iliad*. Both here and at 13. 365 it is her beauty that is noticed: she is Πριάμοιο θυγατρῶν εἶδος ἀρίστην ['the most beautiful of Priam's daughters'] and ἰκέλη χρυσέῃ Ἀφροδίτῃ ['beautiful as golden Aphrodite']. And who would take the most desirable of Priam's daughters at the sack of Troy? I wonder, then, whether Cassandra is there to make us think of Agamemnon's return to Mycenae with her. And this provokes similar thoughts about the allusion to Clytemnestra near the very beginning of the poem (1. 113–15), where Agamemnon compares her unfavourably to Chryseis.

So the overall shaping of Agamemnon's participation in the *Iliad* is very telling for our assessment of him. In the earlier books he is presented in such a way that it is convincing that he should be βασιλεύς of the largest contingent, and should have taken over from Menelaus the coordination and remuneration of the whole expedition. But his *aristeia* in book 11 is his last

---

[18] I am inclined to think that the jibing tone of this allusion is the explanation of ἐπικερτομέων (649). This is to agree with Leaf and to disagree both with Macleod ad loc. and with J. T. Hooker, 'A Residual Problem in *Iliad* 24', *CQ*, NS 36 (1986), 32–7.

major contribution, and even there he is wounded inside 300 lines. After that his sporadic contributions are subdued, when they are not humiliating. The poem never reinstates him. He is, furthermore, presented in an unfavourable light in more detailed ways. He fights brutally, he criticizes indiscriminately, he is incapable of apologizing with any warmth or nobility. Most important, if I am right about the political framework, Agamemnon is not up to providing the kind of recognition, the τιμή, that his associates have the right to expect. He lacks αἰδώς, and he lacks magnanimity.

This brings us close to the initial quarrel with Achilles; but I have vowed (for now) to steer clear of that ever-controversial ground. Let us turn, finally, to the first 120 lines of the *Iliad*, before the quarrel proper breaks out. I grant that I am open to the accusation of presenting this in the light of all that follows it. But no one is exempt from some such predisposition; and those who defend Agamemnon's behaviour here have undoubtedly applied their presuppositions about his kingship or supremacy.

Hardly anyone of those I have read seems to have appreciated what a bad start Agamemnon gets off to.[19] An old man comes to the Achaeans with ἄποινα ['reparation'] to ransom his daughter. It was evidently lucrative, quite apart from considerations of mercy, to ransom prisoners, especially women, as when, for example, Achilles ransomed Andromache's mother (6. 425–8—to her father since her husband was dead). But this father is also a fully accredited priest. After his courteous request, we hear:

> ἔνθ' ἄλλοι μὲν πάντες ἐπευφήμησαν Ἀχαιοὶ
> αἰδεῖσθαί θ' ἱερῆα καὶ ἀγλαὰ δέχθαι ἄποινα.

Then all the other Achaeans shouted their agreement, to respect the priest's claim and take the splendid ransom. (1. 22–3)

αἰδώς ['respect'] is the appropriate response, and everyone feels it, every single one except Agamemnon. His reply, with its first-person pronouns and possessives, and its emphasis on his bed as well as the loom, is worded to bring out his personality. And he

---

[19] A notable exception is J. Th. Kakridis, 'The First Scene with Chryses in the *Iliad*', in id., *Homer Revisited* (Lund, 1971), 125–37.

makes it clear that he is well aware that it is a priest he is taunting with the prospect of bastard grandchildren: he threatens
him with violence μή νύ τοι οὐ χραίσμῃ σκῆπτρον καὶ στέμμα
θεοῖο ['or you will have no protection from your god's staff and
sacred bands'] (28). It seems clear to me that within 35 lines of
the start of the *Iliad* Agamemnon is guilty of ἀναίδεια ['unscrupulousness' or 'disrespect'] towards both man and god. At the
least he is guilty of a serious error of judgement which leads
directly to the death of many of the λαός. Apollo's response is
immediate and terrifying; and there is no delay or dispute on
Olympus.

Yet it is Achilles who has to call the ἀγορή, and propose that
Apollo should be placated. And it is to Achilles that Calchas
looks for protection (78–9):

> ἦ γὰρ ὀΐομαι ἄνδρα χολωσέμεν, ὃς μέγα πάντων
> Ἀργείων κρατέει καί οἱ πείθονται Ἀχαιοί.

I think that I shall anger a man who holds great power over all the
Argives and command among the Achaeans.

It is suggestive that Calchas assumes—rightly—that Agamemnon's response will be anger. Achilles duly promises not to
abandon him, not in the face of anyone,

> οὐδ' ἢν Ἀγαμέμνονα εἴπῃς,
> ὃς νῦν πολλὸν ἄριστος Ἀχαιῶν εὔχεται εἶναι.

not even if you speak of Agamemnon, who claims to be far the best of
the Achaeans. (1. 90–1)

G. S. Kirk in his recent commentary (p. 61) describes the line
and a half as 'a gratuitous addition, this, and mildly insulting,
the beginning of trouble'. But is it gratuitous for Achilles to
make it clear that he knows to whom Calchas is alluding? And
is it the ἀρχὴ κακοῦ? Was that not Agamemnon's rejection of
Chryses?

So Calchas tells what we, the audience, already know to be
the simple truth. And Agamemnon launches into angry abuse:
μάντι κακῶν, οὐ πώ ποτέ μοι τὸ κρήγυον εἶπας ['Prophet of evil,
you have never told me anything to my liking'] (106).[20] We

---

[20] It has been suggested, even in antiquity, that this abuse of Calchas looks back to
the sacrifice of Iphigenia at Aulis, which is nowhere directly alluded to in the *Iliad*. If
so, this is another example of a light-touched allusion to Agamemnon's far from happy
career before and after the time of the *Iliad* itself.

know this to be unfair since Homer has just told us (71–2) how Calchas guided the ships to Troy (and at 2. 323 ff. we shall learn of his optimistic prophecy at Aulis).

If there is a 'beginning of trouble' during the ἀγορή, it is, rather, Agamemnon's command:

αὐτὰρ ἐμοὶ γέρας αὐτίχ' ἑτοιμάσατ', ὄφρα μὴ οἶος
Ἀργείων ἀγέραστος ἔω, ἐπεὶ οὐδὲ ἔοικε.

But you must produce another prize for me without delay, so that I am not the only one of the Argives without a prize (ἀγέραστος), as that would not be right. (1. 118–19)

The magnanimous man would resign himself to the unpredictability of divine interests. Why accept his claim that 'that would not be right'? It is typical of Agamemnon that he should make a new issue out of being ἀγέραστος.[21]

If he is justified in feeling that it is improper, then it is strange that no one does anything to correct this in book 19 when he finally gives up Briseis. Agamemnon remains ἀγέραστος right until the end of the poem, and no one protests. He remains the 'summoner', but the poem more or less discards him. He has been portrayed by Homer in such a way that we are satisfied with his eclipse.

Yet not everyone has seen Agamemnon in this poor light. We might feel condescending towards Spenser when we find him telling Raleigh, about the composition of *The Faerie Queene*, that he went to Homer 'who in the person of Agamemnon . . . ensampled the good governour'. But political and nationalist assumptions no less anachronistic may be found in the scholion on *Iliad* 1. 29–31, which may well go back to Aristarchus, and which reflects the mores of Hellenistic monarchs rather than of Homer. The three lines were athetized because they are indecorous, and because the threat is not one to offend the old man 'for even Chryses would have been glad for her to go to bed with the king'—ἡσμένισε γὰρ καὶ ὁ Χρύσης συνούσης αὐτῆς τῷ βασιλεῖ.[22]

---

[21] Griffin, 'Words and Speakers', 51, observes that the word is unique to him and characteristic of him.

[22] συνούσης is Cobet's attractive emendation of A's εἰπούσης which Erbse leaves in his text, but obelized.

In pointing out the distorting presuppositions of others, I do not pretend that I am free of them myself. My account of Agamemnon is admittedly that of an ἰδιώτης who is incorrigibly insubordinate towards ἄρχοντες. I hope to have illustrated, none the less, how characterization in Homer is not a self-sufficient element which can be extracted by itself. It is indivisible from critical interpretation in all its aspects.

4

Constructing Character in Greek Tragedy

P. E. EASTERLING

A dream of a shadow is man.

Critics of ancient drama are still keenly engaged in a long-running debate about character, despite a readiness on everyone's part nowadays to acknowledge significant differences between play-worlds and ordinary social reality. No one any longer asks the equivalent, in relation to Greek tragedy, of the question 'How many children had Lady Macbeth?', naïvely supposing that the stage figures can be studied as if they were beings with a continuing off-stage existence. And most critics are much more willing to recognize that the old certainties about character and personality can no longer be taken for granted. But there is still plenty of room for disagreement, and in this chapter I try to suggest why this should be so, without pretending to wish away, let alone resolve, the difficulties that arise.

A couple of contrasting examples will provide a starting-point. In 1973 Brian Vickers wrote:

Tragedy is about people, and what they do to each other ... The plays translate the clash of will and motive into forms, which although obeying complex literary conventions, still represent human actions, and convey them with intensity, if we are prepared to accept the conventions. Since they deal with fundamental behaviour they have an immediacy which can affect us as powerfully as any other works of literature. To appreciate it we need only to be able to think and feel.[1]

More recently, Simon Goldhill, defending his use of Barthes's distinction between a *figure* in a text and a *person* with 'a future, a consciousness, a soul', sums up his position as one which recognizes *both* 'the necessity of a (not *the*) concept of character

[1] *Towards Greek Tragedy* (London, 1973), 3.

in literary texts' *and* the fact 'that literary characters cannot be treated simply as individual, real, psychologically endowed people'.[2] Paradoxically enough, these two critics have something in common: both start from the premiss that we know what 'people' are (though to be fair to Goldhill, he draws attention to the fact that the self is differently perceived and constituted at different periods, and he insists on the difficulty of defining such notions as 'personality', 'identity', and 'individuality').

The underlying assumption of these, as of most contributions to the debate,[3] is that 'real people' and the 'real world', as opposed to stage-figures in the world of make-believe, are relatively stable and definable and can serve as some sort of yardstick (for comparison or contrast) when we come to think about theatrical creations. And of course in day-to-day living we have to behave and speak and be treated by others as if everyone knew what constitutes a person in the real world. But as soon as we look critically at these everyday assumptions we find them challenged on all sides: philosophers have long wrestled with the difficulty of defining what a person is;[4] psychologists offer different models of the self which are just as radically problematic;[5] sociologists and anthropologists looking at the interactions of human social life find the notion of 'reality' intimately bound up with that of role-playing.[6] Erving Goffman puts the matter neatly in relation to the theatrical analogy: 'All the world is not of course a stage, but the crucial ways in which it isn't are not easy to specify.'[7] Keir Elam adds the reminder that even our understanding of language is de-

---

[2] 'Goldhill on Molehills', *LCM* 11/10 (1986), 163. On 'figures', cf. M. Pfister, *Das Drama* (München, 1977), 221.

[3] My own included: 'Presentation of Character in Aeschylus', *G & R* 20 (1973), 3–18; 'Character in Sophocles', *G & R* 24 (1977), 121–9.

[4] See e.g. B. A. O. Williams, *Problems of the Self* (Cambridge, 1973); A. Rorty (ed.), *The Identities of Persons* (Berkeley, 1976); M. Carrithers, S. Collins, and S. Lukes (edd.), *The Category of the Person: Anthropology, Philosophy, History* (Cambirdge, 1985).

[5] See e.g. R. D. Laing, *Self and Others* (2nd edn., London, 1969; Harmondsworth, 1971), esp. 33–43, 81–2; J. Lacan, *The Language of the Self*, trans. A. Wilden (Baltimore, 1968); T. Mischel (ed.), *The Self* (Oxford, 1977); R. Harré, *Personal Being* (Oxford, 1983).

[6] See E. Burns, *Theatricality* (London, 1972), 122–43; E. Goffman, *Frame Analysis* (Cambridge, Mass., 1974), esp. 496–576.

[7] *The Presentation of Self in Everyday Life* (Harmondsworth, 1969), 78.

pendent on the dramatic model: he quotes John Lyons's remark that 'the use of [the term 'person'] by grammarians derives from their metaphorical conceptions of the language-event as a drama in which the principal is played by the first person, the role subsidiary to his by the second person, and all other roles by the third person'.[8] One might compare R. D. Laing's comment that the vocabulary of psychology is deeply implicated with theatrical terminology: illusion/delusion/collusion/elusion.[9]

Once we are willing to give more weight to the idea that our working assumptions about 'reality' and 'real people' are in fact quite provisional, we may be able to learn something relevant to the drama—Greek drama included—from sociology and its study of the mechanisms of social interaction. Goffman's book *Frame Analysis* is particularly helpful in this respect. The essential question it addresses is 'What is it that is going on here?', a rephrasing of William James's 'Under what circumstances do we think things real?'[10] This question must always relate to the perspective of those involved; Goffman uses the terms 'strip' and 'frame' to distinguish between 'any arbitrary slice or cut from the stream of ongoing activity' on the one hand and a 'definition of a situation ... built up in accordance with principles of organization which govern events' on the other, in each case as seen from the point of view of the participant (10). Such definitions of a situation are made in terms of what he calls the primary frameworks by which a particular society organizes its understanding (e.g. in the distinctions it makes between natural and social events—say, a thunderstorm as opposed to a fight), and also in terms of secondary frameworks, which fall into two main groups. He borrows from music the term 'key' for the first of these, which he describes as the 'set of conventions by which a given activity, one already meaningful in terms of some primary framework, is transformed into something patterned on this activity but seen by the participants to

---

[8] K. Elam, *The Semiotics of Theatre and Drama* (London, 1980), 133–4. Cf. R. Barthes, 'Structural Analysis of Narratives', in id., *Image, Music, Text*, trans. S. Heath (London, 1977), 104–14.

[9] *Self and Others*, 108.

[10] From 'The Perception of Reality', first published in *Mind*, July 1869, = *The Principles of Psychology*, ii (London 1890), 283–324, at 287.

be something quite else' (43–4). Thus a fight can be staged, imagined in fantasy, described in retrospect, analysed, ritually mimicked; and there is a functional likeness in the keying involved in many different kinds of activity. In, for example, make-believe in its various guises—contests and games, ceremonials, rehearsals, discussions, group psychotherapy, and psychological experiments—the key is what determines 'what it is we think is really going on' (45). The other main type of transformation is the fabrication, 'the intentional effort of one or more individuals to manage activity so that a party of one or more others will be induced to have a false belief about what it is that is going on' (83). Both are of interest to the student of the drama.

As the detail of Goffman's argument, particularly in his chapters on 'The Theatrical Frame' and 'The Frame Analysis of Talk', makes clear, the connection between on-stage and off-stage reality is intricate. Not only do we have to bear in mind the fact that the characters and onlookers of the drama are at the same time flesh-and-blood actors and theatre-goers, we also have to be aware of the extremely complex interplay between dramatic roles and roles in unscripted life; and of the peculiarities of 'the onlooking aspect of the audience activity', which is 'not something that is a staged and simulated replica of a real thing, as is the action on-stage. The off-stage version of onlooking is not a model for the theatrical kind; if anything the reverse is true. Onlooking belongs from the start to the theatrical frame' (130).[11] Elizabeth Burns makes a similar point:

> In relation to the theatre, reality and illusion are shifting terms. They do not denote opposites. Everything that happens on the stage can be called real, because it can be seen and heard to happen. It is perceived by the senses and is therefore as real as anything that happens outside the theatre. On the other hand there is an agreement between all those who take part in the performance, either as actors or [as] spectators, that the two kinds of real event inside and outside the theatre are not causally connected.[12]

This agreement, or 'collaboration' (Goffman, 135–6), is established by means of sets of conventions, which differ from

---

[11] Cf. Elam, *Semiotics*, 88, who distinguishes between 'dramatic' and 'theatrical' levels of reality.

[12] *Theatricality*, 15.

one tradition to another and from one medium to another
(stage, radio, film) but are remarkably similar in their functions. The distinctive features of the Greek tradition, particularly the use of the mask, have perhaps been too much
emphasized, under the powerful influence of John Jones:[13] it
seems that in *all* cases the job of conventions, whether masks or
stylized language or spatial or temporal brackets (stage line,
marked-out acting area, curtains, etc.) is, as Goffman puts it, to
'mark the *difference* between actual face-to-face interaction and
that kind of interaction when staged as part of a play' (138).[14]
It is a difference which enables us to remain aware that
'Oedipus' has not in fact just blinded himself, and that 'Medea'
is not about to kill flesh-and-blood children, a difference that
makes simultaneously possible deep engrossment in the fictive
world represented in the drama and detached critical appraisal
of the kind necessary for awarding prizes to the best actor or for
the best play.[15] The particularly interesting point emphasized
by Goffman (186) is that the techniques used by the audience
in 'following along' and 'reading off' what is happening by
attending to the relevant framing cues are the *same techniques* as
they use in relation to other, off-stage, events which they experience as onlookers.[16] For the theatrical frame, though distinctive, is not unique: there are many respects in which it
resembles other frames, and the mechanisms used for interpreting it are not fundamentally different from those by which
other sorts of 'keying' or 'fabrication' are identified: rituals, for
example, or games, or practical jokes.

If it is true, for the reasons sketched out above, that the world
of the drama is felt by the audience to be 'a lie that is not a
lie',[17] that we perceive its essential difference while 'reading it

---

[13] J. Jones, *On Aristotle and Greek Tragedy* (London, 1962).

[14] Burns, *Theatricality*, distinguishes between these 'rhetorical' conventions, 'the
means by which the audience is persuaded to accept characters and situations whose
validity is ephemeral and bound to the theatre' (31) and what she calls 'authenticating'
conventions, which ' "model" social conventions in use at a specific time and in a specific place or milieu' and suggest 'a total and external code of values and norms of conduct from which the speech and action of the play are drawn' (32).

[15] Cf. Elam, Semiotics, 108.

[16] Cf. Burns, *Theatricality*, 17; Elam, *Semiotics*, 77, 103–5, 173.

[17] Mario Vargas Llosa, interviewed in the *Guardian*, 21 Feb. 1987. This recalls
Gorgias' paradox about the 'deception' (ἀπάτη) of tragedy, in respect of which 'the
deceiver is juster than the non-deceiver and the deceived wiser than the non-deceived'
(23 D-K).

off' *as if* it were real, then there are important implications for
the discussion of character.

First, this approach encourages us to attend to the *dynamics of
action and interaction* rather than look for static 'character portraits' with the notion of a unitary character as our starting-
point. In constructing for ourselves—with or without the help
of a particular staged performance—the meaning to be attributed to the behaviour of the stage figures, we are engaged in an
activity which is *both* familiar from everyday social interaction
and entirely inconclusive: familiar because we use the same
techniques to interpret other frames, and inconclusive because
there is always the awareness that it is a 'counterfactual construct' which, as Elam puts it, 'the spectator allows the *dramatis
personae*, through the actors, to designate as the "here and
now"'.[18] There is never any way of checking our constructions
against some absolute 'truth', and there is no limit to the
number and variety of constructions to be made—by the different actors who play a particular part, by different members of a
given audience, and by all the readers and spectators of different periods and cultures, with their different conceptions of the
self, who attempt to engage with the work as a whole.[19]

This leads to a second point. In practice, of course, the process of engagement and interpretation—the making of the
construction—may be obstructed in all kinds of ways. Unfamil-
iar conventions of style, language, and theatrical presentation
may leave an audience baffled, and again, the world evoked by
the play—the social structure, values, and attitudes implied by
the characters' behaviour—may seem too remote and alien to
be 'construed'. But conventions, like grammars and codes, can
be learned,[20] and at least some sort of shift can be made to
apprehend the thought patterns of different cultures.[21] There is
no need to fall back on a monolithic view of 'unchanging

---

[18] *Semiotics*, 114.

[19] Cf. ibid. 95: 'Every spectator's interpretation of the text is in effect a new *construction* of it according to the cultural and ideological disposition of the subject.' Cf. also
ibid. 170.

[20] Goffman, *Frame Analysis*, 244, notes 'the great capacity of audiences to adjust and
calibrate in order to get on with getting involved'.

[21] For recent attempts in the case of Greek tragedy, see e.g. C. P. Segal, *Tragedy and
Civilization* (Cambridge, Mass., 1982); S. Goldhill, *Reading Greek Tragedy* (Cambridge,
1986).

human nature' in the style of Vickers (or my own earlier articles) in order to explain how it is that texts composed long ago or in a completely different cultural context can be (relatively) accessible: it is plain enough that human nature does change, just as models of personality change, and notions of what it is appropriate and natural for human beings to do (shifting gender distinctions are a good example from our own time). But provided that we can rely on the continuing existence of mechanisms for 'reading off' the actions of others, whether on or off stage, we have at least some hope of being able to *approach* 'what it is that is going on' in drama like that of ancient Greece. Elam makes a similar point:

It is only because our notion of the world and its individuals and properties is founded on a certain epistemological (and thus ideological) order—rather than on absolute and fixed universal laws—that it is possible to have access to other conceptual organizations or worlds. The individual, for example, is not a simple given but a cultural construct: the essential properties ascribed to 'man' are subject to radical changes from culture to culture and from period to period, as, indeed, are the worlds defined as real and possible.[22]

Thirdly, there is the curious paradox to be borne in mind that despite, or even because of, their fictive status, the figures of drama are often felt to be in some way 'more real' than flesh-and-blood persons met in everyday life. This impression has nothing, of course, to do with naturalism: a play about supernatural or emblematic beings enacted by puppets or robots can be just as 'real' as any other kind.[23] What is important is that drama is much more intensely concentrated and meaningfully shaped, 'purer' than ordinary unscripted experience, so that everything the stage figures do and say, and everything said about them, has to be taken as significant, even their names.[24] To quote Susanne Langer: 'We do not have to find what is significant: the selection has been made—whatever is there is significant, and it is not too much to be surveyed *in toto*.'[25] At

[22] *Semiotics*, 108.
[23] Cf. ibid. 107.
[24] On names, cf. Pfister, *Das Drama*, 221–2.
[25] Quoted by Goffman, *Frame Analysis*, 144. Cf. I. Dilman, 'Dostoyevsky: Psychology and the Novelist', in A. Phillips Griffiths (ed.), *Philosophy and Literature* (Cambridge, 1984), 113–14; Barthes, *Image, Music, Text*, 89; Elam, *Semiotics*, 12: 'things serve only to the extent that they mean'.

the same time, because they are counterfactual these intensely engrossing figures are not personally threatening to the spectator, who can observe them as a privileged onlooker and is not required to make an interactive response.[26]

Here, perhaps, is one factor that helps to explain the endless fascination of drama (and indeed of all forms of make-believe, including psychotherapy). The figures who people it, thanks to their special status, have the power to perform a wide-ranging *service* for their audiences.[27] Protected by their very fictiveness, they can cause the spectators to confront the complexities of emotional experience and to face the problems created by external necessity, whether natural or man-made: old age, disease, death, war, economic circumstances, political and familial conflicts, the boundaries of male and female, public and private, sacred and profane. We might call this the dialectical power of drama, if we can include under that heading the capacity to disrupt as well as to explore (the Greeks might also have said to console). The actor/director Bruce Myers put the matter succinctly: 'Who you are and what is the right way to behave: these are the great questions of theatre.'[28] In practice these are hard questions to keep separate, and 'Who you are' of course raises both ontological issues ('What is a man, what is he not? A dream of a shadow . . .') and questions of identity ('Who is Oedipus?'). What is important is that these are all real questions—one more reason for abandoning the idea of drawing a neat dividing line between drama and 'real life'.

The next step is to take a particular Greek play and look at some specimen passages, to see if this general approach is helpful when we confront the detail of a text. But first we should ask how well this way of looking at character accords with the trend of recent critical work on the tragedians. Interestingly, despite wide divergences of emphasis, there is a general readiness these days to recognize that the business of defining character and personality, let alone the self, is problematic, and that there is no single perspective on tragic action that we can safely take for granted. Christopher Gill has argued that two major

[26] Cf. Dilman, 'Dostoyevsky', 108: 'The safety we find in the make-believe character of art enables us to see through, if only for a moment, the make-believe of real life.'
[27] Cf. Burns, *Theatricality*, 34–5; Elam, *Semiotics*, 134.
[28] Interviewed in the *Guardian*, 16 July 1986.

perspectives coexist in tragic texts, the 'character-viewpoint', which invites us to evaluate moral action, and the 'personality-viewpoint', which offers us 'psychologically strange but compelling phenomena that we cannot disregard as unimaginable or dismiss with simple condemnation'.[29] Charles Segal has made use of psychoanalytical studies to trace a relation between dramatic performance and the unconscious of the spectators, with the stage itself functioning as a kind of dream world, a privileged space in which we can 'evade the censor' and see 'our most buried fears and fantasies' acted out.[30] And both he and Simon Goldhill in their different ways have explored the vocabulary of the mind in Greek tragedy, Segal with the emphasis on the 'complex inner life of motives, desires, and fears' which he finds everywhere implicit,[31] Goldhill drawing attention to conflicting viewpoints, shifting perceptions, and differing attitudes 'towards other people, other ideas'.[32] Adrian Poole strikes a comparable note: 'Tragedy teaches us that the objects of our contemplation—ourselves, each other, our world—are more diverse than we had imagined, and that what we have in common is a dangerous propensity for over-rating our power to comprehend this diversity.'[33]

The importance of setting the presentation of character in this broader, more 'philosophical' context is strongly brought out in John Gould's influential article 'Dramatic Character and "Human Intelligibility" in Greek Tragedy'.[34] Taking his cue from D. A. Traversi's work on Shakespeare,[35] he suggests that the dramatic persons are to be seen 'not as human agents

[29] 'The Question of Character-Development: Plutarch and Tacitus', *CQ*, NS 33 (1983), 469–87; 'The Question of Character and Personality in Greek Tragedy', *Poetics Today*, 7/2 (1986), 251–73; cf. his discussion in Ch. 1 above. The quotation is from *Poetics Today*, 266. As Gill points out, the ancient critics strongly preferred a character-viewpoint in their discussion of tragedy; cf. S. Halliwell, *Aristotle's Poetics* (London, 1986), 150–65; C. Gill, 'The *Ethos/Pathos* Distinction in Rhetorical and Literary Criticism', *CQ*, NS 34 (1984), 149–66.
[30] *Interpreting Greek Tragedy* (Ithaca, NY, 1986), 295. For bibliography on psychoanalytic criticism, see 'Pentheus and Hippolytus on the Couch and on the Grid', in the same book (268–93); R. S. Caldwell, 'Selected Bibliography on Psychoanalysis and Classical Studies', *Arethusa*, 7 (1974), 115–34.
[31] *Interpreting Greek Tragedy*, 99.
[32] *Reading Greek Tragedy*, 179–80. See esp. chs. 4 and 7.
[33] *Tragedy: Shakespeare and the Greek Example* (Oxford, 1987), 1.
[34] *PCPS*, NS 24 (1978), 43–67.
[35] *An Approach to Shakespeare* (2nd edn., London, 1957).

in isolation ... but, through their language, as parts of a "world" of metaphor which transcribes and reshapes our experience in a new mould'. He continues:

> I take the paradigmatic force of *Agamemnon* to consist, not of a number of human figures behaving in ways in which, from my experience of myself or of others, I can imagine human figures separately behaving, but in the total image of human existence that the play presents. The play as a whole, that is, is the 'meaning' that is to be humanly intelligible, the play as a whole being an image, a metaphor of the way things are, within human experience—not a literal enactment of 'the way people behave'.[36]

This is a valuable reminder, and all I should want to add is the gloss that 'the way things are' may be something approachable *only* by means of metaphor. Its very elusiveness is what makes the different images representing it so interesting; perhaps 'the way things might be' or 'could have been' would be a more precise formulation.

In other respects Gould's article stands a little apart from recent work. The main thrust of his argument is his claim that the formal aspects of Greek tragedy mark it off as distinctively different from later drama, which is preoccupied, by contrast, with 'the workings of a complex inner personality'.[37] In stressing the stylization associated with the use of masks and special costume, with the presence of the chorus, and with the non-naturalistic form of the texts themselves he seems to give too much weight to one particular set of conventions. This leads him to the rather surprising conclusion that 'it is the function of the existence and use of ... such different forms as rhesis, stichomythia, aria and *amoibaion* that in a marked degree both the action and the stage figures should be seen and felt by us, the audience, as fragmented and discontinuous'.[38] But then his argument shifts to a contrast between Sophocles and Euripides in their use of these formal modes, showing (to very telling effect) how the differences between Sophocles' more fluid and Euripides' more sharply articulated forms affect our reading of the figures in the plays. This is entirely convincing, yet it seems

[36] 'Dramatic Character', 61–2; cf. 48.
[37] Ibid. 45.
[38] Ibid. 50.

to militate against the general claim quoted above, that the use
of the different formal features *in itself* conveys an impression of
'fragmentation and discontinuity'. And in any case, if it is right
to see reality itself as elusive, a different approach to the formal
modes may be more fruitful. Perhaps they could be 'seen and
felt by us, the audience' as suggesting different perspectives
from which a problematic situation might be explored, and
thus as potentially offering a more suggestive model of reality
than a more homogeneous level of discourse might evoke. Certainly in the *Antigone*, which I have chosen as my sample for discussion, the interplay between the lyric exchanges of actors and
chorus (806–82; 1261–1347) and the scenes of iambic dialogue
can be seen as an integrating force, giving further depth and
complexity to the situation created by Creon and Antigone.[39]

It is time to look closely at a particular text. Notoriously,
Antigone is a play that invites judgement of its stage figures: a
great deal of the critical literature in fact reflects the way it
encourages its readers to take sides. Perhaps, though, we should
hesitate to go as far as Gill, who writes that 'the protagonists
stand before us as "characters", as responsible, choosing agents
who luminously explicate their motives for action and invite
evaluation on these grounds'.[40] The 'definition of the situation'
given respectively by Antigone, Ismene, Creon, and Haemon
has to be set against the impression they 'give off' of their
motives and feelings, and both are to be interpreted as part of
the larger pattern suggested by the play as a whole—for
example, in its meditation on the history of the house of Lab-
dacus, with *atē* hovering over the play as Polyneices the raven-
ing eagle hovers over Thebes in the *parodos*; in the language of
Eros and Dionysus and Hades and the bridal chamber of the
Bride of Death; in the mythological analogies of Niobe, Danae,
Lycurgus, and Cleopatra; in the mysterious phenomena of the
dust storm and the corrupted sacrificial offerings; and in the
imagery of wild nature and man's unceasing attempts to control it.

If I now concentrate attention mainly on the issue of motives,

[39] Cf. P. E. Easterling, 'The Second Stasimon of *Antigone*', in R. D. Dawe *et al.*
(edd.), *Dionysiaca* (Cambridge, 1978), 155, on the relationship between the choral odes
and the iambic dialogue.
[40] 'The Question of Character and Personality', 269.

it is not because I want to suggest that this should be the limit of our enquiry, but in order to illustrate the way the text invites us to be actively involved in making constructions.

First there is the scene in which Ismene, challenged by Creon, claims to have shared with Antigone in the burial of Polyneices. The important structural point to note is that the scene is a replay for Creon's benefit of something the audience has itself witnessed. In the Prologue Antigone tells Ismene about Creon's decree, making it clear that she will not hesitate to disobey in order to do what she sees as the right thing by Polyneices: she will be 'a holy criminal' (ὅσια πανουργήσασ[α], 74). Ismene is at first bewildered, and then rejects Antigone's plan as dangerous folly, Her language is strong: 'poor wretch' (ὦ ταλαῖφρον, 39) she calls Antigone, and 'too bold' (σχετλία, 47). 'There is no sense in going to extremes' (τὸ γὰρ | περισσὰ πράσσειν οὐκ ἔχει νοῦν οὐδένα, 67–8). Antigone is in love with the impossible (ἀμηχάνων ἐρᾷς, 90), and 'senseless' (ἄνους, 99). Why? Because the burial is forbidden by the powers that be: Ismene equates the will of the city (44) with Creon (47), with law and the 'vote'—or 'decree' (ψῆφον)—'and powers of the rulers' (59–60), with 'those who are stronger' (63), with the citizens (78–9). She does not dispute the rightness of burying Polyneices; she simply regards it as bound to fail, because she and Antigone are women, and those in control have greater power. She evokes the shadow of the family's troubles, seeing what could happen to Antigone and herself as the worst in the whole horrible sequence. But although Antigone can't win, Ismene will try to protect her by keeping her plan secret: she values what Antigone is trying to do. 'Senseless as you are, you are truly dear to those who love you' (ἄνους μὲν ἔρχει, τοῖς φίλοις δ' ὀρθῶς φίλη, 99).

Now we have Ismene summoned by Creon to answer the charge of conspiracy with Antigone (489–90). Creon says he has seen her indoors, 'raving and not in control of her wits (φρένες)', which to him proves her guilty conscience (491–4). We may want to construct a different explanation for her anguished state (e.g. despair at the news that Antigone has been apprehended) and be tempted to read Creon's reading of Ismene as a sign of paranoia (already suggested by his suspicions of bribery and conspiracy in his conversation with the

Guard). Before Ismene arrives, Antigone claims that the Elders would express their approval of what she has done if they were not muzzled by fear (504–5, 509). The question of *their* response is thus explicitly raised: we are warned to recognize that they may say one thing and mean another. Interestingly, they describe Ismene's distraught state as caused by her feelings towards her sister: 'Here is Ismene, shedding such tears as fond sisters weep: a cloud on her brow shadows her darkly flushing face, raining tears on her lovely cheeks' (526–30)—striking language (especially the rare word ῥέθος, 'countenance'), which is in sharp contrast with Creon's denunciation: 'you who were lurking in my house like a viper, secretly drinking my blood, while I didn't realize I was nurturing two curses (ἄτα), to rise against my throne . . .' (531–3). This looks grotesquely wrong (though ἄτα is ominous and has links both with language used by Antigone, Ismene, and the chorus to characterise the Labdacid inheritance (185) and with Creon's own statement of his civic programme (314)). But Ismene does not contradict Creon; instead she claims to have shared in the burial and to want a share in the punishment: 'I have done the deed' (δέδρακα τοὔργον, 536).

Being a replay of something already presented to the audience, this is bound to provoke questions: Ismene refused to do the deed earlier, so why does she now say she did it—'if Antigone allows my claim (εἴπερ ἥδ᾽ ὁμορροθεῖ)?[41] Is there any sense in which her claim could be serious? She didn't question the rightness of Antigone's intention, and she offered to keep the plan secret, so she could be called an accessory, though she does say (556) that she tried to dissuade her. She goes on to claim that 'the offence is equal' (558)—which Jebb paraphrases as 'and yet,—though I *did* shrink from breaking Creon's law,—I am now, morally, as great an offender as you, since I sympathise with your act'. As to *why* she makes this claim, the constructions made by readers and critics are revealingly varied. Is it a manœuvre to save Antigone, a futile attempt to share her heroism, 'an impulse of a sentimental and

---

[41] Nauck's εἴπερ ἥδ᾽· ὁμορροθῶ is an unnecessary change, which draws attention away from the crucial question: How are we to interpret what Antigone and Ismene now say about what they said and did earlier?

almost hysterical kind'[42]—and so on? As Steiner says, the
debate persists.[43] Antigone's position is just as elusive. Is she
right to claim (555) that Ismene 'chose to live' if that meant life
without Antigone? These were not quite the terms in which
Ismene formulated the argument in the Prologue. And why in
any case does Antigone say what she does? Is she angrily rejecting Ismene's wish to share the deed, or is she protecting Ismene
from Creon, as some critics, starting with one of the scholiasts,
have thought? The point, of course, is that we have no means of
knowing, but the audience is encouraged to think about the implications of the sisters' different versions of something it has
itself witnessed, and only if we are willing to make constructions
from their words can we become involved in the issues raised by
their different points of view. (Not that we shall have to plump
for a simple answer: rejection and protection could even coexist.) The language of the scene seems to encourage this process. At 561–5 Creon says 'One of these two has just been
proved senseless (ἄνουν), the other has been so always', and
Ismene replies that the sense (νοῦς) people have by nature
leaves them when they are in trouble. 'Yours evidently has',
says Creon. One of the questions raised by the scene is surely
'Who *has* got sense around here?' (We are reminded of the end
of the Prologue (99), when Ismene claims that Antigone is
senseless, and Creon later uses the same language to dismiss the
chorus's suggestion that the hand of a god might be seen in the
burial of Polyneices (281).) And the question of who has sense
points up the larger question of the rights and wrongs in the
conflict between Creon and Antigone.

Critics have often noted[44] that this debate is articulated
through insistent emphasis on words for sense, mind, judgement, wisdom, sanity—and clearly this insistence suggests an
interest in the springs of action, the 'inner life'; it is also
dramatically signalled in such a way as to stimulate us to make

[42] R. C. Jebb, comm. on *Antigone* (3rd edn.), introd., p. xxix.

[43] G. Steiner, *Antigones* (Oxford, 1984), 151. This book well illustrates the play's continuing dialectical power; cf. M. Hollis, 'Of Masks and Men', in Carrithers *et al.* (edd.),
The Category of the Person, 222–3, on the issues raised by *Antigone*: 'The trappings are
antique but the puzzle is wholly modern.'

[44] E.g. G. M. Kirkwood, *A Study of Sophoclean Drama* (Ithaca, NY, 1958), 233–8;
R. P. Winnington-Ingram, *Sophocles: An Interpretation* (Cambridge, 1980), 121–2;
Goldhill, *Reading Greek Tragedy*, 175–80.

constructions. When at 176 Creon says it's hopeless to think you will understand any man's soul (ψυχή) and quality of mind (φρόνημα) and judgement (γνώμη) until he has been exposed to responsibility, this encourages us to look at what *his ψυχή* and *φρόνημα* and *γνώμη* will be like, and we are given repeated reminders that this is a crucial question. The scene with Haemon is one example.

It opens with the focus on Haemon, the chorus asking the question 'What is Haemon's state of mind?'[45] Does he come 'grieving for the doom of his promised bride Antigone and bitter for the baffled hope of his marriage' (627–30, Jebb's translation)? Creon takes up the question: 'We'll soon know, better than *seers* could tell us. Surely, son, you aren't enraged with your father, or are we dear to you [your φίλοι] however we act?' (631–4). There could hardly be a more pointed invitation to 'read between the lines' of what Haemon says, and the irony in φίλοι is heavy. When Haemon replies to Creon's long speech he first picks up the chorus's tactful 'wisely (φρονούντως) spoken' (682), with a gnomic evaluation of 'wisdom' (φρένες) (ambiguous, because the definition of 'right thinking' is precisely what is under review), then respectfully evades taking responsibility for a judgement on Creon's words, simply allowing the possibility that a different view might validly be held. His next move is to repeat what he hears people saying in secret—in secret because they are afraid to say it openly to Creon. 'In the dark', Haemon implies, he hears things that are *true*; the idea of the secrecy of the criticism is emphasized by 'in the dark' (ὑπὸ σκότου) at 692 and 'dark rumour' (ἐρεμνὴ . . . φάτις) at 700. In the first scene with the Guard Creon had himself envisaged secret mutterings on the part of people discontented with his edict (289–92). We presumed he was deceiving himself when he accused those people of paying for the burial of Polyneices, but the 'secret voices' remain a possibility—recalled, indeed, by Antigone's claims about what the Elders 'really' think.

Now Haemon spells out what the voices say. The city is distressed (ὀδύρεται): the citizens think Antigone is *most* underserving (ἀναξιωτάτη), suffering *most* evilly (κάκιστ[α]) for deeds *most* glorious (εὐκλεεστάτων). She saved her own brother from

being left unburied, to be destroyed by dogs and birds: isn't
that worthy of golden honour (693–9)? We note the emotional
intensity of the language. Of course its status as 'truth' is inde-
finable since there is *no* off-stage reality to which it refers—and
no representatives of the people come on later to confirm what
Haemon says (Tieresias takes up the issue at a different level).
In any case we know Haemon to be biased in Antigone's
favour. We can't rule out the possibility that what he offers as a
report of public opinion is his own construction designed to influence Creon. 'In the dark' and the 'dark rumour' perhaps
give warning that Haemon's report is not easy to evaluate.
How do we take those superlatives—as evidence of *his* emotion,
or as a strict report of what people are saying? What is important is that the passage offers an alternative reading of Antigone's action for us to think about, and it prepares for
Haemon's debate with Creon about the source of authority. A
disjunction is now emphasized between the city and the ruler—
contrary to the assumptions of Ismene in the Prologue, and of
Creon and the chorus up to this point.[46] Now Haemon claims
that the *whole city* (ὁμόπτολις λεώς, 733) denies Antigone's guilt,
and Creon asks 'Is the city going to tell me how to rule?' (736).

To revert to the point about wisdom. Haemon follows up his
remarks about the voices with an appeal to his father to be willing to accept other views: 'for whoever thinks that he alone is
wise, or that in speech or mind he has no equal—such a person
when laid open is seen to be empty' (707–9).[47] We are
reminded of the question posed by Creon about understanding
a man's soul and mind and judgement (176), and one answer is
now suggested in Creon's case. But it is still provisional: the
language of 'emptiness' is used again at the end of the scene, in
the violent quarrel between father and son, when Haemon
accuses Creon of having empty resolves (κενὰς γνώμας, 753),
and Creon retorts with the claim that Haemon is 'empty of wisdom' (φρενῶν . . . κενός, 754). The issue is taken up again and
again as the play goes on: is it Haemon who is mad, driven by
Eros, or Creon who is mad, like Lycurgus maddened by Diony-

[46] Contrast 736–9 with 44, 59–60, 63–4, 78–9 (Ismene); 209–10, 661–72 (Creon);
211–14 (chorus).
[47] Cf. B. M. W. Knox, *The Heroic Temper* (Berkeley, Loss Angeles, and London,
1964), 75, 103, 110; Winnington-Ingram, *Sophocles*, 127.

sus?[48] It is the mind of Creon, says Teiresias, that has made the city sick (τῆς σῆς ἐκ φρενὸς νοσεῖ πόλις, 1015; cf. 1141).

All the time we are led to make new constructions, and the constructions always lead to larger questions, ensuring that character and action can never be kept tidily separate. And the desire to construct is perfectly compatible with the knowledge that strictly speaking there is nothing there at all.[49] It is the very elusiveness of the 'inwardness' of other people, real or fictive, let alone of ourselves, that gives drama its extraordinary appeal. William James put the point nicely when he remarked, 'The mind is at every stage a theatre of simultaneous possibilities.'[50]

---

[48] Cf. Winnington-Ingram, *Sophocles*, 94, 103–4.

[49] Cf. Barthes, *Image, Music, Text*, 147: 'There is nothing beneath.'

[50] *The Principles of Psychology*, i (London, 1890), 288.

5

Character and Action, Representation and Reading Greek Tragedy and its Critics

SIMON GOLDHILL

Man is an invention.
(Foucault)

THE CHARACTER OF INDIVIDUALITY

The idea of 'human nature' tends to attract the rhetoric of 'essential truth', and rarely with less critical attention than in the study of characterization in ancient dramatic fiction. The disciplines of philosophy, history, and anthropology have established from their differing viewpoints a need to acknowledge the complex problems involved both in understanding such categorizations as 'the natural' or 'the human' in other cultures, and also in recognizing or repressing the cultural imperialism of the interpreter's own system of categorization in such an enterprise.[1] Yet all too frequently writers on Greek drama have ignored the need for the construction of a critical history of individuality, as if the categories of the person were

Thanks to the characters and individuals who read and commented on this chapter, especially Pat Easterling, John Henderson, Neil Croally.

[1] A vast bibliography could be given. Mine would include, for an interesting general introduction, M. Carrithers, S. Collins and S. Lukes, (edd.), *The Category of the Person: Anthropology, Philosophy, History* (Cambridge, 1985). In history, I have learnt in particular from the studies of L. Stone, particularly *Family, Sex and Marriage in England 1500–1800* (London, 1977); J. Goody, J. Thirsk and E. P. Thompson (edd.), *Family and Inheritance* (Cambridge, 1976); A. Pagden, *The Fall of Natural Man* (Cambridge, 1986); M. Foucault, *The Order of Things* (London, 1970); id., *The Archaeology of Knowledge* (London, 1972). On anthropology and cultural studies, apart from many particular case studies, see esp. P. Bourdieu, *Outline of a Theory of Practice* (Cambridge, 1977); E. Saïd, *Orientalism* (London, 1978). On philosophy, B. A. O. Williams, *Problems of the Self* (Cambridge, 1972), and further bibliog. in *The Category of the Person*. On classical material, see the seminal studies of G. E. R. Lloyd, esp. *Science, Folklore and Ideology* (Cambridge, 1983); also e.g. R. Parker, *Miasma* (Oxford, 1983). The French tradition from Gernet through Vernant, Vidal-Naquet, and Loraux has been particularly influential.

cross-cultural *données*. So, to take one example from an influential work, Brian Vickers founds his study of Greek tragedy on
'some simple propositions', including: 'Greek tragedy is about
people ... Human behaviour ...concerns those fundamental
human passions which are reflected to a greater and lesser
degree in the literature of all nations at all periods. In Greek
Tragedy, people love and hate as we do.'[2] This project begs the
question not merely by the repression of the cultural specificity
of the fifth-century Athenian construction of 'love' and 'hate'.
(How can φιλεῖν or ἔρως be simply translated as 'love', as if the
history of courtly love, Romanticism, not to mention Christianity, makes no difference to a modern reader's approach to such
a term; as if, indeed, the interrelations of the sexes in the
ancient world could simply be mapped onto a modern, post-
Freudian emotional topography?[3]) More importantly, perhaps, Vickers also begs the question precisely by ignoring the
way in which what he calls 'love' and 'hate', might affect the
concept of the person (which he takes for granted in his opening
remarks). Vickers imagines a community of humanity both in
his blithe assumption 'as we do'—which 'we'? Do 'we' agree on
what we all do?—and also in the assertion of the common concerns and attitudes of the ancient and modern world. Such an
assumption of community shows how his (humanist) critical
approach can only function through the occlusion of crucial
cultural differences. In this opening section, I wish to outline
some ways in which such an occlusion leads to an inevitable dis-
tortion of the discussion of characterization and individuality.

Nothing less than a complete cultural history—an impossible
task, even if there were enough space for such a project—could
hope to outline adequately what might be called the construction of the self in fifth-century Athenian democracy. Some
briefer remarks here, however, may help sketch the difficulty of
taking the categories of the person as cross-cultural norms. In
my discussion of character in *Reading Greek Tragedy*, I pointed
first to the apparent lack of interest in idiosyncrasies of personality in the public, masked personae of Greek drama—which is

---

[2] B. Vickers, *Towards Greek Tragedy* (London, 1973), 6.
[3] Foucault's *History of Sexuality* (*La Volonté de savoir* (Paris, 1976); *L'Usage des plaisirs*
(Paris, 1984); *Le Souci de soi* (Paris, 1984)) shows one attempt to chart these differences.

so different from, say, the dramas of Ibsen or even Chekhov.[4] The siting of an individual in a community—both the family and the *polis*—also realigns the construction of individuality and the sense of an individual as an agent. Similarly, *ēthos*, as Jones discusses at length, is 'without the ambition of inclusiveness'[5] associated with 'character'; that is, *ēthos* does not attempt, as 'character' often does in modern usage, to express a whole personality or the make-up of a psyche, but rather a particular disposition or set of attitudes that can be seen to be instantiated in a particular course of action. I also attempted in the general discussions in *Reading Greek Tragedy* to suggest some of the ways in which the ideas of, say, masculinity and femininity are deployed in fifth-century Athens, and also what it might mean to be a citizen, a soldier, an Athenian—all of which inform the notion of the self. Rather than recapitulate such analyses here, I wish to look briefly at Vickers's assertion that 'in Greek tragedy, people love and hate as we do', and to follow through some of the implications of such a proposition in his reading of a particular passage which discusses how 'people love'.

In Sophocles' *Antigone*, after the stichomythic exchange between Creon and Haemon, the chorus sing a well-known ode on ἔρως, *erōs*, (*Ant.* 781–801). Vickers comments as follows: 'As he goes off in anger, the chorus make a sublimely irrelevant deduction about Haemon's motives. Love, they say, "twists the minds of the just", love alone has caused this quarrel (781 ff.). They have not really been attending to the play.'[6] The unqualified translation of ἔρως by 'love', as if there were no difference between the externalized and destructive force that the chorus describe, and 'love' as in the Western, Judaeo-Christian tradition (as, for instance, personal fulfilment), is particularly misleading in a play whose conflicts focus on the obligations and duties invoked by the terminology of φιλεῖν and related words.[7] Neither Antigone's commitment to her family ties, nor

---

[4] *Reading Greek Tragedy* (Cambridge, 1986), 168 ff.

[5] J. Jones, *On Aristotle and Greek Tragedy* (London, 1962), 32.

[6] Vickers, *Towards Greek Tragedy*, 537. The emphasis 'love *alone*' is not in the Greek. (It enhances but is perhaps not crucial to Vickers's rhetoric.) Indeed, I am not sure (despite Jebb, Bayfield, *et al.*) that ταράξας (794) must be translated 'stir up' (i.e. Vickers's 'cause') rather than its most common sense of 'throw into confusion'. *Erōs* may be regarded by the chorus as a factor that confuses, rather than starts, the (political, familial) row.

[7] I have discussed this, with bibliog., in *Reading Greek Tragedy*, 79–106.

Creon's argument of obligation to the city finds a place for *erōs*; and that the chorus here turn to explain the young man's actions in terms of *erōs* adds a significant element of motivation to set against the conflicting claims of φιλία. To translate both ἔρως and φιλεῖν as 'love' not only ignores the differences between ancient and modern constructions of affective relations and obligations, but also effaces an important semantic distinction in the dynamics of the play itself.[8] Nor is it by chance that the chorus propose *erōs* as a motivation for Haemon: the ephebe holds a privileged position in the normative narratives of *erōs* as a figure especially open to the force of desire.[9] I wish here, however, to focus on this ode in particular as a prelude to Antigone's *kommos*. For, as Richard Seaford has recently pointed out, the invocation of *erōs* is a typical part of the hymeneal celebrations, and as Antigone processes to her death, she is represented as making a marriage with Hades.[10] The connection of this ode with the following action is important not merely for the recognition of a significant ritual pattern in the play but also, in the context of my argument, because it raises a crucial question of Antigone's status in terms of age and gender. For Antigone is a *parthenos*, and it is precisely with such a category that the overlap of social, psychological, and

[8] For the equally unqualified translation of φιλεῖν as 'love', see e.g. Vickers, *Towards Greek Tragedy*, 543: 'The central situation is, as Antigone says, the fact that she "cannot share in hatred but in love" (523). Creon is remarkable for his hatred and lack of love: his *philia* is shown as false ... Antigone is remarkable for her love and lack of hatred.' Vickers nowhere distinguishes adequately between ἔρως and φιλεῖν.

[9] See esp. P. Vidal-Naquet, *Le Chasseur noir* (Paris, 1981); E. Schnapp, "Éros en chasse", in *La Cité des images: Religion et société en Grèce antique* (Paris, 1984); A. Brelich, *Paides e parthenoi* (Rome, 1969).

[10] R. Seaford, 'The Tragic Wedding', *JHS* 107 (1987), 106–30, esp. 107–8. Seaford also notes (120–1) that the description of Haemon's and Antigone's death also constitutes a precise corruption of the topoi of the representation of marriage. See also N. Loraux, *Façons tragiques de tuer une femme* (Paris, 1985), 61–82; C. P. Segal, *Tragedy and Civilization* (Cambridge and London, 1981), 152–206; and, for the continuation of this theme in later writing, M. Alexiou and P. Dronke, 'The Lament of Jeptha's Daughter: Themes, Tradition, Originality', *Studi Medievali*, 12/2 (1971), 819–63. On the τέλος of marriage becoming the τέλος of death, see A. Lebeck, *The Oresteia* (Washington, 1971), 68 ff.; S. Goldhill, 'Two Notes on τέλος and Related Words in the Oresteia', *JHS* 104 (1984), 169–76. It is worth noting further on this stasimon that whereas for men the possibilities of *erōs* include a pattern of acceptable behaviour (the proprieties of ἐράστης and ἐρώμενος outlined by e.g. K. J. Dover, *Greek Homosexuality* (London, 1978)), there is no equivalent narrative or norm for females in the fifth century —a narrative of *erōs* that is, that does not presuppose transgression. In what circumstances can a woman's *erōs* be acceptable or desirable?

biological discourses can be seen to affect the very construction of (the categories of) the person. Recent studies have outlined how the *parthenos* is conceptualized as a dangerous wild animal, whose wildness must be tamed by the yoke of marriage; whose body must be opened by marriage to prevent the build-up of blood and resultant 'hysterical' diseases; whose *ēthos* is crucially dependent on such a biological and social position.[11] Such a conceptualization of virginity as a dangerous liminal state to be passed through—far more than a physical categorization—is quite different from the evaluation of permanent virginity in Christianity and even from the figure of the *virgo* in Roman culture. What it is to be a παρθένος, *virgo*, virgin, has a (changing) history. The song to *erōs* here, then, cannot be adequately understood separate from the marriage to Hades which is a topos in the representation of the death of *parthenoi*. Similarly, the Hippocratic treatise on the diseases of *parthenoi* talks of a 'love of death' (the verb is ἐρᾶν) as a typical symptom of a virgin whose condition is to be treated and cured by immediate marriage;[12] and hanging, the means of Antigone's death, is also a specific element in the (tragic) way to kill a *woman*.[13] The ephebe Haemon and the *parthenos* Antigone are both constructed within narratives of *erōs* that can be seen to be culturally specific. In what sense can either be said simply 'to love as we do'?

Indeed, it is typical that Antigone's status as *parthenos* is ignored by Vickers throughout the play, with a resultant oversimplification of the conflict of Creon and Antigone. He writes: 'The sex of the offender against Creon's *nomos* is entirely irrelevant to the seriousness of the deed.'[14] For him, Creon's explicit remarks about Antigone's gender are only to show how the tyrant bullies those weaker than himself. (Ismene's similar

---

[11] See in particular G. Sissa, *Le Corps virginal* (Paris, 1986); G. Sissa, 'Une Virginité sans hymen: Le Corps féminin en Grèce ancienne', *Annales ESC* 6 (1984), 1119–39; A. Rousselle, *Porneia: De la maîtrise du corps à la privation sensuelle* (Paris, 1983); Lloyd, *Science*, 58–111; H. King, 'Bound to Bleed: Artemis and Greek Women', in A. Cameron and A. Kuhrt (edd.), *Images of Women in Antiquity* (London, 1983).

[12] κελεύω δ' ἔγωγε τὰς παρθένους, ὁκόταν τὸ τοιοῦτον πάσχωσιν, ὡς τάχιστα ξυνοικῆσαι ἀνδράσιν· ἢν γὰρ κυήσωσιν, ὑγιέες γίνονται (*Virg.* 16).

[13] This phrase is taken from the title of Loraux's study, *Façons tragiques*.

[14] Vickers, *Towards Greek Tragedy*, 533. So too 527: 'My argument will be that Antigone is presented as an admirable, committed character who is never criticized.'

comments on Antigone's femininity are ignored.) Yet it is specifically as a female that Antigone is to care for the dead of her family,[15] and her specifically female opposition to Creon— within the highly polarized attitudes of fifth-century Athens— is unlikely ever to be a simple corrective to a male error.[16] On the one hand, repressing the difference between his and an ancient culture's narratives of *erōs*/love allows Vickers to see a choral ode as 'sublimely irrelevant'; on the other hand, repressing the importance of gender difference within a culture allows him to see Antigone's status as 'entirely irrelevant' to her conflict with Creon. Differences between cultures and differences within a culture are regarded as irrelevant, as Vickers's argument proceeds from and attempts to demonstrate an all-determining common humanity.

The danger of this humanist ideology, then, is the ignoring of the cultural and historical conditions for the social, biological, and psychological categories of the person. The repression of differences in the name of what is supposed to be self-evident and beyond criticism: what we all do and always have done with regard to what can always be called, simply, 'love'. A first requisite, I suggest, for progress on the topic of characterization and individuality is a recognition that the categories of 'character', 'person', 'individual', as well as 'male', 'female', 'mother', 'father', 'tyrant', 'virgin', etc., cannot be treated adequately as cross-cultural norms but must be seen as elements of a cultural discourse which needs to be opened to critical enquiry.

THE INDIVIDUALITY OF CHARACTER

Although the previous section suggests a need to recognize the cultural determinants in which categories of the person are constructed, it does not follow that the figures of dramatic fiction

---

[15] This is especially emphasized by M. R. Lefkowitz, 'Influential Women', in Cameron and Kuhrt (edd.), *Images of Women*.

[16] Cf. F. I. Zeitlin, 'Playing the Other: Theater, Theatricality, and the Feminine in Greek Drama', *Representations*, 11 (1985), 63–94, who writes (72–3): 'The woman ... typically defends its [the house's] interests in response to some masculine violation of its integrity. As a result, however, of the stand she takes, the woman also represents a subversive threat to male authority as an adversary in a power struggle for control that resonates throughout the entire social and political system.'

can be treated simply as 'real people' (even after the recognition of the different possibilities of the ideas of 'reality' and 'people'). A fundamental difficulty for any psychological approach to character in a literary text—even or especially when the characters are embodied by actors on a stage—is their ineradicable *difference* from an individual patient with a subconscious, a history, a family (with subconsciouses and histories). However much one needs a sense of 'human intelligibility' or models of the self or of the person to understand a drama, it does not follow that the same criteria that we use to evaluate or discuss real human behaviour and real human beings can be used without question for analysing 'character' in a text critically. In this section, I wish to discuss some of the problems that arise when the characters of drama are treated as (real) individuals.

John Gould concludes his influential discussion of characterization with a restatement of the difficulty of separating a character from the 'pervasive metaphorical colouring of the whole language of the play'—from 'the world of metaphor' which is the play's text.[17] The implications of this conclusion for the sense of the boundaries of an individual and the boundaries between individuals in dramatic narrative can be further analysed. I shall begin with a moment of self-description from Aeschylus:

> ἰδοῦ δὲ γένναν εὖνιν αἰετοῦ πατρὸς
> θανόντος ἐν πλεκταῖσι καὶ σπειράμασιν
> δεινῆς ἐχίδνης· τοὺς δ' ἀπωρφανισμένους
> νῆστις πιέζει λιμός· οὐ γὰρ ἐντελεῖς
> θήραν πατρῴαν προσφέρειν σκηνήμασιν.

> See the offspring bereft of an eagle father,
> Who died in the coils and skeins
> Of the dreadful viper. Starving hunger
> Oppresses the orphans. For they have not the power
> To bring the prey to the dwelling of the father.
> (*Cho.* 247–51)

As part of an appeal to the gods, Orestes' language stresses the weakness and need of the children. The conflict between

eagle and snake is a common motif since Homer in poetry and
scientific enquiry,[18] and certain associations of the viper—that
the female destroys the male in copulation and that the children eat their way out of the womb in revenge[19]—are strikingly
appropriate to Clytemnestra and Orestes as he approaches the
matricide. Yet it would be quite insufficient to regard this
utterance merely as indicative of Orestes' *ēthos* or even of
Orestes' rhetoric (as part of an emotional scene of recognition).
For the image of Electra and Orestes as children bereft of an
eagle father is deeply intertwined with the earlier—and later—
language of the trilogy. Agamemnon and Menelaus embarked
on the expedition 'like vultures' (*Ag.* 49 ff) and it is an omen of
eagles—the 'winged dogs of the father' (*Ag.* 135)—that promises victory to and delays the expedition at Aulis. The sacrifice
of Iphigeneia, the association of Agamemnon and Zeus, the
very problems of motivation and decision at Aulis are invoked
in Orestes' appeal to Zeus (as Agamemnon's son recognizes his
sister in the shared aim of regaining control over the *oikos*). The
significance of Orestes' remarks is in part determined by the
earlier language of the play, and has significance for the development of the discourse of the drama. Similarly, the image of
Clytemnestra as snake harks back not merely to the language of
monstrosity associated with the queen throughout the trilogy,[20]
but also, in the term πλεκταῖσι, ['woven things', 'coils'] to the
woven coils of the net in which Agamemnon died and the
woven tapestries over which he processed to his death. Thus, in
the next scene of the *Choephoroi* when Orestes, in response to
Clytemnestra's dream of a snake, claims ἐκδρακοντωθεὶς ἐγὼ
κτείνω νιν ['I, turned snake, shall kill her'] (549–50), it is an
incarnation which indicates his double and problematic position precisely by the incorporation of the representation of
Clytemnestra in his self-description. So, finally, the language of

---

[18] See e.g. *Il.* 12. 200 ff; S. *Ant.* 110 ff; Arist. *HA* 9. 1. 609ᵃ; Aelian, *NA* 17. 37.

[19] First mentioned in Hdt. 3. 109. See A. Y. Campbell, 'Aeschylus' *Agamemnon* 1223–
38 and Treacherous Monsters', *CQ* 29 (1935), 25–36, esp. 31–3; E. T. Borthwick, 'A
"Femme Fatale" in Asclepiades', *CR* 17 (1967), 250–4 (who has extensive refs. and bibliog.). See also the good note of A. F. Garvie, in Aeschylus, *Choephoroi* (Oxford, 1986),
ad loc. Aelian, *NA* 1. 24 pertinently comments on the story of the viper: τί οὖν οἱ
'Ορέσται καὶ 'Αλκμαίωνες πρὸς ταῦτα, ὦ τραγῳδοὶ φίλοι;

[20] See esp. F. I. Zeitlin, 'Dynamic of Misogyny in the *Oresteia*', *Arethusa* 11 (1978),
149–84, esp. 164–5.

the hunt,[21] the capabilities and fulfilment implied by the term
ἐντελεῖς ['fully empowered'],[22] and indeed the context of the
paternal dwelling,[23] all help link Orestes' self-image significantly and specifically into the thematic texture of the play's
narrative.

What is recognized here (as Orestes recognizes and is recognized by Electra) is not merely a bounded, unique, and autonomous individual. Rather, the language in and through
which the figure of Orestes is formulated is part of the (figural)
language of the trilogy, part of its specific textual dynamics,
part of its *narrative*. The language does not merely express
(his) 'character', nor does it merely offer access to an indi
vidual 'character'. The representation of a fictional figure is
(over)determined by the fictional narrative in which the figure
plays a part.

If the figures of drama cannot be separated—as bounded
individuals—from the (figural) language of the narrative,
neither can they be separated from the literary tradition in
which they also inevitably play a part. Thomas Docherty out-
lines three functions of the name in the process of characterization. First, 'the name indicates authority of some kind',[24] that
is, it sites a figure within a social or cultural history and context
(Agamemnon (as) king, father, husband, etc.—located also in
the 'heroic world' of the past). Secondly, 'the name is a *locus*
around which characterization actually takes place',[25] that is,
traits and qualities are associated by an audience and by other
characters in the fiction with a proper name. (So 'Agamemnon'
is formed both in the conflicting descriptions attached to the
name by characters throughout the trilogy and in the
audience's (conflicting) attribution of qualities as evinced in
such scenes as the Carpet Scene.) Thirdly, 'the name gives the
reader a point of view on the fiction as a whole—it offers a posi-

[21] On hunting imagery, see esp. P. Vidal-Naquet, 'Chasse et sacrifice dans l'*Orestie*',
in J.-P. Vernant and P. Vidal-Naquet, *Mythe et tragédie on Grèce ancienne* (Paris, 1972).
[22] On τέλος, see, for discussion and bibliog., Goldhill, 'Two Notes'.
[23] On the house, see Jones, *On Aristotle and Greek Tragedy*, 83 ff. I have discussed the
importance of the paternal house in detail in *Language, Sexuality, Narrative: The* Oresteia
(Cambridge, 1984), 99-207.
[24] T. Docherty, *Reading (Absent) Character: Towards a Theory of Characterization in
Fiction* (Oxford, 1983), 73.
[25] Ibid. 74.

tion for the reader to inhabit and from which to see the world of
the fiction and the other characters. Clearly this "position" is
inherently relativistic'.[26] (Here, the consideration of Orestes,
for example, as paradigmatic model is fundamental.) Docherty
is concerned primarily with modern prose fiction and the challenge to secure characterization that such experimental fiction
so often strives self-consciously to maintain. (Docherty also sees
such a challenge as articulated through the reader's continual
return to different modes of authority and identity; hence in
part the formulation of his title, *Reading (Absent) Character*.) One
aspect of naming which Docherty does not consider, however,
is the effect of names—figures—repeated from text to text
within a literary tradition. This is crucial to Greek drama.
When Agamemnon's name is mentioned in Aeschylus' *Oresteia*,
it comes always with a collection of associations in particular
from Homer but also from other poetic traditions. If the qualities of a literary narrative make it difficult to see a character as
simply an individual, so too the relations between texts are also
crucial to the development of characterization.

Let me give one brief example from Sophocles' *Ajax*, which
shows well how a single remark can open a whole vista of allusion. Ajax is a figure who has been much discussed precisely in
terms of the disjunctions and overlap between the Homeric and
Sophoclean representations.[27] In particular, his scene with
Tecmessa and Eurysaces, his son, has been shown significantly
to echo and distort the Homeric scene of Hector, Andromache,
and Astyanax in book 6 of the *Iliad*.[28] The famous suicide
speech ends as follow: τὰ δ' ἄλλ' ἐν "Αιδου τοῖς κάτω μυθήσομαι
[The rest I will narrate to those below in Hades] (*Ajax* 865). In
the *Odyssey*, when Odysseus attempts in Hades to talk to those
below, it is Ajax who in unchanging enmity turns his back and
walks away in silence. Change, specifically with regard to
philein and *echthairein*, is a key issue of the play, brought into

---

[26] Ibid. For further discussion of naming, see Goldhill, *The* Oresteia, s.v. 'naming'.

[27] See esp., for discussion and bibliog., R. P. Winnington-Ingram, *Sophocles: An Interpretation* (Cambridge, 1980), 11–72.

[28] See S. M. Adams, 'The *Ajax* of Sophocles', *Phoenix*, 9 (1955), 93–110; W. E.
Brown, 'Sophocles' Ajax and Homer's Hector', *CJ* 61 (1965–6), 118–21; G. M. Kirkwood, 'Homer and Sophocles' Ajax', in M. Anderson (ed.), *Classical Drama and its Influence: Essays Presented to H. D. F. Kitto* (London, 1965); and esp. P. E. Easterling, 'The
Tragic Homer', *BICS* 31 (1984), 1–8.

focus not only by such explicit remarks as Ajax's reflections in the Deception Speech (646–92), but also by the shifting of position shown by Odysseus—Ajax's most bitter ἐχθρός. Ajax's assertion in Sophocles' play that he will speak in Hades, through its reminder of the Homeric Ajax's famous silence in Hades, not only offers an ironic pointer to Ajax's continuing hatred but also raises the question both of the role of change in the discourse of the play and of the importance of the different construction of heroic behaviour in the Homeric poems and a drama of fifth-century democratic Athens. The silent Homeric Ajax echoes in the Sophoclean Ajax's promise to speak. The characters of Greek tragedy are predominantly, though not exclusively, figures who also appear in earlier poetic traditions. Ajax, like Agamemnon, Orestes, Clytemnestra, *et al.*, must be approached through the reading of other representations of the (named) character. There is always, as Euripides puts it, a 'present and absent Orestes'[29] on stage, and such an awareness of conflicting representations, conflicting traditions, challenges—fragments—the sense of a dramatic figure as a unique and bounded individual.

Already in Homer, moreover, there is an awareness that the heroic figures the poet describes are 'not like men of today'. So too in Greek tragedy, unlike, say, O'Neill or Chekhov, it is important that the figures on stage are not contemporary nor from the city of the audience nor of a similar status to the members of the audience. Greek tragedy focuses on figures from the heroic past, generally in cities other than Athens and of a type other than the adult male citizens who make up at least the vast majority of the audience. What difference does this make to characterization and individuality, specifically with regard to cultural norms? To what degree is the disjunction between the audience and figures on stage manipulated? Jason accuses Media of doing what no Greek woman could have done. The Danaïds claim to be Greek by descent but are scarcely Greek in appearance and dress. Are they so in their behaviour? It is extremely hard to decide in general or in specific cases to what degree the placing of Athenian tragedy in other cities, other times, allows for other modes of representation.

[29] E. *El.* 391–2.

Gould writes apropos of poetry—and characterization in poetry—'it resembles and it does not resemble our experience'.[30] When the characters of fiction are set in an other place and other time, it is especially hard to articulate securely these differences and similarities.

The construction of character in a literary narrative, in a literary tradition, and in a designedly different world, creates, then, in different ways considerable barriers to treating dramatic figures simply as 'individuals' or 'real people'. The complex dynamics of *representation* cannot be removed from the recognition of character and individuality in narrative fiction.

FIGURE AND DISCOURSE

Despite the difficulties of talking about literary representations as if they were 'real people' or 'individuals', it does not follow that a notion of character can be dispensed with. It is out of a desire both to do justice to the workings of the literary text as narrative representation and to maintain the importance of characterization in drama that I have turned to Roland Barthes's terms 'figure' and 'discourse'—which, it seems, have been regularly misunderstood.[31] I return to Barthes here again, however, not so much to put the critical record straight as to stress the advantages and strengths of Barthes's thesis.

Now in the study of character and Greek drama, particularly in the twentieth century, an *opposition* of character and discourse has been regularly developed by critics. An extreme form of the opposition is defended by Tycho von Wilamowitz and his followers for whom any demonstration of character is absolutely subordinate to 'dramatic effect',[32] and a weaker form of the position is seen in numerous critics especially of Euripides, the dramatist who is most often accused of (at least

[30] 'Dramatic Character', 62.

[31] See e.g. J. Moles, 'Review Discussion', *LCM* 11/4 (1986), 55–64; *contra*, S. Goldhill, 'Goldhill on Molehills', *LCM* 11/10 (1986), 163–7. See now also D. Wiles, 'Reading Greek Performance', *G & R* 34 (1987), 136–51.

[32] T. von Wilamowitz-Moellendorf, *Die dramatische Technik des Sophokles* (Zurich, 1969), on which see H. Lloyd-Jones, 'Tycho von Wilamowitz-Moellendorf on the Dramatic Technique of Sophocles', *CQ* 22 (1972), 214–28; E. Howald, *Die griechische Tragödie* (Munich, 1930) is perhaps the most extreme version of 'Tychoism'. See also R. D. Dawe, 'Inconsistency of Plot and Character in Aeschylus', *PCPS* 9 (1963), 21–62.

occasionally) sacrificing consistency or credibility of characterization to a desire for good plots or even just good rhetorical
arguments. Barthes, however, questions the validity of this
opposition of character and discourse. Discourse and character,
he writes, can be seen in 'good narrative writing' as mutually
and inextricably implicative: 'from a critical point of view . . . it
is as wrong to suppress a character as it is to take him off the
page in order to turn him into a psychological character
(endowed with possible motives): *the character and the discourse are
each other's accomplices*'[33] (Barthes's emphasis). There are two
related extreme positions, then, that Barthes eschews. First, the
idea that character can be wholly suppressed in a narrative, as
if (in drama, for example) it makes no difference to which
figure different utterances are ascribed. Secondly, the idea that
a character can be removed from the page, and treated as a real
person, a full, psychologically endowed individual. Barthes develops his criticism of this second position in a positive direction
by outlining a distinction between 'figure' and 'person'. He
writes:

We occasionally speak of [a character] as though he existed, as
though he had a future, an unconscious, a soul; however, what we are
talking about is his *figure* (an impersonal network of symbols, combined under the proper name . . .), not his *person* (a moral freedom
endowed with motives and an overdetermination of meanings); we
are developing connotations, not pursuing investigations; we are not
searching for the truth of [a character] but for the systematics of a
(transitory) site of the text.[34]

It is important that Barthes is not denying that possible
psychological motivation plays a significant role in fiction.
What he is questioning first is the validity of treating characters
as if they were real people off the page, *really* and *absolutely*
endowed with motivations, which, if only we could discover
them, would give us 'the truth' of a character. In innumerable
places in Greek drama, characters raise questions about other
characters' possible motivations, or suggest reasons for their
own behaviour. In innumerable places, too, critics have raised
further questions of characters' motivations. These questions,

[33] R. Barthes, *S/Z*, trans. R. Miller (London, 1975), 178.
[34] Ibid. 94.

these possibilities of motivation, are a crucial part of what I shall be calling the 'discourse of character' in Greek drama, that is, the consideration of human behaviour and its causes that plays such an important role in fifth-century tragedy. Indeed, the question of possible motivations functions as a key element in the discourse of the tragic texts ('the character and the discourse are each other's accomplices'). But what a critic cannot hope to discover, Barthes argues, is a *certain* answer—the truth—to the questions of possible motivation. It is because a character is a 'figure' and not a 'person' that there can be no sure and fixed answer to what a character is 'really feeling', 'really thinking', 'really wanting'—his/her (real) motivation—at any particular moment in a text.[35]

Yet it remains necessary to be able to develop the different connotations of, say, the representations of Electra and Clytemnestra in the *Oresteia*—where the name functions as the node of such connotations. It also remains necessary to be able to discuss, say, the role of Clytemnestra's powerful manipulation of language within the narrative, or Orestes' hesitation before killing his mother—what Barthes terms 'the systematics of a (transitory) site of the text'.

Barthes' use of the term 'figure', then, makes possible the discussion of such necessary elements of characterization as Clytemnestra's hypocrisy, Orestes' hesitation, *but* without requiring or leading to the uncritical position of treating a character as a person 'with a future, an unconscious, a soul'. It enables us to see the questions of motivation as part of the narrative discourse of the play (and not simply as problems to be solved by ever-increasing critical sensitivity).

The terms 'figure' and 'discourse', then, and Barthes's analysis of their interrelation, help avoid two typical and unproductive critical arguments. First, Barthes's position aims to circumvent the rigid opposition of character and discourse—the opposition that sees, for example, Orestes' hesitation before matricide either as only a clue to his character or as only a moment of dramatic effect (to allow the development of the play's discourse). Secondly, Barthes aims in the distinction

---

[35] This is not to suggest that in 'real life' motivations can be absolutely and certainly determined—as Prof. Easterling points out in ch. 4.

between 'figure' and 'person' to avoid arguing endlessly over what Orestes is 'really feeling', 'thinking', as he hesitates and then completes the matricide. If the question of motivation or causation is raised at that point in the *Oresteia*—as I believe it is—it is a question which functions in the discourse of the play *as a question*, and it is not open to a true and certain answer, however close the reading of the text.

Barthes offers important criticisms, then, of particular arguments which have been common in the analysis of Greek tragedy and also offers some indications of possible ways to pursue the necessary discussion of characterization and individuality in narrative fiction. In the following section, I wish further to follow these indications by investigating the idea raised in this section of the 'question of motivation' and its role in the discourse of a play.

THE DISCOURSE OF CHARACTER, THE CHARACTER OF DISCOURSE

In the Greek tragic texts, there are extensive and complex vocabularies for the explanation of behaviour in terms of humans' attitudes— e.g. φρήν, φρονεῖν, σωφρονεῖν, νοῦς ['mind'; 'to have sense', 'to think'; 'to be sensible'; 'mind', 'thought'] (and such terms of transgression as ἄφρων, τολμᾶν ['senseless'; 'to dare']).[36] That σωφρονεῖν, for example, is a common term for political behaviour,[37] and that τολμᾶν can also be used to express the performance of 'deeds of derring-do', suggest that, as with the modern discourse of 'sense' and 'madness', the boundaries between (mental) attitudes and the actions in which such attitudes are seen to be instantiated are far from rigid. None the less, the public, masked personae of Athenian tragedy are regularly said to act and claim to act because of their attitudes and states of mind.

[36] On the variety of this vocabulary in Aeschylus, see e.g., for bibliog. and discussion, D. Sansone, *Aeschylean Metaphors for Intellectual Activity* (Wiesbaden, 1975). On Sophocles, see e.g. A. A. Long, *Language and Thought in Sophocles* (London, 1968), esp. 51 ff. For recent discussion and bibliog., consult F. Solmsen, 'φρήν, καρδία, ψυχή, in Greek Tragedy', in D. E. Gerber (ed.), *Greek Poetry and Philosophy: Studies in Honour of Leonard Woodbury* (Chico, 1984).

[37] See H. North, *Sophrosyne: Self-Knowledge and Self-Restraint in Greek Literature* (New York, 1966), 32 ff.

In *Reading Greek Tragedy* I analysed the use of such vocabulary in three plays. In Euripides' *Hippolytus*, I discuss how the
various figures of the play—including the divinities—utilize the
language of 'sense' and in particular the language of
σωφρονεῖν.[38] The complex and varied usage of this term not
only is crucial to the play's concern with the relation between
human language, morality, and behaviour, but also cannot be
viewed separately from the play's thematic interest in the relation between speech and thought, silence and utterance—that
is, between the inward life and outward expression of a figure.
The evaluation of Hippolytus as a figure both by the characters
of the drama and by the critics of the play in part depends on
analysing the relation between what he says and what that
might indicate about his *ēthos*. In *Antigone*, the political debate is
also formulated in mutual accusations of corrupt mental attitudes, as assertions of madness, senselessness, and failures of
understanding clash.[39] Creon's first speech (163–210) establishes his own story as the narrative of a man's disposition
(φρόνημα) being tested in the circumstances of power. In *Ajax*,
much of the play up to Ajax's suicide is taken up with various
characters' reflections on and doubts about the mental state of
the hero—and in the great Deception Speech, the audience too
is faced with a marked problem of relating the hero's words to
his intended course of behaviour and to his true beliefs.[40] After
the death of Ajax, the debate about his burial revolves around
conflicting evaluations of the hero. In both the *Ajax* and the
Hippolytus, the explicit external influence of divine figures on
the emotional or mental state of the figures of the drama adds a
further element to the dynamics of the relation between external and internal aspects of characterization. In each of these
three plays, it is important to investigate how the 'discourse of
character'—the focus on (the norms and transgressions of)
human attitudes; on the relation between expression, belief,
and behaviour; on the necessity and problems of evaluating a
figure's attitudes—is affected by the character of the discourse
of the play in which it plays a part. Here, I intend to consider
briefly one much discussed moment in Euripidean drama,

[38] *Reading Greek Tragedy*, 107–37, esp. 132–7.
[39] Ibid. 168–79.
[40] See for discussion and bibliog., ibid. 189–92.

where the implications for the study of characterization and
individuality have been inadequately appreciated.

Πε.   ἐκφέρετέ μοι δεῦρ' ὅπλα, σὺ δὲ παῦσαι λέγων.
Δι.   ᾶ.
       βούλῃ σφ' ἐν ὄρεσι συγκαθημένας ἰδεῖν;
Πε.   μάλιστα, μυρίον γε δοὺς χρυσοῦ σταθμόν.

Pe.   Bring me here my armour. You! Stop speaking.
Di.   Ah.
       Do you want to see the women assembled on the mountain?
Pe.   Yes! I would give a great weight of gold to do so.

                                           (*Ba.* 809–12.)

This exchange is often regarded as a turning-point in the
interchanges of Pentheus and Dionysus. After Dionysus' interjection, ᾶ,[41] Pentheus gives up his apparent intention to mount
a military enterprise against the women and agrees rather to
observe them in their Bacchic conclave. For Dodds, this transformation is the key to Pentheus' true nature: 'The question has
touched a hidden spring in Pentheus' mind, and his self-
mastery vanishes.'[42] Winnington-Ingram, too, sees this as a
psychologically revealing reversal of intention: 'An answer
comes back pat; and it is the true answer ... This is, as Professor Dodds remarks, the answer of a maniac.'[43] It is a true
answer and the answer of a maniac because it truly represents
Pentheus' (maniacal?) 'unconscious desire'.[44] Winnington-
Ingram, however, also sees this as a demonstration of Dionysus'
power: the god 'begins to exert some kind of psychic power over
his victim'.[45] Segal also emphasizes a close connection between
a demonstration of Dionysiac power and a demonstration of
Pentheus' real desires: 'Dionysus' speech probes Pentheus'
hidden desires ... Dionysus lays bare and exploits his
opponent's repressed, voyeuristic (and thus infantile) sexual-

---

[41] The sense of this interjection has been much debated. See e.g. E. R. Dodds's
comm. (Oxford, 1944), ad loc.; R. P. Winnington-Ingram, *Euripides and Dionysus: An
Interpretation of the* Bacchae (Cambridge, 1948), 102; C. P. Segal, *Dionysiac Poetics and
Euripides'* Bacchae (Princeton, 1982), 197; O. Taplin, *Greek Tragedy in Action* (London,
1978), 120–1.

[42] In his note ad loc.

[43] *Euripides and Dionysus*, 103.

[44] Ibid. 103.

[45] Ibid. 102.

ity.'[46] For Oranje, however, if this scene represents a 'psychic invasion', it is the god's power alone which is demonstrated as he drives Pentheus mad: 'Pentheus' answer in 812 . . . is one in which madness speaks . . . There seems no reason to suppose that in Pentheus Euripides has conceived a character who was limited by the repression of his own sexuality.'[47] Roux goes so far as to suppose that Pentheus' response to Dionysus (812) is 'dite sur un ton de persiflage'[48]—a sign of Pentheus' continuing resistance to the god.

Is this scene, then, a demonstration of Dionysus' divine power as he drives Pentheus mad—an external force that destroys the θεομάχος ['one who fights with a god']? Or is Dionysus' question merely a 'probe' which allows the repressed desires of Pentheus to find true expression—the king's internal nature that leads him to destruction? Or is it a demonstration of Dionysiac power by the unloosing of such repressed desires—as the god's force somehow 'springs' the king's internal desires? What is at stake in the very formulation of such questions is the recognition of the nature of Dionysiac possession. When does such influence start in the play—all of which occurs under the aegis of the god's prologue? Is the Dionysiac influence over Teiresias, Cadmus, Pentheus, Agave the same in each case? Are the unwilling Theban women in maenadic costume and the willing χορός of Eastern maenads and the willing χορός of Teiresias and Cadmus similar demonstrations of the god's power of transformation and release? The question which motivates the narrative of the *Bacchae*—What is it for Thebes to recognize Dionysus?—becomes also the question of critical discussion or audience response to the narrative, as the different figures of Dionysus' play dress up to worship Dionysus. If Dionysus' 'Ah', then, represents a turning-point in the narrative, it is a turning-point which necessarily implicates an understanding—a recognition—of Dionysiac influence, and it is the security of that understanding, that recognition, which the *Bacchae* itself seems to make problematic. So the different critics' different constructions of the internal and external aspects of Pentheus' transformation are closely involved with their

---

[46] *Dionysiac Poetics*, 197.
[47] H. Oranje, *Euripides' Bacchae: The Play and its Audience* (Brill, 1984), 82–3.
[48] J. Roux, *Les Bacchantes* (2 vols., Paris, 1970–2), ad loc.

recognition of Dionysus—a recognition with implications for the very construction of 'human nature'. (Thus Dodds writes, in a way which makes such implications explicit and clear: 'To resist Dionysus is to repress the elemental in one's own nature.')[49] The question of Pentheus' motivation here cannot, therefore, be separated from the question of Dionysus' power and the recognition of Dionysus (in and by each reader amid the play of disguises and shifting boundaries). This turning-point in the narrative of the *Bacchae*, then, turns on the question of character—and the character of the questions asked of it. And these questions are crucially interwoven with the discourse of the play, its concern for the boundaries and normative controls of human nature.

ACTION AND CHARACTER

This discussion of the close involvement of the discourse of character in the tragic texts leads inevitably towards Aristotle, who suggests in the sixth chapter of the *Poetics* that tragedy without character (*ēthos*) is feasible (although it is evidenced, he claims, only by the most modern work, contemporary with himself).[50] Despite regular modern arguments that Aristotle's (normative) description of tragedy has many failings as an account of our extant drama,[51] recent treatments of the *Poetics* and of tragedy in the light of Aristotle make a brief reconsideration relevant here.

Stephen Halliwell's study of the *Poetics* has illuminated the connections between character (*ēthos*) and action in Aristotle's aesthetic theory, and placed in sharper focus the need to relate Aristotle's aesthetics to his other ethical and normative concerns.[52] For Aristotle, writes Halliwell, character (*ēthos*) necessarily involves the depiction of the ethical choice of an agent:

---

[49] Dodds, comm., xiv.

[50] αἱ γὰρ τῶν νέων τῶν πλείστων ἀήθεις τραγῳδίαι εἰσίν (*Poet.* 1450ᵃ24–5).

[51] Arguments well summed up by Jones, *On Aristotle and Greek Tragedy*, 46: 'Applying Aristotle's *Poetics* to the surviving Greek tragedies . . . has involved commentators in a double process of rejection and re-writing.'

[52] S. Halliwell, *Aristotle's Poetics* (London, 1986), esp. 138–67. For further modern discussions, see e.g. G. Held, 'The Meaning of ἦθος in the *Poetics*', *Hermes*, 113 (1985), 280–93; E. Schütrumpf, 'The Meaning of ἦθος in the *Poetics*: A Reply', *Hermes*, 115 (1987), 175–81.

'Aristotle's understanding of character is essentially ethical, rests on a close relation between character and action, and interprets the behaviour of persons less in terms of individuality than by reference to a set of objective and common standards.'[53] It is practical reasoning, instantiated in action, that indicates a figure's measure against 'things as they might or should be': so, for Aristotle, 'if character is to play a part in tragedy, as it is ideally required to do, there must be no uncertainty or ambiguity about it; we must be able to identify it as a specific dimension of the action, embodied in clear evidence for the ethical disposition of the agents'[54] Despite Aristotle's statement, then, that tragedy can be without character, there remains, Halliwell argues, a place for *ēthos* in (the ideal) tragedy, although Aristotle's emphasis on different formal characteristics of drama also maintains the secondary position of 'character' in his theoretical stance: 'The main tenets of the theory of tragedy, therefore—the stress on unity of action, on pity and fear, and on the nature of the complex plot—confirm that characterization should be integrally involved in the composition of the ideal tragedy, but also show the limit on Aristotle's expectations of it.'[55]

Implicit in this construction of *ēthos* is not merely a privileging of practical reasoning as a sign of disposition, but also a theory of cause and effect. The human agent's ability to evaluate the effects of his possible decisions and the causes of his situation is crucial to the process of practical reasoning. So, too, connections between events—not merely the connections supposed in the process of practical reasoning but also the connections that make possible Aristotle's physical or scientific enquiries—depend on a pattern of 'things as they might or should be', a pattern that instantiates the rationality of τὸ εἰκὸς ['what is likely/probable/generally true']. It is here that Halliwell sees the greatest disjunction between Aristotle's theoretical position and the extant dramas of the tragic corpus: 'It [Aristotle's world] is a world whose causal connections demonstrate "things as they might or should be", not as they simply are, but it is ... remote from the sense of the hopeless, the mysterious

[53] S. Halliwell, *Aristotle's* Poetics, 164.
[54] Ibid. 152.
[55] Ibid. 164.

and the opaque which colours much of the tragic myth we know.'[56]

Aeschylus' *Oresteia* has proved a particularly difficult text to fit into an Aristotelian model, not merely because its view of human action, with its tragic logic of the double bind, seems to offer a paradigm of 'the hopeless, the mysterious and the opaque', but also specifically because its view of a causal pattern of events is marked by an uncertainty that may seem to set at risk an Aristotelian principle of τὸ εἰκός and the practical reasoning that depends on it. I wish to continue this section by investigating briefly one aspect of Aeschylean causality which is germane to the disjunction between Aristotle and the tragic corpus.

If the action of the *Oresteia* involves its figures in a particularly bleak world of compulsion, uncertainty, and grief, the *Oresteia* is also a trilogy which ends, if not with an unqualified resolution of such forces, at least with what many critics have seen as a lauding of the potential of the just city to make sense of man's existence—a view not wholly alien to Aristotle's construction of man as πολιτικὸν ζῷον, a 'political animal'. It is within the context of the praise of the potential of the *polis* that Athene delivers the following lines, which are rarely given their due weight in readings of the final scene of the trilogy:

> ὅ γε μὴν κύρσας βαρεῶν τούτων
> οὐκ οἶδεν ὅθεν πληγαὶ βιότου·
> τὰ γὰρ ἐκ προτέρων ἀμπλακήματά νιν
> πρὸς τάσδ' ἀπάγει, σιγῶν ⟨δ'⟩ ὄλεθρος
> καὶ μέγα φωνοῦντ'
> ἐχθραῖς ὀργαῖς ἀμαθύνει.

The man who meets these heavy ones [the Furies]
Does not know from where the blows of life come.
For his predecessors' errors
Lead him away to them, and silent doom,
Even as he shouts loudly,
Wastes him in hateful rages.

(*Eum.* 932–7)

Contact with the Erinyes, according to Athene, necessarily implies humans' ignorance. The expression 'blows of life'

echoes the description of Zeus' destruction of Troy (*Ag.* 367),
Agamemnon's death at the hands of Clytemnestra (*Ag.* 1343–
6), and Orestes' action of revenge (*Cho.* 312–13); and it is precisely the origin (ὅθεν) of such disasters that humans cannot
know. The reason (γάρ) for this is continuing influence of the
past on the present. 'Predecessors' errors' have a determining
effect on a man's life. Thomson explains this by reference to the
oath against perjury taken in the Areopagus which promised
the destruction of the perjurer's race, family, and children by
the Σέμναι θεαί, the divinities whose powers Athene here is describing.[57] Throughout the narrative of the *Oresteia*, however,
particularly in the choruses' views of past events and in, say,
Cassandra's prophetic analysis of the interweaving of past and
present, the direct but obscure effect of the past on the present
action is invoked. An ignorance of the past leads to an inevitable ignorance of the pattern of cause and effect in which man's
narratives of error and punishment are constructed.

The doom that destroys is silent—which is in opposition to
the man who shouts loudly, or boasts. This image of the
inscrutability of the misfortune in which a man is set also recalls
the Erinyes' own description of their destruction of a sinner
against justice:

κάλει δ' ἀκούοντας οὐδὲν ⟨ἐν⟩ μέσᾳ
δυσπαλεῖ τε δίνᾳ·
γελᾷ δὲ δαίμων ἐπ' ἀνδρὶ θερμῷ,
τὸν οὔποτ' αὐχοῦντ' ἰδὼν ἀμηχάνοις
δύαις λαπαδνὸν οὐδ' ὑπερθέοντ' ἄκραν.

He will call on those who hear nothing, as he struggles
Vainly in the midst of whirling seas.
God laughs at the heated man,
As he sees him who boasted this would never happen,
Weakened by hopeless griefs, and failing to round the headland.

(*Eum.* 558–62)

So Athene's description of the Erinyes' powers echoes their self-
description in the common image of man's vain shouting, lack
of control, misplaced certainty, and inability to understand his
misfortune. Despite Lebeck's claim that in the *Oresteia* there is

[57] G. Thomson, *The Oresteia* (Amsterdam, 1966), ad loc. See Dem. 23. 67; Lycurg,
Leocr. 79.

movement from obscurity to clarity,[58] and despite the trilogy's final lauding of the city's powers and blessings, the goddess of Athens authorizes man's continuing ignorance and uncertainty precisely in the causal pattern of things, precisely in the narratives crucial to practical reasoning and moral agency.

The view of human action represented here seems, then, to suppose man's necessary ignorance and uncertainty, specifically with regard to the continuing but obscure influence of the past. It is the way that humans in the *Oresteia* seem to be inevitably written into a narrative over which they have insecure control or understanding that obscures a pattern of cause and effect in action. It is this very obscurity of causal connection which stands against the Aristotelian requirements of tragedy's action and the embodiment of *ēthos* in tragedy.

MORAL ACTION AND MORAL CHARACTER

The representation of moral choice in tragedy and the expression of *ēthos* through such choice has been articulated against Aristotle's aesthetic and ethical arguments most recently by Martha Nussbaum.[59] Nussbaum argues that tragedy's depiction of moral dilemma and choice corresponds more closely to 'the intuitive position' of 'how it *feels* to be in that situation'[60] than either the Kantian or the Aristotelian approach. Her argument is complex and wide-ranging, and here, where I shall treat one small section of her long work, I am aware that I shall be doing some violence to its place in her overall argument. None the less, Nussbaum's treatment of Aeschylus raises some crucial issues for the discussion of characterization and individuality.

Aeschylus, Nussbaum argues, 'shows us not so much a "solution" to the "problem of practical conflict" as the richness and depth of the problem itself'.[61] She describes 'the conflict situation as a test of character', which also gives 'us new informa-

---

[58] Lebeck, *The* Oresteia, 3.

[59] M. C. Nussbaum, *The Fragility of Goodness: Luck and Ethics in Greek Tragedy and Philosophy* (Cambridge, 1986). For a critique from a perspective different from mine, see S. Botros, 'Precarious Virtue', *Phronesis*, 32 (1987), 101–31.

[60] Nussbaum, *The Fragility of Goodness*, 32.   [61] Ibid. 49.

tion about what the agent's character has been all along'.[62] Agamemnon at Aulis is a paradigmatic 'agent'. He is placed in a position of mutually exclusive, conflicting possibilities, where one course of action must be chosen. He is not responsible for the situation in which he finds himself. It is a double bind, where 'there is open to him no guilt-free course'[63] (on which Nussbaum comments: 'Such situations may be repellent to practical logic; they are also familiar from the experience of life').[64] Furthermore, 'his attitude towards the decision itself seems to have changed with the making of it'[65]—a change for the worse in his apparent enthusiasm for a repellent sacrifice. The 'proper response'[66] of practical wisdom does not stop at a decision, but also involves what is to be learnt in and from a decision, and also an acknowledgement or recognition of what is at stake in the chosen action. Tragedy emphasizes how practical wisdom and practical reasoning should involve a continuing process of 'pain and remorse bound up with ... a seriousness about value, a constancy in commitment, and a sympathetic responsiveness that we wish to maintain and develop in others and ourselves'.[67]

In her search for a coherent moral argument, however, Nussbaum's depiction of Agamemnon as agent also runs the risk of underestimating the complexity of the narrative in which Agamemnon is represented. First of all, the chorus tell of Iphigeneia's sacrifice as part of an extended lyric which has an argument of its own. Nussbaum distinguishes 'the report of Agamemnon's commands' from 'the chorus's own memory', which 'brings with it the only note of compassionate humanity in this terrible scene'.[68] Yet the very nature of the depiction of Agamemnon's command is part of the choral rhetoric which invests their further comments with the power to move through its contrary expression of compassion. So the chorus's representation of Agamemnon's choice is to be set against their unwillingness or inability to see beyond 'things as they are'

---

[62] Ibid. 44. [63] Ibid. 34.
[64] Ibid. 34. [65] Ibid. 35.
[66] Ibid. 42. [67] Ibid. 50.
[68] Ibid. 37.

(66–7) and their final expresssive refusals to comment on the
implications of actions (248–57). Thus the description of Agamemnon's change of mind, on which Nussbaum bases much of
her argument, needs to be read in the light of the Hymn to
Zeus, whose maxims, the chorus implies, Agamemnon is instan-
tiating. The Hymn to Zeus promises σωφρονεῖν ['good sense']
for even the unwilling (180–1), and straightness of mind (175–
6) for the supporters of Zeus. Yet Agamemnon, in putting on
the yoke-strap of necessity with an 'unholy, impious, irreligious
changing-wind of the mind'[69] changes to 'thinking the all-
daring'—the very antithesis of σωφρονεῖν. Are the chorus talking of Agamemnon here only as agent, that is, offering comment on the psychological process of an individual's choice?
Are they not also constructing an argument about divine
influence—an attempt to explain Agamemnon's action in
terms wider than 'practical reasoning'? The chorus's representation of Agamemnon's choice is not merely an (unmedi-
ated) exemplum of moral agency, but part of a narrative
(which affects—constitutes—the representation). The *parodos* is
not simply a story of Agamemnon, but a story of a chorus's nar-
rating of a story of Agamemnon.

If there is a danger of ignoring the narrative of the drama in
Nussbaum's discussion of Agamemnon as moral agent, there is
also a danger of ignoring the literary tradition in which Agamemnon plays a part. 'Agamemnon is allowed to choose',
writes Nussbaum,[70] as if Homer had no influence on the understanding of such a choice, as if there were simply two symmet-
rical alternative courses of action for the autonomous
individual to choose between. So the chorus's comment μάντιν
οὔτινα ψέγων ['blaming no seer'] (186) becomes for Nussbaum
only another psychological insight into the decision-making
process: 'Voicing no blame of the prophet or his terrible message, Agamemnon now begins to co-operate inwardly with
necessity, arranging his feelings to accord with his fortune.'[71]

---

[69] It is noticeable that Nussbaum (ibid. 36), unaccountably translates only one of
the three adjectives qualifying τροπαίαν; together they place a very strong emphasis on
the corrupted state of mind of Agamemnon *as* he puts on the yoke strap. He then
changes from this impiety to utter recklessness. Does this qualify Nussbaum's assertion
of the guiltlessness of Agamemnon before the decision?
[70] Ibid. 34.   [71] Ibid. 35.

Yet the chorus's remark also recalls the opening scene of the *Iliad*, where Agamemnon indeed turns on the μάντις ['seer'], Calchas, with insults and aggression (*Il.* 1. 106–20.). Over the matter of another young girl, Chryseis, and the incipient wrath of another divinity, Agamemnon in the *Iliad* is all too ready to blame a seer—which leads to a disastrous turn in the war for the Achaeans. Over his own daughter, Agamemnon in the *Agamemnon* has no reproach for Calchas—and gives up the girl to start the war. There is an ironic paradox of behaviour here that depends not so much on Agamemnon turning 'himself into a collaborator, a willing victim',[72] as on the juxtaposition and difference of literary representations.

The involvement of the past and the present which I discussed in the previous section is also crucial to a sense of moral agency. Nussbaum mentions 'a background guilt in the situation',[73] but emphasizes 'the contingent and external origin of Agamemnon's dreadful dilemma. It simply comes on him as he is piously executing Zeus' commands.'[74] The guilt of the family is seen by Nussbaum in the circumstances which place Agamemnon, 'a previously guiltless man, in a situation in which there is open to him no guilt-free course'.[75] This opposition of an individual to his family is crucial to maintain the sense of Agamemnon as 'moral agent'. Calchas, however, explains the situation thus:

μίμνει γὰρ φοβερὰ παλίνορτος
οἰκονόμος δολία, μνάμων μῆνις τεκνόποινος.

For there remains, rising up again, a fearful
Deceitful keeper of the house, wrath that recalls, child-avenging.

(154–5)

This remark is an explanation of Artemis' requirement of 'another sacrifice'.[76] It explains the significance of the omen of

---

[72] Ibid. 35.
[73] Ibid. 34.
[74] Ibid. 34.
[75] Ibid. Here Nussbaum is following H. Lloyd-Jones, 'The Guilt of Agamemnon', *CQ* 12 (1962), 187–99, an argument followed up in id., *The Justice of Zeus* (Berkeley, 1971).
[76] On the interconnections between the members of the house of Atreus and their actions that the language of sacrifice forms, see F. I. Zeitlin, 'The Motif of the Corrupted Sacrifice in Aeschylus' *Oresteia*', *TAPA* 96 (1965), 463–505.

the eagles in a way which looks back to the earlier narrative of the house of Atreus and forward to the future events of the trilogy. μίμνει ['there remains'], μνάμων ['remembering'], and παλίνορτος ['rising up again' (from the past)] each express the continuing pattern of events within the narrative of revenge and transgression—a pattern which is established certainly if not immediately. φοβερά ['fearful'] is a leitmotiv of this narrative from the watchman's fear (14) to Athene's recognition of a need for fear in a just society (*Eum.* 691). The 'deceitful keeper of the house' both anticipates Clytemnestra's deceitful claims precisely of faithfully keeping the household (*Ag.* 606–14), and also implies the quarrel and dreadful feasting of Thyestes and Atreus. The final word τεκνόποινος suggests the coming revenge for a child enacted by Clytemnestra, but also the revenge enacted by a child, namely Orestes, and also the earlier punishments of Atreus and Thyestes with their reciprocal acts of violence against generational continuity. Iphigeneia's sacrifice is one of a series of intergenerational crimes of violence. The μῆνις, then, the 'wrath' of gods or god-like humans (which leads to destruction), is qualified by a series of terms and instantiated in a series of ways which interconnect the members of the household. And such an interconnection is Calchas' explanation of why Agamemnon suffers. The determining force which Calchas describes so ominously and even obscurely depends on a view of action within a household that makes it hard to see Agamemnon as an autonomous, moral agent. The belief that 'no personal guilt of Agamemnon's has led him into this tragic predicament'[77] relies, then, on a view of the person as moral agent which may not be capable of doing justice to the representation of Agamemnon—as a figure always already inscribed in the determining narrative of his household.

Yet it would be wrong to conclude this part of the discussion on a critical note. For Nussbaum raises a fundamental issue in her explicit connection of the normative and characterization. Greek tragedians as οἱ σοφοί[78] are placed in a didactic role in the city; the great humanist traditions of education, too, have produced and continue to produce paradigms of behaviour and

---

[77] Nussbaum, *The Fragility of Goodness*, 33.
[78] See my *Reading Greek Tragedy*, 222–3, for the sense of this phrase.

attitude from a reading of the texts of the ancient world. Nussbaum makes it plain both how the discourse of character is part of the normative discourse of Athenian tragedy, and also how the very discussion of such issues cannot but involve the normative system of the interpreters themselves. It is precisely in relating the problems of representation to the analysis of the normative categories of the person in (the study of) Greek tragedy that the discussion of characterization and individuality is to advance.

6

Characterization in Euripides: *Hippolytus* and *Iphigeneia in Aulis*

JASPER GRIFFIN

The question of characterization in Attic tragedy is a fascination and also a complex one. It has sometimes suffered from the assumption that a playwright always behaves, in this regard, in the same way. That is, I think, untrue, and I hope it will emerge from this discussion that in these two plays—one of them among the earliest which we possess from the poet's pen, the other left unfinished at his death—Euripides can be seen to handle the characterization and the psychology of his people in ways which have a good deal in common, but which also are importantly different.

I

In the *Hippolytus* Euripides did something pretty unusual for an Attic dramatist. He wrote a second play on a myth which he had handled already, and instead of concentrating on a different part of the story, as with the two Oedipus plays of Sophocles or with his own two Alcmaeon or Melanippe plays, he treated again exactly the same events as he had dramatized before. What he changed was the colouring and meaning of events. In his first *Hippolytus* play,[1] as is evident both from ancient reports and also from the extant fragments, Euripides versified the good old sequence of the unchaste wife who offers herself to a personable young man, is rebuffed by him, and denounces him falsely to her husband. In Greek myth we find such incontinent ladies as Stheneboea, also known as Anteia, who went through this routine with the young Bellerophon; she, too, was the sub-

---

[1] See the discussion of the plays in W. S. Barrett's magisterial edition of the *Hippolytus* (Oxford, 1964), 10–45; and now O. Zwierlein, 'Senecas Phaedra und ihre Vorbilder' (*Ak. der Wiss., Mainz*, 1987. 5).

ject of a play by Euripides, and Aristophanes lets his Aeschylus, in the *Frogs*, roundly call the pair of them, Stheneboea and Phaedra, a couple of whores (πόρναι).[2] The blameless Peleus, too, was the subject of similar advances from the wife of his host Acastus of Iolcus. Some called her Astydameia, others Hippolyte: under either name she was bad news.[3] Both Bellerophon and Peleus, however, did manage to survive the perils into which they were plunged by the credulous and jealous husbands of these naughty wives.

All societies which shut up their women folk at home feel uneasiness about what they may be getting up to when their husbands are away. We see these misogynist fantasies in the *Thesmophoriazusae*, for instance. The presence of a young man is likely to present an irresistible temptation to the essentially passionate and irrational female nature. It will be convenient to use, as paradigm, the Hebrew story of Joseph and Potiphar's wife:

And it came to pass after these things that his master's wife cast her eyes upon Joseph; and she said, 'Lie with me.' But he refused ... and it came to pass that Joseph went into the house to do his business; and there was none of the men of the house there within. And she caught him by his garment, saying 'Lie with me', and he left his garment in her hand, and fled, and got him out. [She denounced him to the men of her household, and when her husband came home] she spoke unto him according to these words, saying, 'The Hebrew servant, which thou hast brought unto us, came in unto me to mock me; and it came to pass, as I lifted up my voice and cried, that he left his garment with me and fled out.' And ... his master's wrath was kindled ...[4]

I quoted that at length because it shows us, with great clarity and economy, the natural shape of this universal story-pattern. The woman makes her attempt at seduction, and then she denounces the recalcitrant young man to the anger of her husband. The first Hippolytus play of Euripides presented this sequence, it appears, in very much the good old way.[5] Phaedra

---

[2] T. B. L. Webster, *The Tragedies of Euripides* (London, 1967), 109 ff., on Euripides, *Bellerophon*; Aristoph. *Ran.* 1043.

[3] Hes. frs. 208–9 MW; Pind. *Nem.* 4. 54 ff.

[4] Gen. 39. It is fascinating to see how Thomas Mann equips that stark mythical narrative with elaborate psychology in his great novel *Joseph and his Brothers*.

[5] E. frs. 430, 435 N²; Zwierlein, 'Senecas Phaedra', 24 ff., thinks the first Phaedra was not really so bad.

130   *Jasper Griffin*

made a dead set in person at Hippolytus, he veiled his head in
horror, she denounced him to Theseus, perhaps producing
faked evidence of violence, and Theseus caused his death with a
curse. This play, we are told, shocked the Athenians. It certainly was one of the most notorious productions of its always
controversial author, much mentioned by the comic poets.
Then (I think this is the order) Sophocles wrote a play on the
same myth, calling it *Phaedra*, in which he showed how this eminently Euripidean theme of the passionate love of a woman
could be handled in a Sophoclean manner. The contrast of the
Medea with Sophocles' *Trachiniae* will probably give an idea of
the change of atmosphere and ethos. Deianira had always been
infamous as the wife who killed her husband with the poisoned
robe of Nessus: Sophocles presents her as a patient and long-
suffering wife, who has borne without exploding the countless
amours of her husband, but who, faced with his actually introducing a younger rival into her house, resorts to the robe in the
belief that it is not a deadly poison but a harmless love-charm.
A murderous Medea is softened into a womanly and well-
meaning character. Something of the same transformation—
removal of venom—I guess, took place in Sophocles' *Phaedra*:
for he presented her as believing that her husband, who had
gone down into the Underworld and not returned, was dead.
Clearly her action assumes a very different appearance.[6]

It is generally assumed that Euripides wrote his second
Hippolytus out of chagrin at the failure of the first, and to correct
(in the words of the *Second Hypothesis*) 'what was unseemly and
deserving of criticism' in that unfortunate work.[7] 'We may
assume', says Mr Barrett, 'that the failure of his earlier play had
rankled with him.' Scholars indeed generally seem to share the

---

[6] I find the acute and ingenious suggestion of Zwierlein (id., 55–62), that in
Sophocles' *Phaedra* the heroine attempted to poison Hippolytus, impossible to accept. S.
fr. 678 R seems to show that the approach to Hippolytus was not, in Sophicles' play,
made on the stage.

[7] 'It is manifest that this play was written later, as what was unseemly and deserved
criticism has been put right in this play.' Cf. the ancient *Life* (Schwartz, *Scholia in
Euripidem*, 1, 5): 'They say that he married Choerile, daughter of Mnesilochus, and
when he realized her lewd behaviour he first wrote the play *Hippolytus*, in which he
denounces the shamelessness of women, and then divorced her' (an anecdote follows,
with Euripides quoting one of his own plays). All this has alike the look of being
invented: even the order of composition of the plays is only an interence ('it is manifest')
not a fact derived from the didascalic records. Cf. M. R. Lefkowitz, *Lives of the Greek
Poets* (London, 1981), 89–104.

aesthetic and moral attitudes assumed in a fifth-century Attic audience. 'The Athenians were doubtless over-squeamish in their abhorrence of the Phaedra of his first play; but she can have been at best but a distasteful character, and now in her place we have a far nobler and more tragic figure. The economy of the play is improved'—for now we find it natural that Theseus should believe Phaedra and ignore Hippolytus' denials. Above all, 'the greatest advantage lies in the treatment of Hippolytus that is now made possible': in the first play he must simply have been an innocent overwhelmed with unmerited disaster, a spectacle not really tragic, while in the second his chastity is accompanied by 'a narrow unthinking intolerance of common humanity', so that he becomes partly responsible for his own calamity.[8]

I do not myself believe that chagrin at the failure of a play would in itself have motivated Euripides to produce a quite different play on the same theme. He was usually unsuccessful in the competitions—four first prizes only, we are told, in his long career—and he must have been hardened to criticism and even derision long before 428, when we consider what an obviously stock comic subject he already is in Aristophanes' *Acharnians*, produced in the spring of 425. In any case, the explanation is suspiciously mechanical: 'They didn't like the first version, so he produced one which they did like.' Nothing else which we know of Euripides suggests that he attached so much weight to meeting the tastes of the *demos*.[9]

A much better reason, I think, lies in the genuinely artistic challenge which he set himself in the second *Hippolytus*. Let me remind you of the story of Potiphar's wife. There are two high points in it: the woman making her advance to the young man

[8] Euripides, *Hippolytus*, ed. W. S. Barrett (Oxford, 1964), 13 f. 'Da Euripides Phaidra zu entlasten gedachte und das zweite Stück in dieser Absicht schrieb' (W. H. Friedrich, *Euripides und Diphilos* (Zetemata, 5; Munich, 1953), 138). G. M. A. Grube, *The Drama of Euripides* (London, 1941), 177, refers to 'the disgust caused to the Athenians' by the first *Hippolytus*.

[9] 'Euripides was not the sort of poet who would change his opinion or his considered judgement or win over or to gratify the public' (C. F. Kumaniecki, *De Consiliis Personarum apud Euripidem Agentium* (Cracow, 1930), 29). Kumaniecki is, however, in my view wrong to draw the conclusion that what Euripides did was to retain culpable features in his second Phaedra 'he did criticize Phaedra a little ... she cannot be said to be wholly innocent and blameless here' (ibid. 30). What follows here is not part of a biography of Euripides but an attempt to bring out the particular character of the extant *Hippolytus* play.

('Lie with me'), and the woman denouncing him to her husband. An actress contemplating the part nowadays would instantly see those as her two big moments, and so would the Athenian actor who played the leading female role. The same is true of the narrative in the sixth book of the *Iliad* of the affair of Anteia and Bellerophon: she could not induce him to make love to her, so she said to her husband: 'May you die, Proetus, if you do not kill Bellerophon, who tried to seduce me against my will' (*Il.* 6. 160–5). We can, I think, characterize this sequence of scenes. It is vigorous, highly coloured, melodramatic, obvious. I imagine Euripides meditating on his first Hippolytus play, recalled (I guess) to his thoughts by the elegant variant upon it by Sophocles, and deciding that after all it really *had* been a rather unworthy production: not so much for ἀπρέπεια as for the artistic reason of obviousness and crudity in its conception.

Was it possible, then, to write a play on that age-old theme which would be better? That would mean getting away from the traditional schema of the tale. Was it, for instance, possible to create a good play in which Phaedra did not attempt his seduction, and in which she did not denounce him to her husband? As Euripides continued to reflect, he came to be seized by the idea of a play on the theme in which Phaedra should actually not come face to face with either of the two male characters vital to the plot. She should not speak to Hippolytus, and she should not speak to Theseus: the two big and striking scenes would be sacrificed to a subtler conception. It had great attractions. It also had great difficulties. There was presumably the practical difficulty of persuading the actor who was to portray Phaedra that the part was a good one, even with its big scenes excised. More important, there was the problem of making the plot work.

Any well-brought-up Greek aristocrat would be bound to repel the amorous advances of his father's wife. To make the traditional plot work, all the poet needed was a Hippolytus who was a decent young man. As for Phaedra, her motivation presented no great problem: all the world knew that women were prone to that sort of behaviour. That is why one had to keep such a sharp eye on them. But the new play would have to differ from the old in precisely this respect. The new Phaedra was not to declare her passion to Hippolytus: that meant, for one thing, inventing a more elaborate device by which the audience was to learn of it in the first place. An obvious answer was a speech by a god, as no mortal knew the secret, and that in turn suggested the role of Aphrodite and the transformation of the story by placing the blame on the divine rather than on the frailty of woman. But it also set the playwright further problems. Somehow Hippolytus must get the message of Phaedra's passion for him, and also he must react to it in a way which drives her into desperate courses.

The Phaedra of the second play is a respectable matron, not the sort of floozie who traditionally starred in this story-pattern; that is because she is not to be allowed to have the big scene of attempted seduction. Aphrodite decides to destroy her, not for any fault of hers, but in order to strike at Hippolytus. Being respectable, Phaedra suppresses her passion until she reaches the point of collapse and prostration. In the end she allows herself to be forced to reveal her secret: the only way in which she could both declare it and disown her own action in doing so. There is a climax of hints from her sick-bed. First she raves about joining the hunters out on the hills, an area of activity specifically masculine, to which virgin females of myth could aspire but which excluded married women. 'Send me to the mountain: I go to the woods and the fir-trees, where the hounds pursue the dappled deer—O God, I long to whoop on the dogs and fling the javelin', etc. The fit passes, her nurse rebukes her for craziness, Phaedra is overwhelmed with mortification:

μαῖα, πάλιν μου κρύψον κεφαλήν,
αἰδούμεθα γὰρ τὰ λελεγμένα μοι.

Cover my head again, I am ashamed of what I have said. (243–4)

Then the nurse, affectionate and officious, resorts to the device of supplication to extort Phaedra's secret. Phaedra has given a further hint: ὀλῇ. τὸ μέντοι πρᾶγμ' ἐμοὶ τιμὴν φέρει ['My secret will be the death of you; yet it is creditable to me] (329). Finally: δώσω· σέβας γὰρ χειρὸς αἰδοῦμαι τὸ σόν ['I shall give it to you, as I respect the constraining force of your supplication'] (335). But before she can bring herself to utter it, she begins by talking about the destructive passion of her mother Pasiphae for the bull, and of her sister Ariadne for Theseus: τρίτη δ' ἐγὼ

δύστηνος ὡς ἀπόλλυμαι ['And I am the third to come to grief']
(341). In the end she hints at Hippolytus until the nurse utters
the name: 'You said it, not me', she cries (σοῦ τάδ', οὐκ ἐμοῦ,
κλύεις, 352).

What is going on here? What we see is an unusually careful
and detailed depiction of a piece of rather subtle human psychology.[10] Phaedra is resolved not to speak, yet her weakness is
breaking her down. And as we all know, those in love always
have a strong desire to talk about it.[11] Phaedra first reveals her
repressed desire for the hunter Hippolytus in the form of a wish
to join the hunters: the nurse is baffled, but Phaedra has the
relief of having expressed her real desire in a coded form. Then
she encourages enquiry by hinting that her secret is, after all,
creditable. Thus she gets into a position in which she can act as
though forced to speak, although there is sophistry in this, as
life would be impossible if anybody could make anybody do
anything they chose simply by going through the forms of
supplication, a privileged gesture which existed as a recourse
for the desperate to save their lives when on the run or menaced
with death. Even when she has got into that position, Phaedra
still finds it difficult to utter her secret. She works her way
round to it by way of the amorous misadvantures of her mother
and sister: that is to say 'I am not the only one', and also 'It
isn't surprising that it's happening to me'—a device which has
the effect of minimizing the shockingness of her own case and
her own unique responsibility for it.[12] Finally she cannot utter

---

[10] See the perceptive account of R. P. Winnington-Ingram, 'Hippolytus: A Study
in Causation', in *Entr. Hardt*, vi: *Euripide* (Geneva, 1958), 179 f., 193. He says: 'Why
does Phaedra yield [to the Nurse]? There can be no doubt that the fundamental reason
is the deep longing that she has to make the revelation' (179). Malcolm Heath, in his
acute but perhaps at times too hard-headed book *The Poetics of Greek Tragedy* (London,
1987), 146 n. 46, comments: 'I note in passing that Winnington-Ingram's interpretation of Phaedra's submission . . . has not a scrap of support in the text.' I hope to show
what sort of support it has in reality. Good too is B. M. W. Knox, *Word and Action* (Baltimore and London, 1979), 210–11.

[11] e.g. Callimachus fr. 714 Pf.; Asclepiades fr. 847 Gow-Page = Anth. Pal. 5. 7;
'Dicere quo pereas saepe in amore iuvat', Prop. 1. 9. 34. Perhaps after these explicit
parallels one may also refer to universal human experience. Who has not been the recipient, now and then, of confessions from the lovelorn?

[12] On the first point, see Gow on [Theocritus] 8. 59: ὦ πάτερ, ὦ Ζεῦ, | οὐ μόνος
ἠράσθην ['O father Zeus, I am not the only one who has been in love']; on the second,
Agamemnon's apology: ἐγὼ δ' οὐκ αἴτιός εἰμι, | ἀλλὰ Ζεὺς καὶ Μοῖρα καὶ ἠεροφοῖτις
'Ερινύς ['I am not responsible; no, it was Zeus and Moira and the Erinys who walks in

the name, and she ensures that it is the nurse who utters it: another sophistry of the heart for avoiding responsibility.

I have been explaining all this in terms of psychology. A proud and self-respecting person is driven into a corner and eventually finds herself unable to go on keeping her secret. If we were eavesdropping on such a scene in real life, the emotions of Phaedra would be transparent to us, and so would the devices, human and familiar ones, by which she attempts to cope with them. We have all used similar sophistries in such contexts ourselves. Are we right to interpret a scene of Attic tragedy in this naturalistic and psychological way? I shall attempt to support the kind of analysis here offered by looking in turn at Hippolytus.

Euripides, I suggested, was impelled towards the introduction of Aphrodite into his play by the decision that Phaedra should not herself declare her passion to Hippolytus. If Phaedra is a respectable person, not at all a fighter against a god, a θεόμαχος like Pentheus, why has the goddess done this to her? Answer: because of Hippolytus. This young man, with his outdoor name and his noble birth, is very naturally imagined as a hunter. Hunting goes with the outdoor world and with chastity:[13] its goddess is the virgin Artemis. In his devotion to that life and that goddess, Hippolytus has gone too far. He embodies the distaste for the feminine world which is sometimes found in such young men. From the point of view of the shape of the play, a prologue by Aphrodite could be elegantly balanced by the appearance of her divine opposite at the end. Now Hippolytus was Theseus' son by the Amazon queen: he is repeatedly referred to as 'the Amazon's child' (10, 308, 351, 581). In addition he is illegitimate, νόθος, although the usual version seems to have been that Theseus did marry her.[14] A bastard with the

darkness'] (*Il.* 19. 86–7); and the extensive literature on it since E. R. Dodds, *The Greeks and The Irrational* (Berkeley and Los Angeles, 1951), ch. 1—esp. A. Lesky, 'Zur Problematik des Psychologischen bei Euripides', *Gymn.* 67 (1970), 10–26 = *Gesammelte Schriften* (Berne, 1966), 247–63; O. Taplin, above, pp. 75–6.

[13] On the connection see W. Burkert, *Structure and History in Greek Mythology and Ritual* (Berkeley, Los Angeles, and London, 1979), 11 ff.; id., *Homo Necans* (Berlin, 1972), 95 (= Engl. trans. (Berkeley, 1983), 81).

[14] Cf. *RE* Suppl. 13, 1153. 22 ff. νόθοι appear sometimes in the *Iliad*, where their position seems to be equivocal. *Il.* 11. 102: υἷε δύω Πριάμοιο, νόθον καὶ γνήσιον ἄμφω | εἰν ἑνὶ δίφρῳ ἐόντας ['a legitimate and a bastard son of Priam, in the same chariot']. The bastard is significantly called Isos, Equal. At *Il.* 8. 284 we have a splendidly characteristic

pride of a legitimate heir, the nurse calls him (νόθον φρονοῦντα γνήσια, 309). His father alludes to it to his face (962). He himself, at the end of the scene of confrontation in which his father sends him into exile, cries:

> ὦ δυστάλαινα μῆτερ, ὦ πικραὶ γοναί.
> μηδείς ποτ᾽ εἴη τῶν ἐμῶν φίλων νόθος.

O my poor mother, my unhappy birth. May no friend of mine be illegitimate. (1082–3)

Mr Barrett comments on this speech:

Hippolytus fancies, I suppose, that he has had shorter shrift as νόθος than he would have had as γνήσιος; though from no word that Theseus has said could this be deduced . Dramatically, in fact, the outburst is unmotivated—the νοθεία is wholly irrelevant to the action of the play; presumably therefore Eur.'s purpose is to throw subtle light on Hipp.'s psychology for its own sake, to suggest this feeling of inferiority, of otherness, as what lies behind his urge to establish himself in compensation as a paragon of virtues that common man cannot share.

That note is unusual in Mr Barrett's great commentary in its psychological speculativeness. Certainly the speech is striking and invites us to read meaning into it. Hippolytus refers to his birth again at the very end of the play: five lines before his death he tells his father τοιῶνδε παίδων γνησίων εὔχου τυχεῖν ['Pray that your legitimate sons may be like me'] (1455). Like his ambiguous farewell to his patron goddess, 'Easily do you leave our long companionship',[15] that line maintains an exquisite balance between acceptance and bitterness. Neither quality is to be emphasized to the exclusion of the other.

I suggest that while it is true that psychology is to be read into these utterances, they are to be taken with the emphasis on Hippolytus' mother the Amazon: together they create a rather

utterance by Agamemnon to Teucer: 'Be a glory to your father,' ὅ σ᾽ ἔτρεφε τυτθὸν ἐόντα | καί σε νόθον περ ἐόντα κομίσσατο ᾧ ἐνὶ οἴκῳ ['he brought you up in his house, bastard though you are']. Some ancient scholars deleted in the line for its tactlessness (ἀκαιρία); another scholiast points out that bastardy was no reproach in the heroic period (ἀλλ᾽ οὐδὲ ὄνειδος ἦν ἡ νοθεία παρὰ τοῖς παλαιοῖς (Σ6T); so too the D-scholium and also Eustathius ad loc.))

[15] Cf. J. Griffin, *Homer on Life and Death* (Oxford, 1980). Knox, *Word and Action*, 221, 228, is, I think, one-sided to say that the line 'shows Hippolytus' disillusion' and is 'a reproach'.

different pattern of meaning, and one that is not unmotivated
dramatically. The son of such an eminently virginal and outdoor mother (in this play she has not even a name, she is only
'the Amazon'), born out of wedlock to a notorious womanizer
like Theseus,[16] and living in a household with his father's subsequent wife and children, it is surely not surprising that
Hippolytus should have had an attitude of aversion from sexual
matters. He tells us himself that he is quite inexperienced, and
that he knows 'no more of this business than what I hear and
pictures I have seen; and I am not eager to look at them, since
my soul is virgin' (1004–6). That is very unusual for a Greek
man, living in a society in which nobody would have thanked
you, as a man, for retaining your virginity.[17] Euripides needs
his Hippolytus to have not simply the seemly reluctance of a
good young man towards an indecent proposition from his
stepmother, all that was needed in the first play. Now that
Phaedra is a more virtuous character, Hippolytus needs a more
marked hostility to sex: the approach which the nurse makes to
him evokes a vehement outburst of disgust and also threats of
denunciation to Theseus. Although in fact he will not carry out
those threats, they suffice to impel the respectable Phaedra of
this play, concerned as she is with her good reputation, her
κλέος, to suicide and to slander in a new and apparently un-
answerable form:

ἵν' εἰδῇ μὴ 'πὶ τοῖς ἐμοῖς κακοῖς
ὑψηλὸς εἶναι· τῆς νόσου δὲ τῆσδέ μοι
κοινῇ μετασχὼν σωφρονεῖν μαθήσεται.

That will teach him not to be superior to my unhappiness. Taking a
share with me in this sickness he shall learn modesty. (729–31)

---

[16] Barrett, comm., 18 n. 3. Theseus' extensive list of infidelities was made a justification for adulterous thoughts by Phaedra in the first *Hippolytus*, fr. 491 N.

[17] B. Vickers, *Towards Greek Tragedy* (London, 1973), 146, tries to deny any morbid-
ity at all in this: the chastity of Hippolytus 'is not that of a puritan ... but a perfectly
normal consequence of the cult to which he has dedicated himself'. That seems to me
strange as a statement about normal Greeks and at odds with various points in the play
which I mention in this chapter. On the other hand, little seems to me to be gained by
strongly worded statements that Hippolytus appears 'priggish and odious' (Webster,
Tragedies of Euripides, 74). Kamerbeek, too, thinks Hippolytus exhibits 'des traits d'un
priggishness désagréable' ('Mythe et réalité dans l'œuvre d'Euripide', *Entr. Hardt*, vi.
23). Similarly, H. P. Foley speaks of 'the pompus and self-centred Achilles' of the *IA*
(*Ritual Irony* (Ithaca, NY, 1985), 98): that, too, seems to me not only too hostile but also
beside the point. These virtuous young men of Euripides seem to rile modern scholars.

The mixture of motives expressed here is, I think, subtly characterized and worthy of comment. Phaedra has her more pre-
sentable and calculated motive, that of protecting the position
of her children. She also reveals, in her last words, a more
passionate one, which draws its force from her rejected love. He
shall share her suffering, at least, and *that* will teach him to be so
virtuous.

Hippolytus has acquired a particular character, a rather
morbid aversion from sex; the poet has gone out of his way to
suggest that it is connected with his peculiar parentage and his
own awareness of it. That is to be seen as having impelled him
towards the devotion to the chaste goddess Artemis, which in
turn forms part of the striking and significant structure of the
play, the hostile goddesses standing irreconcilable at either end.
Hippolytus might have been more understanding, or even
healthily sceptical, of the nurse's message, but instead he produced a response as violent as the more justified response to a
cruder approach in the first play. That particular Phaedra
needed this particular Hippolytus if the subtler conception of
the second play was to work.[18] Because they both were rather
unusual types, or (more exactly) because Hippolytus was an
unusual type of person, while Phaedra was placed by the plot in
a position which made it very hard for the vital secret to be produced, the poet found himself rounding out their psychologies
with a fullness and a suggestiveness quite unusual in Attic
tragedy.

Let us stop at this point and reflect. First, it is notable that
some persons in the *Hippolytus* did not need to be equipped with
particularly interesting or unusual psychology. Theseus needs
only to be the typical angry and credulous husband: a little less
credulous, indeed, than the general run of such husbands,
because his wife's suicide does seem to place her accusation
beyond doubt. And in fact that is all the characterization he is
given. A typical husband, he believes his wife; a typical father,
he feels remorse on learning that he has destroyed his son by
mistake. Theseus is more or less interchangeable, allowing for
the different stylistic level, with the ordinary chap who killed

---

[18] Cf. R. P. Winnington-Ingram, *Studies in Aeschylus* (Cambridge, 1983), 96: a
similar point about Aeschylus.

his wife's lover and in his own defence delivers the first speech of
Lysias. Euripides, that suggests, has not been suddenly converted to the idea of psychological drama for its own sake.
Rather, he has used the observations of human nature which he
made in life and in literature with more than usual accuracy
and subtlety, because on this occasion the logic of a very particular plot made it more than usually necessary.[19] The implication of that for the general study of Euripides' work is that
such sensitive psychology may indeed be present in other plays,
and it is not in principle a mistake to seek or to find it; but that
we need to consider carefully in each case how far the sort of
psychology we are discussing has a real and discernible function beyond itself, as making some necessary contribution to
the plot or the form of the whole.[20]

Secondly, it is worth suggesting that Euripides derived this,
like so many other things, from Homer. It has been pointed out
that the *Iliad* needs, for its plot to work, an Achilles of a very
special sort. The Achilles of the *Iliad* is not an ordinary hero
with an ordinary fit of anger: such a hero would have been
satisfied, as we are told by Odysseus, Phoenix, and Ajax, with
the compensation offered in book 9. He needs to have a depth
of mind and feeling which is unintelligible to the other characters, and which will on the one hand make it impossible for
him to cope with his own anger, and on the other enable him to
talk to Priam in a tone and with a power which are alike
beyond the range of anybody else in the poem. His Iliadic
opponent Agamemnon also is a particular character, though to
a lesser extent and in a less interesting way. He wavers between
arrogant bluster and impotent despair; and that instability,
that tendency to both of a pair of opposite extremes, is well
tailored to his role in the poem, since he must both insult

---

[19] Thus I disagree with the view of B. Seidensticker, in W. Jens (ed.), *Bauformen der
griechischen Tragödie* (Munich, 1971), 215, that in the play character is wholly subordinate to the clash of ideas on the superhuman level. Nor does the emphasis seem
rightly placed by W. Zürcher, *Personendarstellung bei Euripides* (Basle, 1947), 87 (Phaedra
not an individual but defined by the conflict of ἔρως and αἰδώς).

[20] This has some resemblance to, but is not meant to be identical with, the statement
of Friedrich, *Euripides und Diphilos*, 86, that in such plays as *Andromache* and *Electra*, 'Hier
wie dort sind die psychologischen Besonderheiten ein Mittel, ausgebeuteten Stoffen
neue Möglichkeiten abzugewinnen, und sind insofern Symptome, die das Ende der
Kunstform ankünden.'

Achilles and abase himself in vain before him.[21] It may well be that the carefully tailored persons of the *Hippolytus* owe something to meditation on that aspect of the technique of the *Iliad*.

II

Mention of Achilles and Agamemnon forms a natural transition to the second of my Euripidean plays, the *Iphigeneia in Aulis*. The *Iliad* is, as it happens, a long epic which is particularly interested in depicting a wide range of characters: we have only to reflect how well we know, by the time we reach book 23, that large cast of heroes who behave in ways so characteristic of themselves at the funeral games of Patroclus. I say 'as it happens', because we need look no further than the *Aeneid* to find an epic with hardly any interest in that aim, while even the *Odyssey* has much less of it than the *Iliad*.

Agamemnon appears on stage in several extant plays, but this is the only extant tragedy to give a speaking part to Achilles. It may perhaps be doubted whether Euripides derived important elements of his characterization in the *Hippolytus* from the *Iliad*, but the presence of the Homeric epic cannot be questioned in the *Iphigeneia in Aulis*. The Achaeans are assembled at Aulis; that is mentioned in *Iliad* 2, which also includes the Catalogue of Ships, the very visible model of the *parodos* of the play,[22] as the chorus describe visiting the army and seeing the great heroes who are listed in the Catalogue. The indecisiveness of Agamemnon in the *Iliad*, at one moment bullying and over-confident but at others passive and despairing, underlies the volatile Agamemnon of the tragedy—but those qualities, in *Iphigeneia in Aulis*, spread far beyond him to most of the other important persons of the play.

The person, of course, who is not Homeric is Iphigeneia herself. She was a great figure in tragedy: both Aeschylus and Sophocles had written plays with the title *Iphigeneia*, and her fate is an important motif in the *Oresteia* and, to a lesser extent, in the *Electra* plays; Euripides had also dramatized a later stage of her legend in the *Iphigeneia in Tauris*. The first question, then,

---

[21] See J. Griffin, 'Words and Speakers in Homer', *JHS* 106 (1986), 50 ff.
[22] However much of it is genuine.

was: What remains to be done with this myth, at so late a stage in the history of tragedy? Already in the *Cypria*, the most important of the Cyclic epics, Artemis demanded the sacrifice of Iphigeneia, and so the Achaeans summoned her to Aulis ὡς ἐπὶ γάμον Ἀχιλλεῖ, saying that she was to be married to Achilles. Sophocles developed that hint: Odysseus, the handy man for tricks and lies, went off to Mycenae and induced Clytemnestra to send her daughter to Aulis for the marriage.[23] One development remained: Clytemnestra, in the *Iphigeneia in Aulis*, insists on coming with Iphigeneia—like any good mother planning to be present at her daughter's wedding. Her presence among the tents and ships is strange, as is repeatedly emphasized in the play (825 f., 913 f.)—a way of insisting on the novelty of the idea. That it is an innovation emerges also from 457, where Agamemnon says: εἰκότως ἅμ' ἕσπετο | θυγατρὶ νυμφεύσουσα ['it is not surprising that she came with her daughter for her wedding']. Evidently it *was* surprising, and the poet emphasizes and justifies his innovation.

Two further possible variants presented themselves. One was to unpack the monolithic unity of 'the Atreidae', who in Aeschylus' account of the sacrifice at Aulis act and suffer as one: ὥστε χθόνα βάκτροις ἐπικρούσαντας Ἀτρείδας δάκρυ μὴ κατασχεῖν ['the two Atreidae struck the ground with their staffs and did not restrain their tears'] (*Ag.* 202–4). Following, perhaps, the example rather half-heartedly set in Sophocles' *Ajax*, where the two sons of Atreus are to some extent contrasted with each other though in practice very much the same, Euripides now has Agamemnon and Menelaus reacting quite differently to the position and working against each other. After all, the poet could coolly point out, their interest was by no means identical: one stood to lose a daughter, the other to regain a wife. We may compare the promotion of Pylades, from his traditional subservience to being a more independent character, in Euripides' *Orestes*. The second variant was that of promoting Achilles from the inert position of the man whose name was simply used to lure Iphigeneia, by pressing the question how such behaviour fitted with Achilles' general reputation, in the *Iliad*, in Pindar, and elsewhere, as heroically truthful and

[23] S. fr. 305 Radt.

contemptuous of guile and falsehood. How did Achilles feel
about being part of such a subterfuge? So Achilles becomes an
important character in events, and with the two sons of Atreus
each now playing his own hand the situation becomes highly
complex. Finally, the army itself takes on an alarming life and
will of its own.

When the play begins, Agamemnon has agreed to sacrifice
his daughter Iphigeneia and has sent a message to Mycenae to
summon her, on the pretext that she is to be married to
Achilles. Why did he do it? We are given two incompatible
accounts. According to Agamemnon himself, when he heard
the goddess's demand he was for disbanding the army rather
than complying, 'but my brother, applying every argument,
induced me to commit this crime' (οὖ δή μ' ἀδελφὸς πάντα
προσφέρων λόγον | ἔπεισε τλῆναι δεινά, 94–5). Menelaus, how-
ever, tells a different story. According to him, Agamemnon was
concerned only with retaining his position as Commander-in-
Chief. Rather than see the expedition disbanded, he was perfectly happy to surrender Iphigeneia to her death:

ἡσθεὶς φρένας
ἄσμενος θύσειν ὑπέστης παῖδα, καὶ πέμπεις ἑκών,
οὐ βίᾳ—μὴ τοῦτο λέξῃς—σῇ δάμαρτι.

Well pleased and gladly did you promise to sacrifice your daughter,
and you sent to your wife of your own free will, not under constraint:
don't claim that it was. (359–61)

Some scholars have taken it that one of these accounts is true,
the other false. Thus Wecklein, commenting on the constrained
and unimpassioned speech in which Agamemnon replies to his
daughter's plea for her life, says that it is chilly because we
know from the speech of Menelaus that Agamemnon's real
motive is φιλοτιμία, desire for position, in comparison with
which he does not care about her fate. Wecklein did not like
Agamemnon, but I think this line of analysis an unpromising
one. The fact is that Euripides has not shown us how and why
Agamemnon took his fatal decision, in part no doubt because it
would have been hard to prevent him from entirely forfeiting
the sympathy of the audience as we saw him do it, in part perhaps because it had been handled by Aeschylus, but mostly
because it was a familiar dramatic high point and Euripides is

going to produce a lot more new and exciting ones. He does not explain, either, why Agamemnon did not tell Achilles about the fictitious marriage. Denys Page constructs quite a plausible little history to explain this, based on what Agamemnon might reasonably have expected Achilles to do;[24] but this too, perhaps, is not to the point. As the text of the play stands, indeed, Achilles actually says that if only he had been asked, and not taken for granted, he would have consented to the use of his name to entrap Iphigeneia (962 ff.). Unfortunately that is said in the course of a speech much of which gives grounds for suspecting that it is not by Euripides. The speech is full of unexpected changes of tone and of intention. Now the *Iphigeneia in Aulis* is of all Greek tragedies the one with the largest number of changes of mind,[25] and Euripides clearly was out to exploit them to the utmost in this play. But Page remarks also that the interpolator, too, 'admired emotional inconsistency'.[26] Really life can be very difficult at times.

To return to Agamemnon. Having decided spontaneously, or having been induced, to summon his daughter, he has now thought better of it and written another letter countermanding the first. Too late! His brother Menelaus intercepts the second letter and fiercely denounces him for his change of mind, and meanwhile Iphigeneia actually arrives, with her mother and baby brother. Agamemnon, faced with this new situation, collapses: now that the girl is here, she cannot be saved. Calchas and Odysseus know about the prophecy, and they will denounce any attempt to evade it. Menelaus, meanwhile, has moved in the opposite direction. From demanding that Agamenon keep his word and kill his daughter he passes to sympathy with his brother, pity for the girl, and understanding of the terrible nature of the killing:

ἄφρων νέος τ' ἦ, πρὶν τὰ πράγματ' ἐγγύθεν
σκοπῶν ἐσεῖδον οἷον ἦν κτείνειν τέκνα.

I was young and thoughtless, before I saw the position more closely and perceived what it is to kill a child. (489–90)

---

[24] *Actors' Interpolations in Greek Tragedy* (Oxford, 1934), 179. Further elaboration of the point: Friedrich, *Euripides und Diphilos*, 97 ff.
[25] B. M. W. Knox, 'Second Thoughts in Greek Tragedy', *GRBS* 7 (1966), 229–32 = *Word and Action*, 243–6.
[26] *Actors' Interpolations*, 189.

How are we to explain these changes? Not, I think, or not primarily, in terms of psychology. Since we do not know why Agamemnon ever agreed to the action, we do not know why he
changes his mind for the first time. As for his second change,
deciding that now nothing can be done, that is indeed given an
explanation; but we observe that both now and later in the
play Agamemnon claims that the army is so passionately eager
to leave for Troy that if he tries to save his daughter the
Achaeans will sack Mycenae and kill him and all his family
(528–35, 1264–8);[27] if that is so, then it was futile to cancel the
letter summoning her, and the further change of mind when he
despairs of keeping her away is something of a charade. What
really interests the poet is the contrasting emotions.[28] It is
tempting to burlesque Aristotle on the relation of plot and
character and say that in such a play the emotions, the πάθη,
are the main thing, not the persons; but it is necessary to have
persons for there to be πάθη.[29]

Menelaus' change of heart is given an explicit motivation:
now that it comes to it, he realises what an awful thing he is
doing. That puts him with such obtuse Euripidean persons as
Admetus in the *Alcestis*, who only realizes when his wife is
actually dead what it is that he has done in letting her die (ἄρτι
μανθάνω ['Now I understand'], *Alc.* 940). But the point is evidently the formal, almost geometric, elegance of the way in
which both brothers move, as it were in a stately dance—a
minuet, perhaps—to take up the opposite positions from that in
which they started. The opening scenes of the *Heracles* provide
an illuminating parallel. At the beginning of that play the
family of Heracles, beset by the villainous usurper Lycus in the
absence of the hero, have taken refuge at an altar. Heracles
does not appear to rescue them, and their position seems lost.
Megara, the wife, wants to cut short the agony of useless delay

---

[27] I am reminded of the penetrating comment of M. C. Bradbrook about Shakespeare: 'The difficulty in his case arises from the difference between the realism with
which he presents his characters and the conventional manner in which he motivates
them' (*Themes and Conventions of Elizabethan Tragedy* (Cambridge, 1935), 63–4).

[28] 'In one thing Euripides far excelled Aeschylus and Sophocles, namely in the
representation of the mental movements from which decisions arise' (Kumaniecki, *De
Consiliis*, 121; he refers also to Euripides' accurate representation of *animus titubans*, a
mind indecisive).

[29] Arist. *Poet.* 1450ᵃ15 ff.

and surrender to their persecutor; old Amphitryon insists that hope must be kept up until the very end: 'The best man is he who always puts his trust in hope' (105 f.). Four hundred lines pass, and their death has come very close. Now it is Megara who utters a passionate prayer to Heracles to appear and deliver them, while Amphitryon expresses cynicism and despair. Zeus has been invoked so many times to no purpose, and it is idle to bother with prayer; as for hope, time flies away and does not fulfil our hopes (490–507).

Again scholars have looked for significance in all this beyond what it possesses. Professor Burnett enlarges upon the undeserving character of Megara, for instance.[30] But here again the point is the elegant pattern in itself. As in the *Heracles*, so with the changing attitudes of Agamemnon and Menelaus in the *Iphigeneia in Aulis*, enough of a psychological explanation is given to allow us to find the events humanly intelligible. Tragedy would fail of its effect on an audience if the behaviour of the persons in the play ceased to be such that the audience could follow it as recognizably human (the characters must be, at least in outline, 'like us').[31] But these events in the *Iphigeneia in Aulis* differ significantly from those in the *Hippolytus*. Neither Agamemnon nor Menelaus needs to be an extraordinary man for the purposes of the plot, and indeed neither is extraordinary. They are both rather ordinary blends of selfishness, emotion, weakness, and hoping for the best. Their mutability is all that is exceptional about them—less by our standards, that is, than by the standards of tragedy, where we are used to the iron will of Sophoclean heroes and heroines, and to the overmastering passions of Euripidean characters like Medea and Hecuba. No strong and particular motivation is needed to account for their mutability and their inconsistencies: strong emotions simply follow one another. We watch the process of change with keen interest, and the poet rushes us along from crisis to crisis, but we do not gain a clear idea what sort of individuals these are. Rather, we contemplate and experience a kaleidoscopic succession of emotions, only loosely attached to particular persons.

[30] A. P. Burnett, *Catastrophe Survived* (Oxford, 1971), 156–66.
[31] Cf. P. E. Easterling, 'Presentation of Character in Aeschylus', *G & R* 20 (1973), 3–19.

In a play exceptionally full of changes of mind, the characters who are introduced into the Iphigeneia story by
Euripides, namely Clytemnestra and Achilles, are made rather
more interesting. Everybody in the theatre knew what Clytemnestra was like: the murderous adulteress, paradigm of bad
wives. So Euripides, who in the *Supplices* introduced to the
world a Capaneus remarkable for his democratic ideals and
modest life-style (860 ff.), and in the *Helen* a chaste, monoga-
mous, and home-loving Helen, shows us in the *Iphigeneia in Aulis*
a Clytemnestra who was a paragon of a wife. She says so herself:
συμμαρτυρήσεις ὡς ἄμεμπτος ἦ γυνή ['You will bear witness that
I have been above criticism as a wife'] (1158). In fact, she
pushed complaisance so far as to be a good wife to a man who
had killed her first husband and snatched her baby from her
breast and murdered it (1148–56).[32] This extraordinary story,
apparently unknown except from Euripides, has a special point
which commentators tend to miss: Clytemnestra actually once
put up with the very thing for which she will now become the
killer of her husband. In the *Iphigeneia in Aulis* she warns him:

μὴ δῆτα πρὸς θεῶν μήτ' ἀναγκάσῃς ἐμὲ
κακὴν γενέσθαι περὶ σέ, μήτ' αὐτὸς γένῃ.

Do not, for God's sake, force me to become wicked to you, and do not
be wicked yourself. (1183–4)

We can hardly imagine the nerveless Agamemnon that we see
in this play behaving in the brutal way Clytemnestra describes:
that is just another of these unexplained changes. Nor do we get
a clear view of the reason why Clytemnestra took the killing of
one child in good part but turned difficult over the second. She
does imply at one moment that it was the deceitful way he did
it which made it unacceptable:

Ἰφ. ἄκων μ' ὑπὲρ γῆς Ἑλλάδος διώλεσεν.
Κλ. δόλῳ δ', ἀγεννῶς Ἀτρέως τ' οὐκ ἀξίως.

IPH. Against his will he has slain me for Hellas.
CL. But by deceit, basely, and unworthily of his father Atreus.
(1456–7)

<hr>

[32] Cf. also 633: ὦ σέβας ἐμοὶ μέγιστον, Ἀγαμέμνων ἄναξ ['You whom I revere above
all, my lord Agamemnon']; 726: τί χρῆμα; πείθεσθαι γὰρ εἴθισμαι σέθεν ['What is it? My
habit is to obey you'].

But essentially it is just another change, and the purpose of the mention of the first incident of child-killing is not to explain but to emphasize her reaction to the second.

As for Achilles, he is a problem for us because his big speech (919–74) is so vulnerable to suspicions that it is heavily interpolated. He is made to open it with a passage in praise of his own moderation:

> ἐπίσταμαι δὲ τοῖς κακοῖσί τ' ἀσχαλᾶν
> μετρίως τε χαίρειν τοῖσιν ἐξωγκωμένοις.

I know how to grieve in measure at reverses and to take delight in measure in full-sailed prosperity. (919–20)

A surprise, on the lips of Achilles; but less so on those of an Achilles created by Euripides.[33] The speech goes on to become violently angry: Agamemnon has abused him, and he shall not lay a finger on his daughter. But after all, he adds, if only he'd told me—I'd have allowed the use of my name in a fraud to serve the common good. Not a very coherent oration; it seems that later hands have been at work, exaggerating the unstable purposes which they saw to be characteristic of the play. Achilles finally comes down on the side of saying that he will fight to protect Iphigeneia, even if it means killing Achaean soldiers (1356 f). The plot exaggerates motifs from the *Iliad*: the hero exposes his own side to disaster for the sake of a quarrel over a girl (1354), having suffered ὕβρις at the hands of Agamemnon (cf. *Il.* 1. 203, 214), and his Myrmidons resent being kept back by him from battle (1352–3; cf. *Il.* 16. 200–7). Finally he expresses love for her, once she has expressed her heroic resolution to die for Greece (1406 ff). Page refers to 'the sentimental inconsistency of an Achilleus who is more like a New Comic lover than an Old Tragic warrior'.[34]

It is vital for the plot that Achilles should take the stand that he does, but in this play of shifting resolves he reaches it only by an oblique route. Iphigeneia takes her resolution at a moment when the Achaean cause is menaced, because of Achilles, not

---

[33] Knox comments on *IA* 1024, where Clytemnestra says to Achilles ὡς σώφρον' εἶπας ['How prudently you speak!']: 'Nobody ever had occasion to speak like that to Achilles before' (*Word and Action*, 245). The point is a nice one, even though the epigrammatic formulation should not entirely make us forget Achilles' great speech, full of wisdom, to Priam in *Il.* 24.

[34] *Actors' Interpolations*, 216.

only by frustration but by imminent self-destruction. It is at
that heightened moment of crisis, not just in the fourteenth
week of a long delay, that she finds the spiritual strength to
accept immolation. That change in her, from a frightened girl
begging for life to a heroine who looks down on death, is
exceedingly abrupt: only fifty lines separate the two sides. Aristotle notoriously says that this is a classic example of inconsistency, and of a bad kind: οὐδὲν γὰρ ἔοικεν ἡ ἱκετεύουσα τῇ ὑστέρᾳ
['The girl who begs for her life has nothing in common with the
girl in the later scene'] (*Poet.* 1454ᵃ33). Scholars attempt to
smooth over the transition in one way or another.[35] It is
notable, though, that Achilles, impressed as he is by her resolve,
quite expects her to retract it. 'You may well change your
mind', says he, 'when you see the steel at your throat': so he will
be there, with his armour on, to rescue her if need be (1424 ff).
I think that gives us a hint on the right way to go about this
question.

The sudden resolution of Iphigeneia is not utterly incapable
of being understood in psychological terms. The moment is
emotional and extraordinary, the young girl finding herself
suddenly the focus of attention and the fulcrum of events; and
the impulse to self-sacrifice is one which exists in the real world.
But Euripides is not primarily interested in making it psychologically convincing, except in a more general sense. The world
of the *Iphigeneia in Aulis* is one in which everybody changes his
or her mind, and does so abruptly and from one extreme to the
opposite. Iphigeneia's behaviour is at home in that world: a
place which has enough resemblance to ours for us to understand it, but which also has enough differentness to make us
aware of a distance. Sometimes it is a a *deus ex machina* who
imposes abrupt changes. The end of the *Orestes* is a supreme instance.[36] Apollo tells Orestes:

> ἐφ' ἧς δ' ἔχεις, 'Ορέστα, φάσγανον δέρῃ,
> γῆμαι πέπρωταί σ' 'Ερμιόνην.

The girl at whose throat you are holding your sword, Orestes, yes,
Hermione—your destiny is to marry her. (1653-4)

---

[35] e.g. Kamerbeek, in *Entr. Hardt*, vi. 22; Knox, *Word and Action*, 243-4; Foley, *Ritual Irony*, 77.
[36] Though *Ion* 1400 ff. runs it close.

I allow myself the luxury of a verse from W. H. Auden, 'Five Songs', II:

> But—Music Ho!—at last it comes,
>   The Transformation Scene:
> A rather scruffy-looking god
>   Descends in a machine
> And, gabbling off his rustic rhymes,
>   Misplacing one or two,
> Commands the prisoners to walk,
>   The enemies to screw.

But especially in his late plays Euripides goes beyond that hoary device, and the characters are capable of equally abrupt changes without any divine impulsion. Events rain in upon the characters faster and faster; unexpectednesses and complications multiply, extreme situations suceed each other, men and women are at their mercy. We never quite lose touch with human possibility—even the marriage of Orestes and Hermione might be a success, if one thinks of the love conceived by the kidnapped victim for her brutal captor in *No Orchids for Miss Blandish*—but we are not really meant to follow up such lines of thought. In the *Iphigeneia in Aulis* a dazzling series of exciting and emotional scenes reaches its climax with a change by the heroine which reflects the world she inhabits, and which is in harmony with the way people behave there. We are carried away on a tidal wave of pathos, sentiment, and patriotism, not fretting about strict psychological plausibility.

The poet of the *Hippolytus* shows us that he knows a great deal about the workings of the human heart. That knowledge is one of the weapons in his armoury, along with his rhetorical brilliance, his lyrical gifts, his philosophical interests, his concern for shape and form. Every play must show some of it, or we shall be as unmoved as we should be by a tragedy set among ants. Some plays, for particular reasons, will exploit it particularly; it is not impossible for us to see how and why this happens. Others will subordinate it, some or all of the time, to different aims and interests. That is the lesson which seems to emerge from our consideration of these two strongly contrasting tragedies, *Hippolytus* and *Iphigeneia in Aulis*.

7

The People of Aristophanes

MICHAEL SILK

No one has yet succeeded in constructing a complete and coherent theory of character.

(Mieke Bal, *Narratology*)

I personally would like to bring a tortoise onto the stage, turn it into a racehorse, then into a hat, a song, a dragon and a fountain of water.

(Ionesco, *Notes and Counter-Notes*)

I

Aristophanes is not, in the ordinary sense, a difficult writer, and many of the incidental difficulties which he does pose—say, those involving intricate verbal jokes—are well understood by his interpreters. The diverse creatures who people his plays, however, pose special problems of interpretation. Consider the following representative instances from *Thesmophoriazusae*, which serve to suggest some pertinent questions. The instances are transparently uncomplicated—and therefore convenient to begin with.

Thesmophoriazusae is a striking mixture of (*inter alia*) broad comedy and devotional lyrics. Some of the broad comedy and all of the devotional lyrics are carried by one set of people, the women at the Thesmophoria—some of them in the chorus, some ostensibly among 'the characters'.[1] The women combine

---

[1] Except for the possibility that the 'Lady Herald' may be the chorus-leader (cf. K. J. Dover, *Aristophanic Comedy* (London, 1972), 166 f.), it is customary to assume that the two groups are wholly separate. However, it is not obvious what distinguishes (e.g.) 531 f. (traditionally ascribed to the chorus) from 533 ff. (ascribed to the anonymous 'First Woman'). The groups certainly share the same alignment and indeed the same virtual anonymity: two of the women (we learn incidentally) have typical names (Μίκ(κ)α, 760; Κρίτυλλα, 898), but then so do *choral* individuals elsewhere (e.g. Δράκης, *Lys.* 254; Νικοδίκη, *Lys.* 321; etc.). Need it be assumed that the groups are wholly separate in fact?

two main roles. They are humorous figures, aggressive assailants of Euripides, and they are devotional figures, pious hymn-singers who celebrate the gods in five separate choral songs. The question arising here is simply this: What sort of relationship is there between the two roles, and what sort of entities are the women who play them?

The two central characters of *Thesmophoriazusae* are clever Euripides and his dumb and docile relative Mnesilochus.[2] Early in the play Euripides concocts a plan to get a man disguised as a woman to infiltrate the women's festival. Euripides cannot go himself. His fellow dramatist Agathon has the wit and the performing-skills required, and Euripides asks him to do the job. When Agathon refuses, Mnesilochus offers his services instead—although (on the evidence of his bumbling performance to date) he patently lacks any qualification for such a delicate mission:

> *Ευ.* ὦ τρισκακοδαίμων ὡς ἀπόλωλ' Εὐριπίδης.
> *Μν.* ὦ φίλτατ' ὦ κηδεστὰ μὴ σαυτὸν προδῷς.
> *Ευ.* πῶς οὖν ποιήσω δῆτα;
> *Μν.*   τοῦτον μὲν μακρὰ
>   κλάειν κέλευ', ἐμοὶ δ' ὅ τι βούλει χρῶ λαβών.
> *Ευ.* ἄγε νυν . . .

> EU. Poor, poor Euripides! done for!
> MN. My dear cousin, don't give up.
> EU. What can I do?
> MN. Tell him to go to hell: how about using me?
> EU. Well, in that case . . . (209–13)[3]

The comic possibilities of Mnesilochus' failure duly form the basis for most of the subsequent action. Euripides, one notes, never actually suggested that Mnesilochus should take the part. That—one might say—is because it won't work, and Euripides would be too clever to suggest it. Why, then, does the clever Euripides accept such an implausible offer at all? And why does the dumb and docile Mnesilochus suddenly thrust himself into

---

[2] The name Mnesilochus, as is well known, is not used in the text, but derives from ΣR. This notwithstanding, it is both convenient and harmless (cf. the use of the name Homer), whereas the alternatives (the favourite English alternative is 'Kinsman') tend to be frigid and distracting.

[3] Quotations from Aristophanes follow the text of Sommerstein, but for *Thes.* (as here) the text of Hall and Geldart (OCT).

the part in the first place?—a part which, while all goes well, he proceeds to perform with gusto and some considerable invent-iveness. It is not an answer to say, 'The plot requires it.' This moment is itself part of the plot; and anyway that kind of answer only converts the first set of questions into a second set: Why is it acceptable, on the level of what we call character, for the plot to 'require' it? In these various examples we seem to observe inconsistencies of behaviour in varying degrees on the part of the women, Euripides, and Mnesilochus. Why, and how, are such inconsistencies acceptable?

Consider again the women in *Thesmophoriazusae*. Their duality produces (or is produced by) not only inconsistencies of behaviour in the ordinary sense, but also inconsistencies of linguistic behaviour. There is a moment in the play when, after Mnesilochus in disguise has spoken up for Euripides (466–519), the women react furiously. One of them threatens, obscenely, to shave his (supposedly her) pussy (χοῖρος, 538), a threat to which Mnesilochus responds with understandable alarm ('Please, ladies, not my *pussy!*', 540). Up to this point the women have been fairly restrained in their language, not only in the songs with all their religiosities ('come thou, mighty maiden . . . come thou, dread lord of the sea', 317 ff.), but in the dialogue too. The sudden use of the word χοῖρος represents, for them, a stylistic switch: the level suddenly drops. If asked to 'explain' this switch, we might point to the speaker's anger, as if the change were explicable in terms of a real individual's real emotional reaction. Such a rationalizing explanation is cer-tainly available in this case. But stylistic switches abound in Aristophanes, and most of them are not explicable in such terms. One case in point, among many others, is a comparable vulgarism early on in the play, this time on the lips of Euripides. Mnesilochus, who is again the recipient of the ob-scenity, purports not to be able to remember who Agathon is. Euripides puts him wise:

> Mv.   μῶν ὁ δασυπώγων;
> Ev.   οὐχ ἑόρακας πώποτε;
> Mv.   μὰ τὸν Δί' οὗτοί γ' ὥστε καί μέ γ' εἰδέναι.
> Ev.   καὶ μὴν βεβίνηκας σύ γ', ἀλλ' οὐκ οἶσθ' ἴσως.

> MN.   The one with the untidy beard?

EU. Haven't you ever seen him?

MN. No—not consciously, anyway.

EU. Well, you must at least have fucked him—not consciously, of course. (33–5)

Up to this point Euripides, like the women later, has spoken in a restrained idiom. His remarks to Mnesilochus have been equable in tone, and there is nothing now to suggest that his mood has changed. Nor is there anything in his characterization to come which would suggest that obscenity is a fundamental trait of his, as it is, by contrast, of Mnesilochus'. This vulgarism, certainly, is hardly open to rationalization.[4]

In Aristophanes the stylistic level of a speaker's (or a singer's) words switches frequently and, often, drastically. In interpreting his plays we tend to rationalize such switches, or (failing that) to explain them away as 'comic effect'—thus resorting to a tautology which in a sense points to the true explanation of the phenomenon and yet, in itself, explains nothing. The fact is that both our rationalizings and our ascriptions of 'comic effect' presuppose what is not the case: that, irrespective of any contrary indications, the speakers, and the singers, of Aristophanic comedy must ultimately conform to realistic norms.

For a stylistic idiom to be compatible with realism, it must involve a range of expression which is *consistently* related to a vernacular language, a language of experience, a language of

---

[4] On Aristophanes' stylistic switches, cf. my discussion in 'Pathos in Aristophanes', *BICS* 34 (1987), 78–111. Regarding the tone of βινεῖν, H. D. Jocelyn, *LCM* 5 (1980), 65–7, has argued interestingly that (unlike e.g. English 'fuck') the word is not obscene, partly on the grounds of its distribution within Attic comedy (esp. its use by females), partly on the grounds of its supposed occurrence in a Solonian law (Hsch. s.v. βινεῖν = Solon, *Test. Vet.* 448 Martina). He suggests that the word, instead, had an 'intimate' tone. Against this: (i) the overwhelming occurrence of the word is in low literature (largely comic—cf. the representative citations in LSJ—but note also Arch. 152. 2 West, Hippon. 84. 16 West): if this (given the sense of the word) does not suggest obscenity, it is not clear what would. (ii) 'Intimacy' is not actually incompatible with obscenity: it is a known feature of current English (certainly British English) usage that the obscene 'fuck' is used by some couples (including female members of couples) in intimate contexts, and one recalls D. H. Lawrence's thoughts in this general area (see e.g. 'A propos of *Lady Chatterley's Lover*', in D. H. Lawrence, *Phoenix II*, ed. W. Roberts and H. T. Moore (London, 1968), 514). (iii) The presence of an 'intimacy' in a law, however, seems appreciably less likely (even) than that of an obscenity. (iv) But in any case the actual source of the 'Solonian' citation is as uncertain as its detail (on which Jocelyn himself remarks (67): 'this entry [in Hsch.] is obscure and has been much emended'). All in all, Jocelyn's challenge to the established view can only be called insubstantial.

life. Either the idiom is felt to amount to a 'selection of the language really spoken by men', as Wordsworth called it;[5] or alternatively it involves a broadly consistent stylization, like (for instance) the stylization of Greek tragic language, which does not constitute anything like a language of life, but is, nevertheless, fixed and conventionalized at a set, comprehensible distance from some hypothetical and more naturalistic idiom, which *would* pass for a language of life *à la* Wordsworth. In the latter case, specifically colloquial vocabulary, phraseology, syntax, and so on, will tend to be excluded, not capriciously or opportunistically in one play or in one part of one play, but *throughout* the play or plays. And the same principle of consistency applies to the more conspicuous, if still limited, presence of archaisms, conventional tropes, and the other familiar features of an elevated language.[6] This principle of consistency is complicated, but not subverted, by a gradation of stylization into different levels—like the levels represented by song and speech in Greek tragedy, or narrative and direct speech in many novels, or the direct speech of one character and the direct speech of another character in much narrative fiction and much drama too. In Aristophanes, the inconsistency within a given speaker's range of idiom points the opposite way. The style in which his people are made to express themselves is incompatible with any kind of realism; and more fundamentally, as this consideration of style serves to suggest, the people of Aristophanes *per se* are not strictly containable within any realist understanding of human character at all. Their linguistic and their non-linguistic behaviour[7] may cohere, but in neither case on a realist premiss. And as such, these beings are distinguishable from their counterparts in the central tradition of Western fiction, in drama or outside it.

[5] Preface to *Lyrical Ballads*, ed. R. L. Brett and A. R. Jones (rev. edn.; London, 1965), 244 (1802 variant).

[6] Cf. Arist. *Poet.* 22; M. S. Silk, 'LSJ and The Problem of Poetic Archaism: From Meanings to Iconyms', *CQ*, NS 33 (1983), 303.

[7] *Pace* the curious pretence (current among some literary theoreticians) that linguistic behaviour ('text') is everything. 'Outside of language there is neither self nor desire', says one theorist (J. Frow, 'Spectacle Binding: On Character', *Poetics Today*, 7/2 (1986), 238). In drama (which includes silent films and ballet), as in life (which extends to deaf and dumb illiterates etc.), this is self-evidently untrue. Cf. (in the classical context) the welcome discussion by D. Wiles, 'Reading Greek Performance', *G & R* 34 (1987), 136–51.

This whole non-Aristophanic tradition we may call *the realist tradition*. It is the tradition within which 'l'effet du réel'[8] is not so much characteristic as ultimately decisive. In agreeing to call it 'realist', one is using 'realism' not (like many literary historians[9]) as a period term, but to designate 'a perennial mode of representing the world' in its 'consequential logic and circumstantiality', a mode which has no 'single style' and whose actual style, or styles, in any given age vary according to cultural norms, and whose 'dominance at any one time is a . . . cultural option'.[10] So defined, the realist tradition is the tradition canonized by Aristotle's theory and Menander's practice, and the tradition which reaches its fullest expression in the nineteenth-century novel. And so defined, the tradition includes instances of the two contrasting types of fiction, the narrative and the dramatic: narrative fiction, with (typically) its 'omniscient' narrator who can tell us about a character, as well as seeming to show us that character in action; and dramatic fiction, which presupposes the individual human presence of the actor—whose performance, furthermore, introduces a variable which (except in a marginal case like oral-epic recitation) has no equivalent in the narrative sphere. The differences between narrative and drama are large and important, but, for present purposes, inconsequential.

Within the realist tradition we encounter a wide variety of ways of representing fictional people. Sometimes we feel called on to comprehend these people as 'characters', sometimes (to use Christopher Gill's distinction) to empathize with them as 'personalities'.[11] Some presentations seem to expand or diffuse

---

[8] The phrase was coined by Roland Barthes in an essay itself entitled 'L'Effet du réel' in *Communications*, 11 (1968), 84 ff. For Barthes the stress is on 'effet', not on 'réel', because of the structuralist anxiety to see literature as removed from reference to real life. However, the fact that all fictional characters (like everything in literature) are *constructed* apart from real life (which is what we mean by 'fictional') does not affect their referential capacity to evoke that outside reality. Cf. G. D. Martin, *Language, Truth and Poetry* (Edinburgh, 1975), 68–106.

[9] Most commonly of nineteenth-century, as opposed to earlier, fiction, but also of 'modern' as opposed to 'ancient' fiction (so, for instance, among classicists, G. M. Sifakis, *Parabasis and Animal Choruses* (London, 1971), 7–14, esp. 9). See further the refs. in nn. 10 and 12 below.

[10] J. P. Stern, *On Realism* (London, 1973), 32, 28, 52, 79, 158. On the history of the term 'realism', see R. Wellek, 'The Concept of Realism in Literary Scholarship', *Neophilologus*, 45 (1961), 1–20.

[11] See n. 21 below.

single traits, some seem to produce 'rounded' characters. The presentation may impinge as two-dimensional or as three-dimensional; as more or as less inward-looking; as a matter of status at least as much as of temperament; as a matter of types or as a matter of individuals. And interpreters may have good reason to draw attention to the differences between the presentations of (say) the Greek tragedians and Eugene O'Neill, or Shakespeare and his predecessors, or Euripides and *his* predecessors, or (most commonly) the modern European novel and *its* predecessors.[12] But all such presentations have one thing in common. The people presented have what we may see as a constant relationship with 'reality'—with the world outside as we perceive it or might be presumed to perceive it—because they stand at a constant distance from that real world.[13] They impinge as sentient beings, each with a tendency to be (in Aristotle's language) 'appropriate', 'lifelike', and 'consistent'.[14] At its most clear-cut this tradition produces figures in which we detect a wealth of recognizable detail, with each detail corresponding to some possibility of life, and each detail connectible with or continuous with some other—even *each* other—detail, and the product of the details a recognizable yet also unique creation. It is within this tradition, and only within this tradition, that characters can be seen to do what we call 'develop'.[15] Such development (it might be argued) implies a progression from one perceived state to another via shifts of emphasis between the identifiable details—perhaps like phonetic changes taking place via a continuum of allophones.[16] Within this tradition development is possible, though most certainly not invariable or even always usual: it is most characteristic of the nineteenth-century novel, though we seem to see it first attested in eighth-century BC epic, in the shape of Homer's Achilles.[17]

[12] As (variously) J. P. Gould, 'Dramatic Character and "Human Intelligibility" in Greek Tragedy', *PCPS*, NS 24 (1978), 43–67; K. Newman, *Shakespeare's Rhetoric of Comic Character* (New York, 1985); J. Jones, *On Aristotle and Greek Tragedy* (London, 1962), 239–79; I. Watt, *The Rise of the Novel* (London, 1957), 9–34.
[13] Cf. Stern, *Realism*, 55.
[14] Arist. *Poet.* 15; see Lucas ad loc., and most recently, S. Halliwell, *Aristotle's Poetics* (London, 1986), 159–65.
[15] It is not uncommon to find the capacity 'to develop and change' virtually equated with 'character' *per se* (as by Newman, *Shakespeare's Rhetoric*, 1).
[16] On which see e.g. M. L. Samuels, *Linguistic Evolution* (Cambridge, 1972), 126.
[17] See M. S. Silk, *Homer, The Iliad* (Cambridge, 1987), 83–96.

Aristophanes (I suggest) does not strictly belong to this tradition. There are, it is true, some Aristophanic characters that lend themselves reasonably well to a realist interpretation. Take Strepsiades in *Clouds*. He is a recognizable type, in opposition to his equally typical son Pheidippides. The son is a corruptible, extravagant young urban sophisticate:

> Φε. ὡς ἡδὺ καινοῖς πράγμασιν καὶ δεξιοῖς ὁμιλεῖν,
> καὶ τῶν καθεστώτων νόμων ὑπερφρονεῖν δύνασθαι.
> ἐγὼ γάρ, ὅτε μὲν ἱππικῇ τὸν νοῦν μόνῃ προσεῖχον,
> οὐδ' ἂν τρί' εἰπεῖν ῥήμαθ' οἷός τ' ἦ πρὶν ἐξαμαρτεῖν.
> νυνὶ δ', ἐπειδή μ' οὑτοσὶ τούτων ἔπαυσεν αὐτός,
> γνώμαις δὲ λεπταῖς καὶ λόγοις ξύνειμι καὶ μερίμναις,
> οἶμαι διδάξειν ὡς δίκαιον τὸν πατέρα κολάζειν.

PH. How nice to be *au fait* with everything clever and chic, and have the chance to look down on traditional values. In the days when all I could think about was racing, I couldn't put two words together without making a gaffe. But now ... [Socrates] has got me out of that, and I spend my time on subtle ideas, arguments, preoccupations, I think I can show that it's morally right to whack your father. (1399–1405)

The father is a thrifty, crude old peasant, crafty but not brainy, and deeply conservative:

> Στ. πῶς οὖν ἀπολαβεῖν τἀργύριον δίκαιος εἶ,
> εἰ μηδὲν οἶσθα τῶν μετεώρων πραγμάτων;

ST. So how can you be entitled to get your money back, if you don't know about meteorology? (1283–4)

> Στ.   ὡς ἐμαινόμην ἄρα,
> ὅτ' ἐξέβαλον καὶ τοὺς θεοὺς διὰ Σωκράτη.

ST. How mad I was, then, when I actually threw the gods out—all because of Socrates! (1476–7)

It is not difficult to list the leading characteristics of the two figures (in this instance they are inseparably matters of status and temperament), or to see how, with Strepsiades in particular, actions and words are aligned to each other: how they are evocative, that is, of various character-traits *as a continuum*. The old man's coarse language, for instance, is suggestive of an earthy background *and* of a certain intellectual mediocrity *and* of a fundamental antipathy to the Socratic Enlightenment. All three characteristics, accordingly, are shown to belong together:

Σω. ὦ μέγα σεμναὶ Νεφέλαι, φανερῶς ἠκούσατέ μου καλέσαντος.
     ἤσθου φωνῆς ἅμα καὶ βροντῆς μυκησαμένης θεοσέπτου;
Στ. καὶ σέβομαί γ’, ὦ πολυτίμητοι, καὶ βούλομαι ἀνταποπαρδεῖν
     πρὸς τὰς βροντάς· οὕτως αὐτὰς τετραμαίνω καὶ πεφόβημαι·
     κεἰ θέμις ἐστίν, νυνί γ’ ἤδη — κεἰ μὴ θέμις ἐστί — χεσείω.

so. O most holy Clouds, you have hearkened to my call in visible form. [*To St.*] Did you hear their voice in the awesome thunder's roar?
st. Yes, and I'm in awe, all right, O most honoured ones, and I'm so nervous and shaken up I feel like farting back at the thunder. Maybe it's right and maybe it's wrong, but the fact is I need a shit this minute. (291–5)

Furthermore, Strepsiades even begins to develop. He learns from experience. He sees his past in a new perspective, and is therefore able to identify what went before as his mistake ('how mad I was', 1476), like (say) Cnemon in *Dyscolus* (713) or Creon in *Antigone* (1272). These are real, if minimal, instances of development. They are distinct, for instance, from the differential revelation of character we encounter in (say) *Bacchae* with Pentheus, who begins as strident autocrat and ends as susceptible psychopath, but (we infer) was actually ('really') both all the time. The development of a Strepsiades, a Cnemon, or a Creon, of course, is slight compared with the development of (say) an Isabel Archer:

Madame Merle was already so present to her vision that her appearance in the flesh was like suddenly, and rather awfully, seeing a painted picture move. Isabel had been thinking all day of her falsity, her audacity, her ability, her probable suffering ... She pretended not even to smile, and though Isabel saw that she was more than ever playing a part, it seemed to her that on the whole the wonderful woman had never been so natural. (Henry James, *The Portrait of a Lady*, ch. lii)

Such a complex response as Isabel's here, with its intricate mixture of positive and negative feelings, presupposes a fully explored personal history, which presupposes, in turn, a development over a substantial period of fictional time, even (as with James's novel) a period of years. Full development, one might say, requires at least the time-span of a Shakespearean tragedy (or an *Iliad*)—the span sufficient, for instance, to show us a 'progress' like Macbeth's from a guilty recklessness ('come what come may', I. iii; 'If it were done when 'tis done, then 'twere well | It were done quickly', I. vii) to the several stages of moral dissolution that follow ('I am afraid to think what I have done', II. i; 'What man dare, I dare', III. iv; 'I have almost forgot the taste of fears', v. v.). A Greek tragedy (or New Comedy) tends, instead, to centre on an expanded moment of crisis and the magnification of an individual's response to it. Such patterns, nevertheless, are obviously conducive to the presentation of character-development, however embryonic; and it is symptomatic that they should be as generally uncharacteristic of Aristophanic comedy as they are characteristic of Greek tragedy.

Most (perhaps all) of Aristophanes' characters belong in *some* degree to the realist tradition, and some of them (like Strepsiades) might be construed—without too much forcing of the evidence—as belonging wholly to it. However, most (perhaps all) of them partake also of a different mode of representation, which, for lack of a better term, I propose to call *imagist*. Words used in images—that is, words used tropically, and especially words used metaphorically—disrupt the terminological continuity of their context.[18] Like words used literally, they evoke some reality.[19] Unlike words used literally, they evoke their reality through discontinuity. Verbal sequences that involve imagery rarely consist entirely of disruptive terminology (an exception is the ancient allegory). Commonly, the image is part disrupt*ive* terminology (the 'vehicle'), part disrupt*ed* terminology (the 'tenor').[20] Aristophanes' characters, similarly, have their realist elements, or moments, or sequences, disrupted by imagist elements, or moments, or sequences. And though realist elements, or moments, or sequences, remain, the presence of the disruptive serves to differentiate the representation as a whole from realism proper. In the discontinuities of imagist presentation, accordingly, it is reasonable to see a factor of decisive importance.[21]

---

[18] See M. S. Silk, *Interaction in Poetic Imagery* (Cambridge, 1974), 6–14.
[19] Cf. Martin, *Language*.
[20] Cf. Silk, *Interaction*, 8–14.
[21] This analogy between character and image is (as far as I know) my own. Various

To avoid any misunderstanding at this stage in the argument, it should be noted that some of Aristophanes' characters, especially some that we may think of as his 'non-fictional' characters, invite comparison with images on quite different grounds. Take Socrates in *Clouds*. This figure may or may not have traits comparable with those of the historical Socrates. What he certainly has is exaggerated traits—recondite scientific interests, pretensions to authority, spokesmanship of new deities, an indifferent attitude towards the two arguments, Right and Wrong—which collectively amount to a cartoon of the new intellectualism. But what sort of cartoon is it? Not the emblematic, metonymic kind (as Uncle Sam is a metonym for the USA or John Bull for England). Rather the metaphorical kind—like the lumbering cart-horse which the cartoonist Low regularly used to represent the Trades Union Congress in Britain between the wars, or the infant of tender years he once used to represent the human race in the new atomic age ('Baby play with nice ball?'). So in *Clouds* the new Enlightenment is personified as a mad scientist, called (for convenience) Socrates. So (more transparently) in *Knights* the relation

critics and theorists have suggested that there is a tendency towards discontinuous characterization in *comedy in general*: e.g. N. Frye, *Anatomy of Criticism* (Princeton, 1957), 170; and notably L. Pirandello, *L'Umorismo* (1908), who suggests that serious writing 'composes' a character 'and will want to represent him as consistent in every action', whereas 'the humorist . . . will *decompose* the character . . . and . . . enjoys representing him in his incongruities' (quoted from the trans. by A. Illiano and D. P. Testa, *On Humor* (Univ. of N. Carolina Studies in Comp. Lit., 58; Chapel Hill, 1974), 143). Discontinuity in Aristophanic characterization has been discussed, but without what I take to be the necessary emphasis, e.g. by Dover, *Aristophanic Comedy*, 59–65. Remarkably, theories of character as a whole tend to ignore the fact that there is such a thing as discontinuous presentation at all. This is the case with such diverse and wide-ranging discussions as C. C. Walcutt, *Man's Changing Mask: Modes and Methods of Characterization in Fiction* (Minneapolis, 1966); P. Hamon, 'Pour un statut sémiologique du personnage', in R. Barthes *et al.*, *Poétique du récit* (Paris, 1977), 115–80; S. Freeman, 'Character in a Coherent Fiction', *Philosophy and Literature*, 7 (1983), 196–212; J. Frow, 'Spectacle Binding'; S. Chatman, 'Characters and Narrators'; U. Margolin, 'The Doer and the Deed: Action as a Basis for Characterization in Narrative'; C. Gill, 'The Question of Character and Personality in Greek Tragedy' (all four essays in *Poetics Today*, 7/2 (1986), 189–273). Structuralist-semiotic attempts to 'dissolve' character into 'text' are no exception (see e.g. J. Weinsheimer, 'Theory of Character: *Emma*', *Poetics Today*, 1 (1980), 195; cf. Hamon, 'Pour un statut'; Margolin, 'The Doer'; Frow, 'Spectacle Binding'): *all* character is simply subjected to a common reinterpretative principle. Margolin, however, briefly considers the phenomenon of texts (e.g. the *nouveau roman*) which frustrate expectations of 'a unified stable constellation' of '[character] traits or trait-clusters' ('The Doer', 207).

between the people and their leading politicians is represented metaphorically as the relation between an old man (labelled Demos, as he might be in a modern cartoon) and his slaves, old and new.

Whatever else he is, Euripides in *Thesmophoriazusae* is partly an image of this kind. For instance, despite his original disinclination to disguise himself, Euripides in fact goes through three disguises, the last of which is the disguise of the old madam. Why *that* disguise? Because Euripidean tragedy (in Aristophanes' eyes) is a new and morally subversive kind of drama, fascinating but disturbing: lower in tone than the heroic tragedy of an earlier age (its heroes in rags were notorious),[22] more seductive in its persuasive techniques. This is all summed up in the representation of Euripides himself as an old hag bringing on a girl to seduce the forces of law and order (here the Scythian policeman) and thereby distracting and (literally) disarming them. More generally, the Euripides of this play is an image in the same sense: he is a personification of the 'real' Euripides' own plays. Among the other salient characteristics of those plays (as seen by Aristophanes) are melodramatic emotional moments, flashy ideas, modishly difficult thoughts, and a penchant for the unexpected. Accordingly, throughout this play the character Euripides is melodramatic ('today will tell if Euripides is to live on or die', 76 f.), full of flashy ideas ('brilliant and up to your best standard' [Mnesilochus], 93) given to modishly difficult thoughts ('you can't *hear* what you'll soon be here to *see*', 5 f.), and, 'by introducing something new and clever' (1130), constantly doing the unexpected.[23] In these respects Euripides is evidently, in my terms, a figure belonging to the *realist* tradition. Irrespective of his relation to the historical Euripides or to the historical Euripides' plays, his characterization endows him with the set and stable features of a realist character—albeit a realist

[22] See e.g. *Ran.* 939–44, 954 (lowering the tone); 842, 1063 (rags); 771–6 (persuasion). The mode of transference seems to recall the technique of the (later) ancient biographers of Greek authors: 'the smallest hints of personality in conventional statements [in their works] could be developed into character traits [in their authors]' (M. R. Lefkowitz, *The Lives of the Greek Poets* (London, 1981), ix).

[23] For these as characteristics of Euripidean drama, see (e.g.) *Ran.* 1330–63 (melodramatic moments and constant surprises: the Euripidean predisposition towards the unexpected is summed up in the word στρέφειν, 957); and 892–9 (modish thoughts and flashy ideas); cf. Stanford on both passages.

character comically stylized by its construction around a few limited traits.

The representation of Euripides as 'unexpected', in the image of the unexpected twists and turns of his plays, brings us back to imagist presentation in the sense that primarily concerns us. Images, characteristically, work by discontinuing the context they presuppose. Imagist characters, accordingly, act discontinuously, and unexpected behaviour, verbal or visual, is therefore their imagist prerogative. In the particular instance of Euripides in *Thesmophoriazusae* a version of discontinuity is *also*, ingeniously, converted into a realist character-trait. It is almost as if one were to act on Aristotle's instruction that an inconsistent character should be portrayed as *consistently* inconsistent.[24] However, as the examples already considered suggest, the point (in these Aristotelian terms) is that imagist characters are *in*consistently inconsistent.

The mobile, continuous characters of the realist tradition do, or can, develop: they do, or can, do so by gradual movement between their particular traits. The imagist characters of Aristophanes are fundamentally different. If and when they change, they change abruptly and, perhaps, entirely—like the women at the Thesmophoria, dropping their respectability and picking it up again; like the clever Euripides, abruptly accepting Mnesilochus' offer to help (which *might* be explicable in terms of Euripides' own traits of character); or like the stooge Mnesilochus, suddenly assuming the role of hero by making that offer (which is not apparently explicable in such terms). In short, the realist tradition, at its extreme, permits character-development, whereas the Aristophanic mode of representation involves, at *its* extreme, a binary principle: instead of development, it permits inversion or reversal. Imagist representation, it will be gathered, accepts a merely sequential view of time. In the realist tradition, by contrast, time is perceived as a (literally) *con*sequential matter, as an Aristotelian process of events that follow the laws of 'probability or necessity'.[25]

---

[24] Arist *Poet.* 15.

[25] Arist. *Poet.* 7. To dissociate Aristophanes and development is not to ascribe a non-developmental tendency to comedy as a whole, as S. K. Langer did in *Feeling and Form* (New York, 1953), 335 f. Different again are the 'semantic reversals' which are reasonably taken to be a sign of inner 'psychic process' (i.e. of one form of realist characterization) by Newman, *Shakespeare's Rhetoric*, 11.

It is usual to discuss 'character' in Aristophanes in terms of alternatives which belong to the realist tradition rather than the imagist. Are his characters (for instance) 'types or individuals'? Such a question is eminently discussible in respect of Menander, and it is discussible in respect of Aristophanes the more his characterization approximates to the Menandrian-realist. It is therefore a more appropriate, and a more meaningful, question to ask of Strepsiades in *Clouds* than it is of (say) Philocleon in *Wasps*. That old man begins his play as a sort of caricature of Athenian legalism—and ends it as a sort of personification of the self-expressive life-force, abusing, drinking, and dancing. When we first see him, he is totally lacking in self-confidence, pining in captivity (317). Later on, he exudes total self-confidence ('much the most outrageous of them all', 1303). He is, no doubt, both an individual and a type at different times, perhaps even at the same time, but that formula is not illuminating: the important thing is his capacity to reverse. In this connection it is revealing to note that various interpreters of Aristophanes, from Süss to McLeish, have sought to identify his characters with a neo-Aristotelian set of character-types derived from the *Ethics* and elsewhere: notably the εἴρων (the dry wit, who understates himself), the ἀλαζών (the charlatan, who overstates himself), the βωμολόχος (the buffoon).[26] What these attempts show is that the 'types' cannot be consistently equated with Aristophanes' *characters*, but may be equated with their *functions*. Beyond a certain point, in other words, the analysis is bound to resemble a Proppian analysis of narrative functions,[27] in which a given function may be seen to be transferred from one character to another. So whereas Mnesilochus, for instance, begins *Thesmophoriazusae* as the buffoon, in the later stages of the play the buffoon's function is transferred from Mnesilochus to the Scythian, while Mnesilochus himself acts as a sort of 'dry wit' in his speech at the women's assembly, when he catalogues the vices of the sex from (purportedly) a woman's point of view. The transferability of such 'functions', however,

---

[26] Arist. *EN* 2. 7, 4. 7 f.; *EE* 3. 7; *Rhet.* 3. 18: see W. Süss, *De Personarum Antiquae Comoediae Usu et Origine* (Bonn, 1905); id., 'Zur Komposition der altattischen Komödie', *Rl. M.* 63 (1908), 12–38; K. McLeish, *The Theatre of Aristophanes* (London, 1980), 53–6, 74 f. The three types occur as a set in the *Tract. Coisl.*: see R. Janko, *Aristotle on Comedy* (London, 1984), 39, 216–8, 242.

[27] See V. Propp, *Morphology of the Folktale* (Bloomington, 1958).

is largely, if not entirely, a corollary of imagist discontinuity. The application of these types to the discussion of Aristophanes, therefore, leaves a plausible realist interpretation of his characters as unattainable as ever.

It is a necessary, though not a sufficient, condition of imagist representation that it should involve figures whose appearance is decisive for their being. It follows that if such figures are disguised, they change. In life we suppose that this is not true. In this kind of art, however, it has the appearance of truth—hence the wonderful repeated joke in the second half of *Thesmophoriazusae*, that by appearing to be Menelaus, Euripides can rescue Mnesilochus, if Mnesilochus appears to be Helen; and by appearing to be Perseus, Euripides can rescue Mnesilochus, if Mnesilochus appears to be Andromeda. Mnesilochus himself makes the principle explicit:

> ἔα· θεοί, Ζεῦ σῶτερ, εἰσὶν ἐλπίδες.
> ἀνὴρ ἔοικεν οὐ προδώσειν, ἀλλά μοι
> σημεῖον ὑπεδήλωσε Περσεὺς ἐκδραμών,
> ὅτι δεῖ με γίγνεσθ' Ἀνδρομέδαν.

Thank heaven! There's still hope. My man won't let me down. He just shot past as Perseus. It was a sign that I must be Andromeda. (1009–12)

The topic is prefigured, programmatically, by Agathon, earlier on in the play. The writer must 'identify with', and therefore disguise himself as, his own parts:

> ἐγὼ δὲ τὴν ἐσθῆθ' ἅμα γνώμῃ φορῶ.
> χρὴ γὰρ ποιητὴν ἄνδρα πρὸς τὰ δράματα
> ἃ δεῖ ποιεῖν πρὸς ταῦτα τοὺς τρόπους ἔχειν.
> αὐτίκα γυναικεῖ' ἢν ποιῇ τις δράματα,
> μετουσίαν δεῖ τῶν τρόπων τὸ σῶμ' ἔχειν.

I wear the clothes that fit in with my projects. A playwright, you see, must tailor his own life-style to the dramatic task in hand. If it's a play about women, his own physical being has to have something of their style. (148–52)

Role-playing, disguise, and identification, of course, can and often do figure within the realist sphere. In the imagist tradition, however, they have a distinctive significance.

II

Realism of some kind seems to dominate fictional writing in the Western world from Aristophanes' own day to the beginning of the present century. More precisely: outside Aristophanes the best examples of imagist representation seem either to belong to the twentieth-century avant-garde or to be naïve—perhaps in the ordinary sense of that word, or else in Schiller's sense, whereby (say) Homer is naïve, and the word tends to imply *early*.[28] We do indeed find hints of imagist representation in Homer, especially in the *Iliad*, where (with the notable exception of Achilles) characters have fixed qualities which they either live up to or fail to live up to, and where the prospect of any such failure is felt as a threat to—because a reversal of?— personal integrity. So Hector, besought by Andromache to hold back from the fighting where he will risk his life and her future, grants the validity of her fears but points to the constraints of public opinion *and his own nature*:

ἦ καὶ ἐμοὶ τάδε πάντα μέλει, γύναι· ἀλλὰ μάλ' αἰνῶς
αἰδέομαι Τρῶας καὶ Τρῳάδας ἑλκεσιπέπλους,
αἴ κε κακὸς ὣς νόσφιν ἀλυσκάζω πολέμοιο·
οὐδέ με θυμὸς ἄνωγεν, ἐπεὶ μάθον ἔμμεναι ἐσθλὸς
αἰεὶ καὶ πρώτοισι μετὰ Τρώεσσι μάχεσθαι,
ἀρνύμενος πατρός τε μέγα κλέος ἠδ' ἐμὸν αὐτοῦ.

Woman, all this is on my mind as well as yours. But I am too much in awe of the Trojan men and the long-robed Trojan women to skulk away from battle like a coward. Nor is that what my own heart bids me do, for I have learned always to be valiant and fight among the leading men of Troy and win great glory for my father and myself. (6. 441–6)

'Yes,' says Hector in effect, 'you are right: I *will* be killed. But what else can I—*being me*—do? *Ich kann nicht anders.*' His obstinacy, however, is prompted not by any sort of Lutheran conscience, but by a consciousness that cannot conceive of—and is not conceived in terms of—a flexible response.[29]

---

[28] Friedrich Schiller, *Über naive und sentimentalische Dichtung* (1795–6). Examples from 'carnival' literature might be adduced to support the correlation between imagist and naïve. There are, however, some surprising counter-examples of sophisticated imagism: the Duke in Shakespeare's *Measure for Measure* is one.

[29] The reference is to Luther's speech at the Diet of Worms, 18 Apr. 1521.

Perhaps the simplest, and certainly the most naïve, type of imagist representation is found in the fairy-tale. The ugly frog who changes into a handsome prince is a typical instance. The character is represented as an unchanging being—except that it can go into binary reverse and become its own opposite. Compare the transformation of Demos from ugly old man to handsome younger man at the end of *Knights*.[30] Compare, too, similar transformations in surviving forms of traditional popular culture like the pantomime.

In our own century many writers, especially dramatists, have opened up the possibilities of imagist representation in a more self-conscious, experimental way, by reacting against·the whole realist tradition as no Greek of Aristophanes' day either needed to or could. Against familiar stabilities and traditional expectations of development the new age puts a series of challenging questions. Sometimes the challenge is mounted on behalf of what many would think of as a marginal artistic tendency—stream of consciousness, surrealism, the absurd. For Strindberg, it is associated with a neo-realist perception that modern people, 'living in a transitional era more hectic and hysterical' than earlier ages, are, and should be represented as, 'more vulnerable, . . . torn and divided'.[31] For Pirandello, questions give way to new answers: 'My drama lies entirely in this one thing . . . in my being conscious that each one of us believes himself to be a single person. But it's not true . . . each one of us is many persons.'[32] Accompanying and often underlying these new positions is the rejection of the 'substantial unity of the soul' by influential thinkers like Nietzsche and Freud.[33] Marx-

---

[30] Despite the arguments of L. Edmunds, *Cleon, Knights, and Aristophanes' Politics* (Lanham, 1987), 43–4, it may be assumed that when Demos is pronounced 'handsome' (καλὸν ἐξ αἰσχροῦ, 1321) the ordinary associations of this phraseology would point to some sort of rejuvenation. It is true that (e.g.) at Xen. *Smp.* 4. 17 we learn that old men can be called handsome (καλοί) too, but only by way of a refined qualification to the everyday perception that 'good looks soon pass their prime'—i.e. that 'beauty' and 'youth' do belong together, as of course they do in a host of familiar contexts from Homer (e.g. *Od.* 6. 108) to Aristophanes himself (e.g. *Lys.* 647).

[31] From Strindberg's preface to *Miss Julie* (1888), trans. E. M. Sprinchorn, in B. F. Dukore (ed.), *Dramatic Theory and Criticism* (New York, 1974), 567.

[32] The father's words in *Six Characters in Search of an Author* (1921), trans. F. May (London, 1954), 25.

[33] The phase, 'substantial unity of the soul', is used (as a target) by T. S. Eliot in 'Tradition and the Individual Talent' (*The Sacred Wood* (London, 1920), 56).

ist theory too produces its alternative to the realist tradition,
above all in the work of Brecht. In *Der gute Mensch von Sezuan*,
for instance, 'the "good woman" Shen Te assumes a mask of
harsh oppressiveness and turns into the businessman Shui Ta,
so that each of her twin personalities recalls the possibility of
the other'.[34] As early as *Die Dreigroschenoper* (1928) Brecht is
seen to be exploring norms of imagist representation. At the
final peripeteia of the drama, for instance, we find the arch-
criminal, Macheath, suddenly snatched from the gallows by
royal decree and raised to a peerage, exchanging his crude
curses on the police and farewells to fellow criminals and
lavatory attendants for the lofty operatic observation that the
greater the need, the more imminent the rescue—this frog
having become a prince after all.[35]

In classical Greek drama as we have it, imagist characterization is much more characteristic of comedy than of tragedy; but
the 'progress' of comedy (in the fourth century), as of tragedy
(in the fifth), is clearly towards the realist mode. If one is prepared to extrapolate backwards from that tendency, it might
be conjectured that early drama, tragedy as well as comedy,
contained various imagist elements. One likely context would
be the chorus—the stylized speaking or (especially) singing
group, which both forms of drama eventually found to be
incompatible with their aspirations towards realism, and
sought to eliminate. The Aristophanic chorus, certainly, is—
still?—markedly imagist. In no extant Aristophanic comedy, in
fact, 'does the chorus have a consistent and unalterable dramatic character'.[36] The women in *Thesmophoriazusae*—in or out
of the chorus—actually constitute a modest specimen of group
variability. The chorus in *Wasps* begin as creaky old men, turn
into fierce wasps, and end as earnest commentators on the
action.[37] The chorus in *Peace*, as the play's most recent editor
observes, actually has 'four or five distinguishable identities' in
the space of five hundred lines.[38] But in tragedy too the identity

---

[34] R. D. Gray, *Brecht* (London, 1961), 66.
[35] 'Die Mordgesellen, Abtrittsweiber, | Ich bitte sie, mir zu verzeihen. | Nicht so die
Polizistenhunde . . .'; 'Ja, ich fühle es, wenn die Not am grössten, ist die Hilfe am
nächsten': Bertolt Brecht, *Versuche 1–12* (Berlin, 1959), 217–18.
[36] Sifakis, *Parabasis*, 32.
[37] *Vesp.* 230 ff., 403 ff., 1450 ff.: cf. Silk, 'Pathos in Aristophanes', 87–90, 110 f.
[38] Aristophanes, *Peace*, ed. A. H. Sommerstein (Warminster, 1985), xviii.

Michael Silk

of the chorus is often—in realist terms—elusive: the 'Theban elders' in *Antigone* are a classic case in point.[39] More fundamentally, though, it may be that imagist characterization is originally implicit in the very rhythms of Greek drama—in the alternative reversals from happy man to sad man (common in tragedy) and sad man to happy man (usual in comedy). That Aristotle should have interpreted such patterns as essentially and primarily sequences of *action* testifies to his overwhelming concern with classic tragedy and his own penchant for realism.[40] And that latter prejudice, no doubt, *is* broadly justified by classic tragedy as we know it, where the imagist presence is a marginal one. Outside the chorus, in fact, it is chiefly visible in the dramatic experiments of Euripides. His *Medea*, for instance, reveals *both* the progressive realist who explores the woman's inner agonies about killing her children *and* the avantgarde anti-realist who offers us her transfiguration from oppressed victim to divine agent of vengeance at the end.

III

The obvious positive feature of imagist presentation of character is discontinuity; and if one seeks confirmation of the plausibility of an imagist reading of Aristophanes—a reading that sees discontinuities of characterization as essential, not incidental—one will find it above all in the evident kinship between such discontinuities and others elsewhere in the text or texture of Aristophanic drama.[41] I have already instanced Aristophanes' stylistic shifts and reversals as symptomatic of the mode of character-presentation that they contribute to. With the word 'imagist' in mind, we can hardly overlook the fact that no mechanism is more characteristic of Aristophanic writing in general than metaphor, the discontinuous stylistic feature *par excellence*[42]—just as nothing is more characteristic of his verbal humour than the surprise joke (παρὰ προσδοκίαν).[43]

[39] See M. S. Silk and J. P. Stern, *Nietzsche on Tragedy* (Cambridge, 1981), 267 f.
[40] See Arist. *Poet.* 6; and (on the endings of tragedies and comedies) cf. M. S. Silk, 'The Autonomy of Comedy', *Comparative Criticism*, 10 (1988), 27-9.
[41] Cf. Silk, 'Pathos in Aristophanes', esp. 103-8.
[42] See esp. J. Taillardat, *Les Images d'Aristophane* (Paris, 1965).
[43] 'The instances of comic surprise in Aristophanes are legion' (W. J. M. Starkie, *The Acharnians of Aristophanes* (London, 1909), p. lxvii). It may be noted that the ancient

An equivalent discontinuous tendency is apparent in the organization of his dramatic fictions. This is what we commonly discuss under the heading of 'breaches of illusion'; and no one can dispute the propensity of Aristophanes' characters to be the carriers of these 'breaches' *without undermining their own peculiar mode of existence*. 'Master, shall I tell you one of the usual jokes that always get the audience laughing . . .': whatever else is true of such an opening to a play, it is certainly true that it alerts us to a kind of character-presentation which is not going to be that of a Menander (let alone a Henry James).[44] One notes, however, the frequency of such moments in twentieth-century avant-garde drama, including that of Brecht.[45]

Going deeper into Aristophanes, one could also relate his character-presentation to the discontinuities of his plot-construction, notably those associated with the loose connection of episodes in the latter parts of many of his plays. Here too Brecht offers a valuable point of reference—the Brecht of theory even more than the Brecht of practice. As he repeatedly urges us to see in his theoretical writings on the theatre, seemingly unrelated aspects of drama in fact hang together—above all, aspects of his own innovatory 'epic theatre' as against aspects of the traditional dramatic, or 'Aristotelian', theatre. In particular he allows us to sense a connection between Aristotelian theatre's 'evolutionary' treatment of character and its 'linear development' of plot, as against the concern of his own epic theatre with 'jumps' and 'curves'. Traditional theatre means *growth*; his own means *montage*, where, in place of a 'natural' whole, the individual events are tied together in such a way that 'the knots show'.[46]

---

theorists who established the principle of humour παρὰ προσδοκίαν themselves tended to interpret it very narrowly, as e.g. did Demetrius (*Eloc.* 152), who classified it as merely one among many humorous mechanisms (ibid. 137–62).

[44] *Ran.* 1 f.: cf. Sifakis, *Parabasis*, 7–14.

[45] A representative example from *Die Dreigroschenoper*: the address to the audience in the theatre by Macheath's rival, Peachum, explaining the thinking behind the royal pardon for Macheath ('. . . wir haben uns einen anderen Schluss ausgedacht . . .': Brecht, *Versuche 1–12*, 218).

[46] Bertolt Brecht, *Schriften zum Theater* (Frankfurt, 1963–4), ii. 117, vii. 67. The relevance of Brecht's theory to Aristophanes' practice is briefly, but properly, stated by Sifakis, *Parabasis*, 21, 113 n. 46; cf. W. Görler, 'Über die Illusion in der antiken Komödie', *A & A* 18 (1973), 44–57; K. von Fritz, *Antike und moderne Tragödie* (Berlin, 1962), x–xxviii; H. Flashar, 'Aristoteles und Brecht', *Poetica*, 6 (1974), 17 ff.; D. Bain,

One might, with profit, lay still more stress on a different affinity. The tendency of Aristophanes' imagist characters to reverse themselves surely belongs to a vast pattern of reversals, inversions, and oppositions in Aristophanic comedy as a whole. *Thesmophoriazusae* again offers an apt instance with (among much else) its women playing at being men (ecclesia and all); one man (Mnesilochus) playing at being a woman *ad hoc*; another man (Cleisthenes) who habitually takes that role; a member of the dominant sex (Mnesilochus) taken captive by the weaker sex (women), but himself reversing roles when he kidnaps their 'baby'. Within the action of the play we have a whole series of reversal tableaux, like the weak man Cleisthenes being put down by the strong women ('stand aside—I'll do the interrogating', 626); or the vocal representative of the dominant sex (Euripides) being forced to ask for terms from the supposedly weaker women; and another member of that weaker sex (the dancing-girl) overcoming another member of the stronger sex (the Scythian), who (as a laughable foreigner) is an inversion of establishment domination in his own right. Within such a series of reversals and inversions, details like the women's sudden coarseness, or Mnesilochus' sudden assumption of the strong man's role and Euripides' eager response to it, fall into place, unnoticed. Everywhere we meet (as Bakhtin says of the medieval carnival) 'the relativity of prevailing truths and authorities . . . the peculiar logic of the "inside out" '.[47]

Furthermore, all such reversals and inversions belong to a still larger system of fundamental oppositions, notably those expressed in agonistic terms, around which so many of the plays are constructed: men and women (as *Thesmophoriazusae*), men and gods (as *Birds*), peace and war (as *Acharnians*), new and old (as *Clouds*), young and old (as *Wasps*). The oppositions, of course, may be subject to inversion themselves. In *Wasps*, for

---

Actors and Audience (Oxford, 1977), 3–5. Before Brecht, Pirandello had anticipated the connection between discontinuous character and discontinuous dramatic form: the 'decomposed' and 'incongruous' characters of 'the humorist' (see n. 21 above) are related to 'all that is disorganised, unravelled and whimsical, all the digressions which can be seen in the works of humor' (*On Humor*, 144 f.).

[47] M. M. Bakhtin, *Rabelais and his World*, trans. H. Iswolsky (Cambridge, Mass., 1968), 11. On inversions in *Thesmophoriazusae*, cf. F. Zeitlin, 'Travesties of Gender and Genre in Aristophanes' *Thesmophoriazusae*', in H. P. Foley (ed.), *Reflections of Women in Antiquity*, (New York, 1981), 169–217.

instance, the normal pattern whereby the young resist the orthodoxies of their elders (cf. the end of *Clouds*) is reversed, so that the son Bdelycleon labours in vain to reduce his father to order, the imagist corollary of which is that the old man *becomes* 'young' in his own right.[48] And pervading all the plays is the opposition between higher and lower, serious and non-serious, a particular version of which we find alluded to in a contrasting pair like Euripides and Mnesilochus, and another version in the stylistic switches discussed earlier. This, arguably, is the opposition from which, above all, Aristophanic comedy gets its bearings.[49]

IV

This discussion of imagist representation can hardly be regarded as comprehensive, either in a theoretical sense or in respect of Aristophanes. I hope to have answered one question: the inconstancies of behaviour which the people of Aristophanes exhibit are acceptable because they presuppose Aristophanic 'norms' of discontinuity both on the level of character and elsewhere. And I hope, in answering it, to have shed some light on the possibilities (and actualities) of character-presentation in general. At the same time, various other questions have been left unconsidered. Their existence should at the very least be acknowledged, if only as a gesture towards the ideal of a comprehensive treatment.

In the first place, my discussion of Aristophanes has been essentially behaviourist. I have concentrated on the words and actions of his people and have generally evaded their minds and thoughts. As imagist beings, can they actually be said to have minds and thoughts? In realist representation, characters are assumed to have minds and thoughts which work like those of real people in real life. Real people have experiences, whether *we* know about them or not; they have habits that imply responses to those experiences; and in general they have

---

[48] νέος γάρ εἰμι ['I'm only young, you see'] (1355). On the implications of this 'becoming', see Silk, 'Pathos in Aristophanes', 109–11.

[49] Cf. Silk, 'The Autonomy of Comedy', 16; O. Taplin, 'Fifth-Century Tragedy and Comedy: A *Synkrisis*', *JHS* 106 (1986), 163–74.

memories of their experiences. Fictional people, necessarily, have experiences only when we know that they do, and responses and memories only when these are made public in some way. Within this limitation, however, the characters of realist fiction impinge on us as sentient beings: so far as we see and know them, they act from their minds (experiences, responses, memories), and their behaviour is referable to their minds. Are we to make any such reference with imagist characters, and if so, when and why? Picture Mnesilochus taking his decision to help Euripides, and it is hard to deny imagist characters any mental capacity at all. Think of Xanthias' anti-illusionary question to Dionysus at the start of *Frogs*, and it is hard to see what sort of experiences, responses, or memories such a being needs to be, or can be, credited with.

Secondly, it is easier to say (as I have said) that Aristophanes' presentation of character is both imagist and realist than to assess the relative strength of each element in any given dramatic sequence. The general principle (I would say) is clear enough. And this is that Aristophanic comedy presupposes a non-realist sense or logic of human *being* and *behaving*. As such it admits realism in so far as realism suits its own logic.[50] However, the particular problem, as it concerns particular sequences, remains unsolved. For instance (thinking back to the previous unanswered question), we might ask: Do we credit the character Xanthias with a mind ('of his own') when he talks to Dionysus 'in character', but not when he makes anti-illusionary remarks like the one at the start? Do we in fact—can we conceivably—switch mentalist assumptions on and off like a tap in this way? Is the truth that even when we credit Xanthias with a mind, we always do so on some non-realist terms, which remain to be specified?

Finally, a comprehensive discussion must certainly come to terms with the evaluative implications of the modern experiments in imagist representation, whose diversity and sophistication suggest that while we may argue for the superiority of realism, we cannot simply assume it. As John Gould reminds us in his discussion of tragic character, realist character in fiction—from Greek tragedy to Eugene O'Neill—is a construct,

---

[50] Cf. Silk, 'The Autonomy of Comedy', 23–7.

not a hidden pre-existing reality.[51] This is hardly to devalue realist characterization, since our sense of a human character in life, arguably, must always be as much of a construct as a response to a hidden reality itself.[52] And certainly it does not justify us in describing realist characters as 'systems of rule-governed equivalencies' (like Philippe Hamon) or, more simply, as 'predications' (like Todorov).[53] But it does encourage us to see that the constructional quality of imagist representations does not in itself invalidate their claim to serious attention.

[51] See n. 12 above. Gould (I hasten to add) is at pains to *contrast* Greek tragedy and O'Neill, and he does not give them any common 'realist' label, as I do.

[52] See e.g. E. Goffman, *The Presentation of Self in Everyday Life* (Garden City, NY, 1959); J. Lacan, *Écrits* (Paris, 1966), 93 ff.; cf. Easterling's discussion in ch. 4 above. A similar conclusion about (realist) characterization is reached by Newman, *Shakespeare's Rhetoric*, 127 f.

[53] Hamon, 'Pour un statut', 144; T. Todorov, *Grammaire du Décaméron* (The Hague, 1969), 27–30.

8

The Role of the Interlocutor in Plato's Dialogues
Theory and Practice

LUCINDA COVENTRY

ἔστι δὲ ἴσως τὸ διαλεκτικώτερον μὴ μόνον τἀληθῆ
ἀποκρίνεσθαι, ἀλλὰ καὶ δι' ἐκείνων ὧν ἂν προσομολογῇ
εἰδέναι ὁ ἐρωτώμενος.

And perhaps the more dialectical manner is to give
answers which are not only true, but made in terms of
what the respondent agrees he knows.

(Meno 75d 5–7)

I

When Socrates sets responsiveness to the interlocutor beside devotion to the truth as a distinctive feature of dialectic, he gives
expression to the idea underlying the importance of characterization in Plato's work. It is essential to dialectic as Plato portrays it that argument should not be unvarying, indifferent to
the participants, but should rather be sensitive to the individual respondent in any dispute. The respondent is repeatedly
urged to say only what he believes;[1] Socrates in turn is bound to
take account of these beliefs in his argument. Such sensitivity to
the respondent may have the result that Socrates' success in
enquiry varies according to his interlocutor, as is suggested by
the comment which Glaucon adds to his encouragement as
Socrates prepares to defend his assertion that philosophers
should rule: καὶ ἴσως ἂν ἄλλου του ἐμμελέστερόν σοι ἀποκρινοίμην

---

[1] See e.g. *Cri.* 49c11–d1; *Gorg.* 495a7–9; *Rep.* 1. 350c5; and the discussion, with
further instances, in G. Vlastos, 'The Socratic Elenchus', *Oxford Studies in Ancient Philosophy*, 1 (1983), 27–58.

['And perhaps my replies may be more in harmony with your questions than someone else's'] (*Rep.* 5. 474a8–b1).[2] So too, the very form which Socrates' arguments take is influenced by the character, ability, and position of the respondent.[3]

Accordingly, the choice and characterization of interlocutors for a dialogue must be important to Plato; for it is intimately related to the development of the argument, and so to the precise thought expressed. Equally, for interpreters, understanding a dialogue calls for consideration of arguments and interlocutors together, just as in a Socratic enquiry both a thesis and its supporter are tested at once.[4] The appropriateness of Plato's style of composition to his philosophy appears partly in the fact that in both, different strands are closely related and throw light on one another, without its being possible to identify one as the fundamental element from which all explanation must start.[5] Thus, of Plato's ethics and his epistemology, neither should be regarded as more basic than the other; understanding is enhanced by seeing their appropriateness to each other and to the whole philosophy of which they are equally fundamental aspects. The same is true of argument and characterization as elements in the composition of a dialogue. Neither can be treated as the key to understanding of the other and of the dialogue as a whole; but the significance of each is most fully grasped in comprehending their relation to each other and their appropriateness to Plato's concerns in the work.

II

Socrates' remark in the *Meno* concerning the importance of responsiveness to the interlocutor is made in the context of a contrast between dialectic and eristic. In the recurrent

[2] Cf. *Tht.* 185c and *Euthyd.* 282c, where Socrates acknowledges that his interlocutors' replies have made his task easier. A helpful respondent need not violate the requirement of sincerity; Parmenides believes that the youngest disputant will be the most suitable respondent on both grounds (*Parm.* 137b6–7).

[3] For an analysis of the relation between particular arguments and the figures to whom they are addressed, see C. H. Kahn, 'Drama and Dialectic in Plato's *Gorgias*', *Oxford Studies in Ancient Philosophy*, 1 (1983), 75–121.

[4] See *Prt.* 331c3–d1, 333c7–9.

[5] The difficulty of deciding on a suitable starting-point for the study of Plato has long been acknowledged; see e.g. Albinus, *Introductio* 4–6.

confrontations portrayed in the dialogues between Socrates and the representatives of rival methods of discourse and argument, this contrast is embodied; and these encounters play a large part in making clear the depth of Plato's concern for the personal nature of dialectic. The practitioners of rhetoric and sophistry whom Socrates faces are portrayed as deficient with regard to both of Socrates' requirements for dialectic; and a connection is drawn between their indifference to the truth and to their individual respondents.

In the *Euthydemus*, the eristic brothers Euthydemus and Dionysodorus are represented from the outset as indifferent to the truth: their skill lies in refuting any statement, true as well as false (272a8–b1). Their equal lack of concern for their respondents is epitomized in Euthydemus' dissociation of himself from Socrates at 296. Socrates has expressed a fear that statements made without proper qualification may lead to difficulties in the argument: ἀλλ' ὅπως μή τι ἡμᾶς σφήλῃ τὸ "ἀεί" τοῦτο ['But I am afraid this "always" may trip us up'] (296a9); to which Euthydemus retorts that any difficulty will affect Socrates alone, not the two brothers: οὔκουν ἡμᾶς γ', ἔφη, ἀλλ' εἴπερ, σέ [' "Not us, at any rate," he said, "but if anyone, you." '] (296b1).[6] Typical of the brothers' combative approach to argument (Socrates' initial description of them, at 271c–272b, is rich in words of conflict and competitiveness[7]), this dissociation and opposition excludes the adaptation to a particular interlocutor's needs and abilities which Socrates demands from dialectic.

Dionysodorus manifests the twofold indifference of the eristics in a particularly telling way as he and his brother begin to demonstrate their skill by questioning the young Cleinias.

---

[6] R. S. W. Hawtrey, *Commentary on Plato's Euthydemus* (Philadelphia, 1981), ad loc., notes that Euthydemus repeats Socrates' ἡμᾶς ['us'] while changing the reference to exclude Socrates himself; this emphasizes the effect of dissociation. Cf. *Meno* 75d1–3, where the opposition ἐμοὶ μὲν εἴρηται ... σὸν ἔργον λαμβάνειν λόγον καὶ ἐλέγχειν ['I have made my statement ... it's your job to exact an account and refute me'], typical of eristic, is contrasted with the co-operative ἐγώ τε καὶ σύ ['you and I'] of dialectic. It is, of course, characteristic of Socrates to maintain that both difficulties and advances in argument are shared by all the participants: see e.g. *Charm.* 166d4–6; *Gorg.* 505e6.

[7] At 271–2, note: παγκρατιασταί, παγκρατιαστά (271c7, 8); παγκρατιαστικῇ (272a5); παμμάχω (271c7); μάχεσθαι (271d1, 3, 272a8); μάχην, μάχη (272a2, 6); ἀγωνίσασθαι (272a2); ἀντᾶραι (272a7).

Whatever answer the boy makes to Euthydemus' first question, Dionysodorus predicts to Socrates, he will be refuted (275e5–6). Cleinias is treated here with the lack of concern for his beliefs and understanding from which Socrates also suffers later as the sophists' respondent. Euthydemus insists that Socrates should answer the questions put to him without ensuring that he understands them, or understands them in the same sense as the questioner (295b–c).[8] In the same way, any interest in the particular reply chosen by Cleinias is ruled out in advance (whereas Socrates has just urged him to make the reply which he thinks true: ἀπόκριναι ἀνδρείως, ὁπότερά σοι φαίνεται (275e1)). For the sophists' purposes, Cleinias' answer is simply material for the refutation which is their ultimate concern; and from this perspective, his understanding of the question, and his intention in answering, are irrelevant. At the same time, Dionysodorus' prediction clearly echoes and confirms Socrates' charge that the brothers are ready to refute any statement regardless of its truth or falsity. Dionysodorus is no more interested in the truth of the answer to be refuted than in the beliefs which prompt Cleinias to make it. Socrates' later analysis (277e–278b) of the sophists' opening questions and their ambiguities indicates how attention to the sense in which the respondent interpreted the question and intended his answer could lead to an increased understanding of the subject under discussion.[9] The brothers' failure to recognize the search for truth as a purpose in argument beyond that of victory over an opponent is of a piece with their lack of interest in the identity of their respondent and his understanding of the issues.[10] They lack the devotion to truth which will lead Socrates to his death (an outcome alluded to, in a burlesque tone suited to that of the dialogue as a whole, at 285a–c); and this deficiency is inseparably

---

[8] See the comments of Hawtrey ad loc.

[9] Cf. *Gorg.* 454b9–c5, where Socrates connects the progress of the argument with understanding his interlocutor's intention.

[10] Their indifference to the identity of the respondent extends to that of the questioner. If the sense in which a question is understood makes no difference to the course of the argument, then it does not matter either who asks or who answers it. Accordingly, from 277b onwards, Euthydemus and Dionysodorus put questions interchangeably. Socrates' recognition of, and resignation to, this approach to argument is reflected in his request at 282d7–8: σφῶν δὲ ὁπότερος βούλεται . . . ἐπιδειξάτω ['one of you demonstrate, whichever wants to'].

linked to their failure to show Socrates' concern for the respondent's well-being (275a–b, 277d2–4, 283b–c) and for mutual understanding between the disputants (295b–c).

Given the important place of sensitivity to the respondent in comparisons between dialectic and rival methods, Socrates' apologetic comments in the *Gorgias* on his unwonted long speeches (μακρολογία, 465e–466a, 519d–e) can be seen as more than an acknowledgement that he is speaking out of character.[11] Rather, they make an important contribution to the dialogue's contrasting representations of dialectic and of rhetoric.[12] In insisting that he is driven to make long speeches by Polus' incomprehension (465e5–6) and Callicles' refusal to cooperate (519d6–7, e2), Socrates represents even his departures from the brevity (βραχυλογία) of dialectic, with its constant reference to the interlocutor, as springing from that adaptation to the respondent's needs and character which is portrayed as typifying dialectic, and which rhetoric, in contrast, is seen as lacking. Rhetorical μακρολογία is dictated by the speaker's inclinations, not by the needs of the respondent—so Polus asks indignantly: οὐκ ἐξέσται μοι λέγειν ὁπόσα ἂν βούλωμαι; ['Shall I not be allowed to say *as much as I want to*?'] (461d8–9).[13] Plato makes Socrates adapt the standard rhetorical plea that one's adversary compels one to speak, so as to express a truth concerning the nature of dialectic about which he cares deeply.[14]

In the *Gorgias*, moreover, a further dimension of the relation between the *Meno*'s two requirements for dialectic can be discerned. Socrates insists explicitly on the merits in an enquiry of

---

[11] Contrast E. R. Dodds' *comm.* (Oxford, 1959), 17, 232.

[12] Compare the effect, at 463e1, of Socrates' comment that he is speaking obscurely—a fault with which he has previously charged Gorgias (451d9–e1). Socrates' acknowledgement that his own argument shows a characteristic whose unconscious use he criticizes in the rhetorician suggests that as in the case of μακρολογία, he is exploiting this feature deliberately for an end consonant with the nature of dialectic—in this case, the use of enigmatic pronouncements to stimulate the interlocutor's thought.

[13] Cf. *Prt.* 334c5–6: μακρὰ λέγειν, ἐὰν βούλῃ . . . καὶ αὖ βραχέα ['to speak at length, *if you so wish* . . . and concisely in turn']; and Protagoras' acknowledgement, at 335a, that adaptation of his style to his interlocutor's needs would be detrimental to his own interests.

[14] See esp. 519d5–6, ὡς ἀληθῶς δημηγορεῖν με ἠνάγκασας ['you have really forced me to play the orator'] (also 505c2–3: κινδυνεύει ἀναγκαιότατον εἶναι ['it seems to be absolutely necessary'], of Socrates' monologue); cf. Dem. 18. 256; Lys. 3. 3.

argument with a single interlocutor, taking into account that interlocutor's beliefs and objections (471d–472d, 474a, 475e). In addition, however, the insistence on dialectical responsiveness to the interlocutor is an element in Plato's representation of dialectic and rhetoric as mirroring the ways of life for which the practitioners of each argue.[15] In the dialectician's readiness to adapt his style of argument to his interlocutor is mirrored the acknowledgement that one is part of a whole, and must take into account one's relation to other parts, for which Socrates contends; while the lack of flexibility with which rhetoric is charged finds its counterpart in the self-regarding career advocated by Callicles.

Now it is part of Socrates' concern in his arguments with Gorgias to convince the rhetorician that a form of discourse cannot be morally neutral. Rhetoric and dialectic are not simply alternative methods of discussing life, but are themselves elements in particular ways of life; it is a mistake to suppose that the choice of one or the other does not commit the agent morally.[16] It is for this reason that Socrates can represent the dispute as a comparison at once of opposing ways of life and of opposing methods of argument.[17] Thus it is appropriate to this dialogue in particular that the truth concerning Socrates' central question, how best to live, should be represented as necessarily attained through a method of argument which is in accordance with this truth and is in fact an element in the fulfilment of its requirements. Socrates' failure to convince Callicles is thus enacted in the latter's refusal to participate in the co-operation of dialectic; the necessity of abandoning the principle of close interaction between disputants gains an

---

[15] Compare the appropriateness of Socrates' orderly approach to argument, possibly foreshadowing the method of collection and division (see Dodds, comm., 17, 226–7), to the view which he advocates of the universe as a κόσμος governed by ἰσότης γεωμετρική, an ordered whole governed by geometrical equality.

[16] Cf. *Cra.* 387b8–9, where λέγειν is agreed to be a πρᾶξις.

[17] With 472c4–6 παραβαλόντες οὖν παρ' ἀλλήλους σκεψώμεθα εἴ τι διοίσουσιν ἀλλήλων ['let us compare them with each other and consider whether they differ at all'] (referring to Socrates' and Polus' rival ἔλεγχοι, but immediately followed by an emphatic statement of the importance of the question how one should live)—compare 500d2–4: εἰ ἔστιν τούτω διττὼ τὼ βίω, σκέψασθαι τί τε διαφέρετον ἀλλήλοιν καὶ ὁπότερον βιωτέον αὐτοῖν ['if these are two distinct ways of life, consider how they differ from each other and in which of the two we should live'].

added bitterness from that principle's intimate relation to the position which Socrates maintains.[18]

The close connection between style of argument and philosophical position which emerges so clearly from the *Gorgias* means that even Socrates' more incidental remarks concerning the conduct of an enquiry should be treated as not merely casual, but related to the concerns of the work in which they occur.[19] Thus Socrates' insistence in the *Meno* that the dialectician should speak the truth in terms comprehensible to the respondent gains added point in the context of the dialogue's exploration of the nature of ἐπιστήμη ['understanding']. Plato represents ἐπιστήμη as a form of cognition which, contrary to the implications of Meno's initial question, ἔχεις μοι ἐιπεῖν; ['Can you tell me?'] (70a1), or of his reliance on Gorgias (71c–d), cannot be attained simply by memorizing what one is told. The learner must be less passive than Meno suggests, making an effort which extends beyond memorizing to understanding what is learned.[20] As such understanding involves grasping the significance of an item of knowledge not just in isolation, but in its relation to other items, it is easy to see that, from the point of view of the respondent, a successful enquiry calls for expression of the truth in familiar and intelligible terms.[21]

[18] T. H. Irwin, 'Coercion and Objectivity in Plato's Dialectic', *Revue internationale de philosophie*, 156–7 (1986), 49–74, maintains that Socrates' success is not diminished by Callicles' obduracy: 'since Socrates' aim was to argue for the truth of his position through Callicles' agreement, not to persuade Callicles, failure to persuade Callicles is no objection to the argument. For Socrates has secured what he wanted, Callicles' agreement to the crucial claims that define the outlook of a rational agent' (70). While I agree that Callicles' refusal to co-operate does not constitute an objection to Socrates' argument as such, I still hold that Socrates' success in establishing his conclusion must be to some extent undermined when he is forced to abandon the style of argument which has been so closely connected with his beliefs throughout the dialogue.

[19] Note, for instance, that in *Rep.* 10 Socrates' initial dismissal of his reluctance to criticize Homer (ἀλλ' οὐ γὰρ πρό γε τῆς ἀληθείας τιμητέος ἀνήρ ['But we must not show more respect to a man than to the truth'] (595c2–3)) encapsulates the philosopher's recognition that no human affair is ἄξιον ... μεγάλης σπουδῆς ['worthy of serious attention'] (604b12–c1), which is central to the criticism of poetry.

[20] On ἐπιστήμη in Plato as understanding, see J. M. E. Moravcsik, 'Understanding and Knowledge in Plato's Philosophy', *Neue Hefte für Philosophie*, 15–16 (1979), 53–69; S. Scolnicov, 'Three Aspects of Plato's Philosophy of Learning and Instruction', *Paideia*, 5 (1976) [Special Plato Issue]; and on the *Meno* in particular, see e.g. K. V. Wilkes, 'Conclusions in the *Meno*', *Archiv für Geschichte der Philosophie*, 61 (1979), 143–53.

[21] Cf. R. Demos, 'On Persuasion', *Journal of Philosophy*, 29 (1932), 225–32, on the importance of integrating new ideas with the background of one's existing knowledge and beliefs.

The treatment in the dialogues of the theme of Socrates' consistency casts light on the manner in which, for the questioner as well, adaptation of his argument to suit his interlocutor is necessarily involved in his attempt to express and extend his understanding of a constant truth. One expression of the fundamental opposition between Socrates and Callicles appears in their different attitudes to the charge of always saying the same things: it is a reproach in Callicles' eyes, but for Socrates the reverse is true (*Gorg.* 491b5–8). Socrates is proud to admit that he says ταὐτὰ ... περὶ τῶν αὐτῶν ['the same things ... about the same things'] (490e9–11); in this he reaffirms his earlier emphasis on the importance of consistency (481d–482c). Callicles interprets this claim in the sense of literal verbal consistency and the use of the same examples: (ἀεὶ σκυτέας τε καὶ κναφέας καὶ μαγείρους λέγων καὶ ἰατροὺς οὐδέν παύῃ ['you never stop talking about cobblers and fullers and cooks and doctors'] (491a1–2); Alcibiades gives a similar account of his assertion that Socrates ἀεὶ διὰ τῶν αὐτῶν τὰ αὐτὰ φαίνεται λέγειν (*Smp.* 221e5–6). Alcibiades' encomium, however, follows a speech in which Socrates leaves behind his accustomed examples; despite the attribution of the speech to Diotima, the contrast is such as to suggest that the consistency which matters to Socrates is other than verbal.

Verbal repetition can in fact be represented as a fault; and as a fault which detracts from Socratic consistency. Socrates' complaint in the *Phaedrus*, that a written text ἕν τι σημαίνει μόνον ταὐτὸν ἀεί ['always says just one and the same thing'] (275d9), looks initially very like his own claim always to say ταὐτὰ περὶ τῶν αὐτῶν; from his confrontations elsewhere with sophists and rhetoricians, it can be seen how they differ. The manner of 'saying the same things' which is a fault shared by rhetoricians with written texts is exemplified when Polus, in reply to Chaerephon's question as to the nature of rhetoric, delivers what has every appearance of being a prepared encomium (*Gorg.* 448c), kept ready—like Hippias' discourse on Simonides (*Prt.* 347a6–b2)—for production at any opportunity.[22] Such repetition,

---

[22] Another variety of rhetorical repetition, the use of stock themes and commonplaces regardless of whether they are applicable on a particular occasion, receives its most extreme illustration in the *Menexenus*. On repetition as a feature of rhetoric reaching its height in funeral speeches, see N. Loraux, 'Socrate contrepoison de l'oraison funèbre', *L'Antiquité classique*, 43 (1974), 172–211.

paying no attention to the particular question asked, is of no
assistance to a bewildered listener, as Socrates points out at *Protagoras* 329a. Nor, however, does it assist the speaker himself in
his grasp and expression of the truth. The rhetorician who
repeats a prepared speech, in failing to answer a particular
question, fails to engage at all in conversation with the questioner. Socratic consistency, however, calls for the ability to
maintain a constant position in successive arguments, rather
than avoiding argument by repeating a verbally constant *non
sequitur*. Moreover, if understanding involves the comprehension of a truth's relation to other ideas, it is both exercised and
extended in discerning the form of expression best adapted to
meet a particular question springing from a particular set of
beliefs and interests. The verbal repetition which Socrates criticizes masks a deficiency in the type of understanding which
Socratic consistency reflects. The nature of understanding is
such that the flexibility of dialectic is necessary to Socrates' consistency; and thus responsiveness to the interlocutor is no additional feature of dialectic's truthfulness, but an essential part of
it.

The contrast in this respect between rhetoric and dialectic
has a still further dimension. Rhetoric is portrayed as deficient
in sensitivity to an individual respondent's needs; yet it is at the
same time a form of discourse in which the speaker is crucially
concerned with the impression made on his audience.[23] With
an irony typical of Plato's treatment of rhetoric, the rhetorician
is seen, in substituting the persuasion of an audience for the
pursuit of truth and the responsiveness to the interlocutor
which is bound up with it, to submit after all to dependence on
another. Accommodation of others' needs is not avoided by
abandoning the pursuit of truth; it reappears in a debased, par-
odic form, becoming a matter of dependence rather than
voluntary interaction.[24]

---

[23] On the different positions of audience and interlocutor in rhetoric and dialectic,
as well as on the equal importance ascribed in dialectic to the interlocutor and the discourse itself, see R. Burke, 'Rhetoric, Dialectic and Force', *Philosophy and Rhetoric*, 7
(1974), 154–65.

[24] Cf. the representation in *Rep.* 10 of the poet as dependent on the whim of his
audience by reason of his lack of knowledge (602b1–4). In contrast, the ἐπιεικής ['good,
reasonable man'] whose concern is to secure the rule of reason in his soul, is simply
strengthened in this resolve by the presence of an audience (603e–604a).

The different positions of audience and interlocutor, and the different forms of attention paid to each, thus become part of Plato's ironic treatment of the autonomy claimed by poetry and rhetoric. These art-forms are seen as attempting to exist as autonomous τέχναι, with aims and standards of their own, distinct from those of philosophy; but Plato represents the attempt as resulting, not in autonomy, but in increased dependence. Rhetoric and poetry become, not arts to be judged on their own terms, by distinct standards, but heteronomous pursuits, dependent for their existence, and for the form which they take, on genuine τέχναι.[25] Plato represents the attempt to engage in a pursuit independent of the goals and standards of philosophy as self-defeating—not merely the wrong choice, but not even the choice of a valid alternative. He expresses this idea of the heteronomy of such pursuits partly through his treatment of their goals; a pursuit inspired by aims other than those of philosophy is portrayed as finding these aims impossible to fulfil.[26] Failing to fulfil the ideals of philosophy, the rhetorician also fails, both in his art and in the life which corresponds to it, to attain the goals which he attempted to substitute for them; he is left, ironically, with a debased version of the ideals which he rejected. In the *Gorgias* in particular, Socrates' interlocutors are so treated as to emphasize their failure in their own terms as well as their inadequacy in comparison with Socrates.[27] In part, this emerges in respect of the relation to others which the interlocutors envisage. In the life corresponding to the practice of rhetoric, Callicles advocates the pursuit of self-advantage, unhampered by the philosopher's concern for the well-being of

[25] Rhetoric is πολιτικῆς μορίου εἴδωλον ['the image of a part of statesmanship'] (*Gorg.* 463d2), cleverly mimicking δικαιοσύνη ['justice']. In *Rep.* 10 Socrates applies to the activity of μίμησις ['representation'] language similar to that which he uses to describe the intermediate, dependent status of particulars: τινὶ μὲν τρόπῳ γενέσθαι ἂν τούτων ἁπάντων ποιητής, τινὶ δὲ οὐκ ἂν ['to prove to be a creator of all these things in one sense, but not in another'] (596d3–4). See also A. Nehamas, 'Plato on Imitation and Poetry in *Republic* 10', in J. M. E. Moravcsik and P. Temko (edd.), *Plato on Beauty, Wisdom and the Arts* (New Jersey, 1982), 47–78.

[26] Cf. the suggestive remark of J. Annas, *An Introduction to Plato's Republic* (Oxford, 1981), 297: the timocratic man fails to live up to his ideals 'because they are inadequate'—not because he is attempting to meet the impossibly high standards of philosophy.

[27] See the discussion of this theme by A. Spitzer, 'The Self-Reference of the *Gorgias*', *Philosophy and Rhetoric*, 8 (1975), 1–22 repr. in K. V. Erickson (ed.), *Plato: True and Sophistic Rhetoric* (Amsterdam, 1979), 129–51.

others. Socrates points out to him, however, that he cannot be as independent as he supposes; he is and will remain reliant on the caprice of the *dēmos* (481d–e, 513a–b).[28] So the voluntary consideration of others which is a part of Socrates' position reappears as a caricature in the dependence which Callicles tries unsuccessfully to avoid. A similar dependence afflicts the rhetoric which reflects and is a part of this way of life. A means of attaining power over others (452d–e, 456a–c), exercised without regard for the needs of individuals in argument, rhetoric none the less subjects its practitioner, in his concern for appearance, to the whim of his audience. Consideration of others, both in life and in discourse, is, Plato suggests, unavoidable; but it may take the form of a fruitful, voluntary interaction or of a reluctant dependence according to whether it is chosen as part of the life of philosophy or results ironically from a vain attempt to live independently of philosophy's demands.

<h1 style="text-align:center">III</h1>

Plato's interest in the interlocutor's role in dialectic, seen as one among the closely related elements of his philosophy, is matched by the practical importance of characterization in his writing. The characterization of interlocutors has a significant contribution to make to the presentation of his concerns in a dialogue. Some of Socrates' interlocutors, in their character and their influence on the course of his arguments, may be less congenial to his purposes than others.[29] For Plato, however, even these apparently less satisfactory figures are chosen as suited to some design. In any dialogue, it is necessary to consider the relation of the interlocutors' characters to the questions at issue and Plato's manner of treating them. Thus in the

[28] Callicles' failure to avoid dependence on common opinion is foreshadowed when he quotes such opinion in the opening words of the dialogue (447a1–2), just as the sentiment there expressed is suggestive of the form of hedonism to which he will be represented as committed, despite his distaste for some of its consequences.

[29] See the comment of Glaucon's quoted in the first para. of this chapter. While rhetoric is represented as inherently self-defeating, in an imperfect world dialectic too may become so, in that confrontation with an obdurate interlocutor may necessitate a compromising of its principles. This is suggested by the wry tone of Socrates' comments on his concessions to Polus and Callicles (*Gorg.* 465e, 519d–e) and to Meno (*Meno* 76d–e).

Phaedrus, for instance, both the general portrayal of Phaedrus' character and his influence on the course of the conversation can be seen to have a particular appropriateness to the dialogue's concerns.

Why, then, did it suit Plato to make this docile but unexceptional figure Socrates' respondent? To begin, the choice of interlocutor is clearly in keeping with the tone of the dialogue; its pervasive irony could not be maintained if Socrates were confronted with the passionate opposition of a Callicles. Nor is this so superficial a consideration as it might appear; for the tone is bound up with Plato's concerns in the *Phaedrus*. It is partly through its irony that the dialogue, while not avoiding the deficiencies of written texts to which Socrates draws attention, at least escapes the charge of failing to acknowledge its own inadequacy. Constantly qualifying itself through ironic presentation, the *Phaedrus* avoids to some extent the misleading fixity and appearance of adequacy in a written work which suggests that it is the one true account of its subject and that reading it is sufficient for complete understanding. The earnestness underlying the dialogue's irony is suggested by Plato's treatment of his chief symbol of philosophic seriousness, Socrates' death. Apparently absent from the *Phaedrus*, this theme is in fact, as in the *Euthydemus*, adapted to the dialogue's tone. Philosophic asceticism and readiness to face death appear mythologized in the fable of the cicadas, forgetting to eat and drink in their wonder at the Muses (259b–d). This lighthearted treatment of a theme whose contrasting presentation in the allusions of the *Gorgias* contributes to that dialogue's passion reflects the way in which Plato's irony springs from the depth of his concern. It is because Plato is so much in earnest about the ideas in the *Phaedrus* that he cannot allow his presentation of them to appear definitive; and so, because of the depth of his convictions, the dialogue must have its peculiar lightness of tone.

The appropriateness of Phaedrus' character to the dialogue's tone is thus no trivial matter; but there are further, more specific reasons why his character, and its relation to that of Socrates, make him a suitable interlocutor. Phaedrus and Socrates have been seen as prefiguring and enacting the relationship between philosophic lovers portrayed in Socrates' second

speech.[30] In particular, the emphasis on reciprocity and sharing between the lovers, and on the kinship between their souls,
may be thought to be illustrated by the representation of Socrates and Phaedrus in the dialogue's opening pages. Here, the
suggestions of a similarity in character between the two
(especially 228a–b) are reinforced by their repeated inter-
change of roles. Phaedrus and Socrates take it in turns to play
the part of guide (227c1, 229a7, 230c5); at 236b9–c6, Phaedrus
comments on the recurrence of the situation of 228a–c, with the
parts played by himself and Socrates reversed. Now it is true
that the theme of sharing and reciprocity is a significant one in
the dialogue; and true also that it is associated with the relationship between Socrates and Phaedrus. Phaedrus' last
words in the dialogue apply the idea of sharing between friends
to his own friendship with Socrates: κοινὰ γὰρ τὰ τῶν φίλων
['friends' possessions are shared'] (279c6–7); his first remark,
too, introduces the theme in his claim that he and Socrates
share an acquaintance in Acumenus (227a4–5).[31] However,
further consideration of Socrates and Phaedrus suggests that
their sharing, and the resemblance between their characters, is
far from complete. Plato has indeed associated their relationship with the love described in the palinode; but he presents it
as at best a very imperfect example, and the result is far richer
than a simple effect of illustration.

The portrayal of the relationship between Socrates and
Phaedrus, as similar to the ideal of the palinode but far from
adequate in comparison with it, is connected, like the dialogue's tone, with the closing discussion of speech and writing.
Plato is disturbed by the tendency of immutable written texts to
appear definitive, and so to conceal their lack of true βεβαιότης
['stability'] and σαφήνεια ['clarity'] (277d8–9)—the inability of
any single formulation to capture the entire truth, and its
worthlessness if it fails to stimulate the reader's thought and

[30] See e.g. A. Lebeck, 'The Central Myth of Plato's *Phaedrus*', *GRBS* 13 (1972), 267–90.

[31] This example is typical of Plato's practice of introducing in an apparently casual and trivial remark themes which acquire depth as the dialogue progresses. Phaedrus' claim has an additional significance of its own: it suggests in advance that whatever Socrates' relationship with Phaedrus may be, he is not the kind of lover who, as the first two speeches tell us (232c–d, 239b1–3, e5–6), tries to keep his beloved from forming other friendships.

understanding. In contrast with the authors of such works, Plato is aware that the desired βεβαιότης and σαφήνεια may not necessarily be found even in the oral discussion which is given preference over writing. To suppose otherwise would be to pay undue attention to formal considerations, and thus to fall into an error similar to that of the unreflective readers of texts. Orally delivered speeches, as Socrates acknowledges at 277e, can share the deficiency of written texts typified by their failure to instruct by allowing questions and explanation; and even in the argument which is contrasted with such speeches, the form of words used must be recognized as being of value not in itself, but only in so far as it assists the attainment of understanding. This, I believe, is one reason for the final description of the concluding argument as itself play (πεπαίσθω, 278b7). On one level a reminder to the readers that the dialogue is a written text, sharing with other such texts their largely playful character (277e6), the expression can be read also as a warning to Phaedrus not to ascribe undue authority to the particular form which the argument has taken, but to recognize the essentially subordinate character of any formulation in the search for understanding.[32]

Plato's concern prompts him to produce a text which, unusually, wears its lack of βεβαιότης on its surface. The dialogue's irony is an important factor in creating this effect, keeping the reader from taking entirely seriously ideas which it is equally impossible wholly to dismiss.[33] This is most noticeable in Socrates' second speech (though, for an example taken from elsewhere in the dialogue, note the irony of 275b–c, where Socrates ascribes to the respectable authority of the ancients the interest in a statement's truth rather than its source which he recommends to Phaedrus). The effect of the palinode's mythical character is enhanced by the inclusion within it of jarring or humorous elements. While far from outweighing entirely the

---

[32] Cf. K. von Fritz, 'The Philosophical Passage in the Seventh Platonic Letter and the Problem of Plato's "Esoteric" Philosophy', in J. P. Anton and G. L. Kustas (edd.), *Essays in Ancient Greek Philosophy* (New York, 1971), 408–47. Von Fritz argues (411–12) that the treatment in *Letter* 7 of the deficiencies even of spoken language 'merely draws the ultimate consequence of what is said in the *Phaedrus*'.

[33] C. J. Rowe, 'The Argument and Structure of Plato's *Phaedrus*', PCPS, NS 32 (1986), 106–25, comments on the ironic elements in the myth: 'It is as if [Plato] were simultaneously challenging us to believe and to disbelieve' (125 n. 62).

power and beauty of the speech so as to suggest that it should not be taken seriously at all, such elements do discourage whole-hearted acceptance of it as a completely serious and exact account. With a characteristic audacity, Plato applies this technique even to his handling of the central image of the charioteer and horses. From its introduction, the image is so treated as to reinforce the explicit statement that this is a likeness, not to be taken literally (246a4–6), nor necessarily even to be seen as the only likeness possible. The soul, Socrates has argued immediately beforehand, must be ἀγένητον ['ungenerated'] (245d–246a); but in introducing the image, he dwells three times on the horses' ancestry (246a7, b2–3)—a repetition which suggests deliberate emphasis on the discrepancy between the soul and the image used of it.[34] The effect is heightened by the bizarre character of the image itself—verging on the ludicrous, if the horses and charioteer can be taken to be not merely winged, but covered with feathers.[35] It is a mark of the power of Plato's writing in the speech that such treatment even of its central image qualifies but does not destroy the reader's acceptance.

This effect of qualifying, avoiding a single settled judgement, can be seen also in the treatment of Socrates' first speech; and here the reasons why it is important to Plato emerge more clearly. It is crucial that two opposing judgements should both be seen to be true of this speech. It is both a δεινὸς λόγος ['terrible speech'] (242d4–5), false and pretentious (242e5–243a1), and a legitimate part of an enquiry into the nature of love, justified in both its method and its content (265e–266a). These descriptions should both be regarded as applying truly to the speech—but not in the sense that each expresses certain of its qualities, and that these faults and merits should be weighed

---

[34] R. Hackforth, *Plato's* Phaedrus (Cambridge, 1952), 68 n. 2, suggests that the expression ἀγαθοὶ καὶ ἐξ ἀγαθῶν ['good and of good ancestry'] may have become stereotyped, meaning no more than 'wholly good'. It is the repetition of such expressions within so short a space, and in this particular context, that suggests to me that Plato was in fact alive to their full meaning and exploited the apparent inappropriateness.

[35] See G. R. F. Ferrari, *Listening to the Cicadas* (Cambridge, 1987), 265 n. 20. Elsewhere, however, Ferrari reverts to the more usual translation, 'winged'; this may result from the difficulty of deciding whether in fact the team are intended as winged, feathered, or both. This vagueness on Plato's part may be deliberate, further discouraging the reader from acquiescing entirely in the use of the image by making it hard even to determine precisely how it is to be envisaged.

against one another in forming a single consistent judgement. Rather, part of the point of Plato's treatment of the speech is that no one judgement, combining both the views of it which Socrates expresses, should be possible. The dialogue contains two opposing assessments of the speech, each of which, when uttered, and from the perspective from which it is made, is not true on balance, but simply true. Such a presentation of a single speech is clearly a matter of structural economy; but it also makes a major contribution to the peculiarly unsettling character of the *Phaedrus*, its discouragement of any statement which is too definite and unqualified.

In style and thought, Socrates' first speech shows close similarities to the work of Isocrates.[36] This similarity suggests that Plato's treatment of the speech may have further relevance for his opinion of Isocrates, as the rhetorician appears at the end of the dialogue (278e–279b). The presentation of Isocrates here reflects Plato's sense of the danger in an appearance of adequacy, in mistaking a promise for its fulfilment.[37] Just as the apparent completeness and finality of a written text can inspire belief in its adequacy, discouraging the questioning thought which could lead to true understanding, so it was all too easy for the superiority which Isocrates showed over other rhetoricians (279a3–7) to be seen as sufficient in itself, rather than as an indication that he was capable of rising still higher (279a7–9). Isocrates illustrates the possibility of a misleading similarity between a philosophical and a rhetorical character. Socrates' concluding judgement, ἔνεστί τις φιλοσοφία τῇ τοῦ ἀνδρὸς διανοίᾳ ['the man's mind shows a certain philosophical ability'] (279a9–b1), encapsulates this idea. While Socrates sees in the rhetorician φιλοσοφία τις, in the sense of signs that the young man may be capable of advancing to true philosophy, Isocrates regarded his present thought as φιλοσοφία, philosophy, and as such remained satisfied with it. In this context, the connection of Isocrates with Socrates' first speech becomes pointed. The

---

[36] See e.g. M. Brown and J. Coulter, 'The Middle Speech of Plato's *Phaedrus*', *Journal of the History of Philosophy*, 6 (1968), 217–31, repr. in Erickson (ed.), *Plato*, 239–64; E. Asmis, 'Psychagogia in Plato's *Phaedrus*', *Illinois Classical Studies*, 11 (1986), 153–72.

[37] Cf. Asmis, 'Psychagogia', 172: in comparison to Lysias, 'Isocratean rhetoric holds out a promise of better things. But the promise unfulfilled is a far greater danger than Lysianic rhetoric ever was.'

speech, in its twofold character, is a reminder of the fluidity and hesitancy of judgement which would be needed to keep an Isocrates from satisfaction with the apparent sufficiency of his attainments.

It is in this light, I believe, that Phaedrus' character and his relationship with Socrates should be regarded. In his portrayal of Phaedrus, Plato offers a more extended illustration of those characteristics represented by Isocrates. Comparison with Socrates repeatedly reveals an apparent likeness accompanied by, and drawing attention to, an inadequacy on Phaedrus' part.

In comparison with other young men with whom Socrates converses, Phaedrus is portrayed not just as promising in general terms, but as showing specific similarities to Socrates. On the other hand, he is far from the affinity with Socrates of Theaetetus which is reflected in their close physical likeness (*Tht.* 143e7–9). Nor, again, is he like Callicles in holding beliefs comparable to those of Socrates and Plato but given an opposite interpretation.[38] Phaedrus' similarities to Socrates do not cover a radical opposition, but rather constitute a pale reflection. Where the same description is applicable to both, it is in a shallower sense that it applies to Phaedrus. Incomplete comprehension, inadequate realization of a concept or a quality's potential, is the distinguishing feature of Phaedrus, rather than development in a direction totally opposed to that of Socrates.[39] As with Thaeatetus, the relation is reflected in physical details. As Phaedrus shares occasionally in Socrates' constant habit of going barefoot (229a3–4), so he exhibits, to a lesser degree and in a shallower version, intellectual characteristics of Socrates.

Central to this representation is, obviously, the love of λόγοι ['discourses'] which the two are portrayed as sharing. The sharing is modified by the very different forms of discourse which they have in mind. When Socrates reveals that the λόγοι of which he is an ἐραστής ['lover'] are those of collection and division (266b3–4, echoing and modifying 228c1–2), and that

---

[38] See Dodds's comm. on *Gorgias*, 267, 269, for comparisons of Callicles' ῥῆσις with passages from the *Laws* and *Politicus*.

[39] The closest parallel is with figures such as Nicias in the *Laches*, who repeat Socratic views without fully understanding them. The presentation of the characteristic in Phaedrus is, however, more extended.

it is in the footsteps of the dialecticians that he follows (266b5–7), rather than in those of Phaedrus carrying Lysias' speech (230d5–e1), Plato is, in his accustomed manner, treating a theme with increasing depth; but he is also drawing attention to the difference between the philosopher and the admirer of rhetoric which coexists with their similarity as lovers of discourse.

Phaedrus' and Socrates' shared love of discourse, together with the difference in the forms of discourse which each values, underlies the detailed comparisons between them in the dialogue's opening pages. Verbal echoes invite the reader to make comparisons from which emerges Socrates' suspicion of the particular forms of discourse which inspire Phaedrus' enthusiasm. Thus if Phaedrus claims as an ἰδιώτης ['amateur'] to be unable to memorize the speech which took Lysias so long to write (227d6–228a3), Socrates too is an ἰδιώτης—when it comes to improvising speeches (236d5). Phaedrus is right to remark that when he compels Socrates to speak, he is following Socrates' own example (236c, 228a–c); but his words also reveal a significant difference. When Phaedrus urges Socrates not to speak πρὸς βίαν ... μᾶλλον ἢ ἑκών ['under compulsion rather than willingly'] (236d2–3), the echo of Socrates' earlier comment that Phaedrus ἔμελλε καὶ εἰ μή τις ἑκὼν ἀκούοι βίᾳ ἐρεῖν ['would speak by force even if no one was willing to listen'] (228c3) underlines the fact that Socrates must really be compelled to speak, while Phaedrus, though feigning reluctance, was in fact prepared to constrain an audience.[40] The contrast underlying the parallels emerges, of course, most obviously when Socrates responds to Phaedrus' concealment of Lysias' speech (228d–e) by veiling his head before speaking himself (237a4–5, 243b6–7).

The resemblance between Socrates and Phaedrus is, then, less close than it might initially appear; and so too the apparent reciprocity in their relationship is qualified. They may exchange the role of guide in the literal sense (though even here Socrates is in some respects more knowledgeable than Phaedrus: 229c1–4); but in the sense of exerting influence, they are far

---

[40] Contrast *La.* 187e–188a: in a philosophical discussion, it is Socrates who exercises the constraint.

from interchangeable. Socrates claims that Phaedrus does influence him—but in the direction of his enthusiasm for rhetoric.
(The repetition εἰπόμην . . . ἑπόμενος ['I followed . . . following']
at 234d5, where Socrates describes how the sight of Phaedrus'
reaction to Lysias' speech affected his own, recalls the alternate
leading and following earlier in the dialogue.) The alternating
guides are thus not of equal worth; Phaedrus' guidance is a
further instance of his shallow reflection of Socrates.

Repeatedly, comparison shows Phaedrus to possess a shallower version of a characteristic exhibited by Socrates, a version which can, however, be confused with the deeper
manifestation on account of a superficial resemblance.[41] The
same danger thus appears as in the case of Isocrates—that of
taking the reflection for the reality, remaining satisfied with a
position which only resembles what could be attained. (It is
perhaps significant that it is Phaedrus who claims that his relationship with Socrates exemplifies the sharing typical of
friendship, while the exaggeration in Socrates' remarks on their
similarity—as at 228b7—suggests irony. Phaedrus is in danger
of satisfaction with his position, less keenly aware than Socrates
of the difference which still remains between them.) Socrates'
description of Phaedrus as vacillating (ἐπαμφοτερίζῃ, 257b5) is
as much a warning as a statement of fact.[42] It is too easy for
Phaedrus, as for Isocrates, to regard his development as complete; Socrates must remind him that he is in fact at a moment
of decision, with a possibility of choosing to advance. Like
Isocrates, Phaedrus is both a figure to whom Plato's concern
with the avoidance of fixity should be addressed, and himself an
expression of this concern.

Phaedrus has, moreover, besides this general appropriateness
to the dialogue, an influence on its structure. Plato makes the
conversation develop in a manner suited to his interests partly
by giving Phaedrus his particular character. This is most
obvious at the turning-point of 257, in the rich significance

---

[41] A further example: at 228d4–5, Phaedrus introduces the notion of following a
proper order which becomes so important later in the dialogue. In this case, however,
observing the proper order means following the sequence of thought in Lysias'
speech—which Socrates criticizes precisely for its lack of the ἀνάγκη λογογραφική that
he requires (264b).

[42] Cf. C. J. Rowe, *Plato: Phaedrus* (Warminster, 1986), ad loc.

both of the transition in the conversation and of the way in which it effected.

Socrates calls attention here to the idea of Phaedrus' influence by remarking on his effect on the palinode: it has its particular poetic style διὰ Φαῖδρον ['on account of Phaedrus'] (257a5–6). Socrates' comments on his own performances, and especially his disclaimers of responsibility, should of course be read cautiously; but there is truth in his assertion of Phaedrus' influence here, as is suggested by the repetition of the phrase τά τε ἄλλα καὶ τοῖς ὀνόμασιν ['especially in its language'] from Phaedrus' praise of Lysias' speech (257a4–5, 234c7). The speech has taken into account Phaedrus' taste for fine expression; Socrates is rewarded for this by Phaedrus' judgement that it was more beautiful than the preceding one (257c2). Phaedrus' influence extends further, however; for the turn now taken by the conversation results from his reaction to the palinode, passing quickly as he does from the comment on its beauty to consider again Lysias and his writing. In this respect, the ensuing discussion as well as the palinode is διὰ Φαῖδρον.

Phaedrus' response is, from Socrates' point of view, unsatisfactory. Failing to ask a single question about the speech, he illustrates exactly the situation described by Socrates at 277e8–9 in the reference to speeches which are ῥαψῳδούμενοι ἄνευ ἀνακρίσεως καὶ διδαχῆς ['recited without questioning and instruction']. His failure to learn is in this case underlined by his continuing to wish, though with little hope, for another speech from Lysias.[43] In keeping with this, he continues to regard speeches as produced in a competitive spirit (ἀντιπαρατεῖναι, 257c4), assessing their quality in comparison with one another, whereas Socrates was seen in his concluding prayer considering the adequacy of his speech in relation to its subject. This deficiency in the standards by which Phaedrus judges is reflected in the reasons which he ascribes to Lysias (257c) and others (257d5–8) for hesitating to write—reasons which lack the depth of those which Socrates will offer. The considerations which Phaedrus sees as influencing the decision

---

[43] Phaedrus thus confirms Socrates' response at 243e2 to his claim that Lysias will be forced to write a reply to the palinode: this will be true, so long as Phaedrus remains what he is. (Note also the play here on the contrast between speaking and writing: it is a *written* speech that an unreformed Phaedrus will exact from Lysias.)

whether or not to write operate on the level of the non-lover's
σωφροσύνη θνητή ['mortal self-possession'] (256e5).

However, this unsatisfactory response also effects a transition
necessary to the dialogue. On one level, Phaedrus' failure to ask
any questions about the speech indicates his inadequacy. A
detailed discussion of the palinode, however, would be inap-
propriate; for it would risk ascribing to the speech too great an
authority. By representing Socrates and Phaedrus as engaged
in analysis of Socrates' second speech, Plato could easily suggest
that such analysis was of greater importance in itself than he
would in fact allow. It could appear that the speech was the one
correct account of its subject, such that the understanding of it
reached by detailed interpretation constituted also complete
understanding on that question. The questioning which should
lead the listener beyond satisfaction with the account given
could degenerate into discussion of that account for its own
sake. Thus it might seem that the only remaining task was to
analyse the definitive exposition which had been provided,
giving precise interpretations of its details, without envisaging
the possibility of a new account with an entirely different structure.[44]

Such ascription of excessive authority to any one account is
decried in the case of written texts. It is represented, moreover,
as a rhetorician's attitude to speeches. Discussion of a speech is
particularly likely to degenerate in this way when one of the
participants is an admirer of rhetoric such as Phaedrus. Plato
suggests this when he depicts Phaedrus as eager to discuss Socrates' first speech (242a5–6); Socrates has already imagined
Phaedrus studying Lysias' speech with its author (228a7–b1).
As a result of the new direction given to the conversation by
Phaedrus at 257c, the palinode, in contrast, receives no such
treatment; lost from sight at the beginning of the discussion
which ensues, it reappears not as an authoritative treatment of
love whose content is to be analysed, but as an example of

---

[44] Cf. Socrates' opinion of allegorical interpretations of myths (229–230a). Socrates
dismisses the attempt to translate myths into rationalizing narratives which correspond
to them in every detail. The search for such correspondence ignores the fact that one is
dealing with accounts different in nature and approach, not with two versions of an explanation which has the same structure in both. Cf. also the remarks of A. de Marignac,
Imagination et dialectique (Paris, 1951), on Plato's avoidance of the suggestion that any
one image corresponds precisely to the reality which it is meant to convey.

method (262–6). Even as such, it is altered in description. Socrates' summary at 265b2–5, for example, does not correspond exactly to the opening of the speech as given. It is more systematic, and includes new material in the explicit ascription of each form of madness (μανία) to a god. Not only is the speech considered from the perspective of method rather than that of content, therefore; such of its content as must be included in the discussion appears in a new form, undermining further any impression that its account is definitive.

This is not to say that the speech is wholly devalued, or that its only role is as an example for use in the discussion of rhetoric, which could then be seen as the main section of the dialogue. Rather, it is essential that this speech, like that preceding it, should be seen in two lights. It is a valid and valuable portrayal of the nature of the soul, its activities and experiences (245c2–4); but it is also a portrayal which is of no greater value or authority than another, different in conception, from the perspective of which it is no more than an example of method, more or less satisfactory. Its position can be understood not by attempting to subordinate one of these views to the other, but by admitting their equal truth. This dual status is reflected in Socrates' description of the speech both as εἰς ἡμετέραν δύναμιν ὅτι καλλίστη καὶ ἀρίστη ['the most beautiful and the best that my powers allow'] and as being made in a particular style, διὰ Φαῖδρον (257a3–6). It is a good and beautiful speech, an expression of the truth, as Socrates claims (245c4); yet it is also conditional, an account given in particular circumstances to a particular listener. Different circumstances and listeners would call for different accounts; but their being different need not in itself keep each from being truthfully described as καλλίστη καὶ ἀρίστη.

As a character who can both call forth a speech in the style of the palinode and dismiss it with a brief comment, Phaedrus thus influences the course of the conversation in a manner ideally suited to the fluidity required by Plato's concerns in the dialogue. It is typical of Plato's ability to achieve several effects at once that this influence should be potrayed as being of such a kind that Phaedrus' inadequacy can be perceived. From this example of an unsatisfactory response, the reader can learn something of what would, in contrast, be required from an ideal interlocutor. At the same time, the conditional quality which coexists with the value of both parts of the conversation is the more keenly felt by reason of the deficiency in the figure who influences them.

Phaedrus, then, is far from embodying the dialectician's ideal partner, just as his relationship with Socrates reflects only very imperfectly the reciprocity of philosophic love as described in the palinode. This imperfection, however, renders him better suited to a dialogue in which Plato is passionately concerned to convey the idea that the worth of any discourse lies in its power to assist in the understanding of a reality for which no one account is sufficient, and that such value as a discourse may possess must therefore be lost if it is seen as unqualified. The *Phaedrus* is a disturbing dialogue, resistant to any single, settled interpretation. Phaedrus' contribution, through his character and Socrates' response to it, to this disturbing quality, is typical of the way in which characterization takes its place in Plato's art, combining with other elements to reflect and express his deepest convictions.

9
Ēthos in Oratory and Rhetoric

D. A. RUSSELL

To be sure, goodness is a blessed thing for any occasion, wonderful equipment for life. I've been talking to this gentleman only for a small part of the day, and now I'm devoted to him. Someone's going to say: 'Words are the persuasive thing, especially the words of clever people.' Well, why then do I detest other people who speak well? It's the speaker's personality that carries conviction, not his words.

(Menander, *Hymnis*, fr. 407 K)[1]

The effect produced by any narrative of events is essentially dependent not on the events themselves but on the human interest which is directly connected with them.

(Wilkie Collins, *The Woman in White*, Preface)

I

Orators and their teachers the rhetoricians knew all this very well and spared no pains to make the spoken word accord with and convey the personality. Their practice and theory are central to any attempt at understanding the Greek approach to character and characterization.[2] They do however present the literary critic with some special problems. On the one hand, oratory was such an important part of Greek life that the need to provide instruction in it became the main motive force of classical, and later of humanistic, education. The conceptual

[1] νὴ τὴν Ἀθηνᾶν, μακάριόν τι χρηστότης | πρὸς πάντα καὶ θαυμαστὸν ἐφόδιον βίῳ. | τούτῳ λαλήσας ἡμέρας μικρὸν μέρος | εὔνους ἐγὼ νῦν εἰμι. "πειστικὸν λόγος", | πρὸς τοῦτ' ἂν εἴποι τις, "μάλιστα τῶν σοφῶν." | τί οὖν ἑτέρους λαλοῦντας εὖ βδελύττομαι; | τρόπος ἐσθ' ὁ πείθων τοῦ λέγοντος, οὐ λόγος. |

[2] Apart from the standard histories and manuals of rhetoric the classic work is W. Süss, *Ethos: Studien zur älteren griechischen Rhetorik* (Leipzig, 1910). Despite some unsatisfactory terminology and classification, it is full of useful insights, esp. on the earlier orators and rhetors.

framework of rhetoric thus provided the standard interpretative and critical method that was applied to all kinds of literature. There should be no doubt that this approach was
congenial to Greek minds throughout antiquity; and it follows
that when we turn, in thinking about literary characterization,
to Lysias and Demosthenes, we very properly feel that we have
arrived at the heart of the Greek literary experience. At the
same time the peculiar conditions of the orator's work have to
be kept clearly in mind. To begin with, he usually has a single
and well-defined aim. This is either to secure acquittal or conviction or to win a majority for a policy or, in epideictic, to display the qualities of his subject or the mood of an occasion. In
all three kinds, but especially in the first two—the forensic and
the deliberative—he has to deal with *ēthos* in three different
ways: he has to project his own personality acceptably, study
the personal traits of his audience so as to please and not offend,
and represent the qualities of his opponents or other persons
who appear in the course of his narrative. In all this, he must
not let himself be led into the psychological enquiries that the
historian or the poet would embrace. He has to make himself
out to be a good, reliable person: there is no place for confession
or self-analysis, unless it can be seen to produce sympathy. He
has to treat his audience with respect; if he plays upon their
weaknesses, he must not alienate them. And all the other characters must be unambiguously good or bad. If the good have
failings, they are venial; if the bad have virtues, they are trivial.
Naturally, 'good' and 'bad' in these contexts do not have a
narrowly moral connotation; in most non-philosophical Greek
thinking, acceptability and the reverse are largely determined
by origin, social status, profession, or political sympathies. It is,
I think, a consequence of this need for the unambiguous portrait that, although every piece of litigation and every political
initiative is historically unique, the personalities we find in the
orators are normally recognized types, not individuals seen in
the round. The orator can feel sure of the reaction of the
audience to a person whom he categorizes for them. Instinctive
attraction or repulsion by an individual cannot be relied upon,
because not all the audience will feel the same, and they need to
be given reasons for their feelings. This applies both to the
speaker and to the persons who play a part in his story; since

the argument is likely to depend on probability ($\epsilon\hat{\iota}\kappa\acute{o}s$), it is natural that the agents should be seen to be the kind of persons who can be expected to behave in a certain way. So what the orator needs to know, as Plato and Aristotle were well aware,[3] is a generalized psychology: what sorts of things different sorts of people do, and what different sorts of audiences like or dislike.

I shall devote most of this chapter to giving some examples of oratorical characterization. But there are two further general considerations which must be mentioned first. One rests on the special circumstances of Athenian courts in the classical period. Litigants plead in person, but such is the sophistication expected by juries (who seem to become more educated and literary as the fourth century goes on)[4] that professional speech-writers ($\lambda o\gamma o\gamma\rho\acute{a}\phi o\iota$) earn a good living and much fame. Such a speech-writer—Lysias is the most celebrated—has to put himself in his client's place, make him say nothing inconsistent with his visible personality, and at the same time make him a representative of an acceptable type. The situation in Rome was different. There, the *patronus* spoke in his own person, and it was his standing and authority that mattered. This is probably why Roman rhetoric has relatively little to say about the *ēthos* of the speaker. Secondly, we need to interrogate the texts that are in front of us. What exactly are they? Obviously not verbatim reports of what was said in court or in the assembly: too much is taken for granted, speakers seem to anticipate later speeches, and the work is surely too highly polished to be quite real. Two motives for publication and preservation suggest themselves: the desire to promulgate or defend a policy, and the need to advertise a speech-writer's skill or put up a model for imitation. The very existence of the speeches we have is evidence that one or other of these motives has operated. We read a text intended for posterity. We are among the intended audience, not eaves-droppers on a distant scene of tension. And suppose the speech was never delivered at all, but intended from the first as a pamphlet or a model? There are indeed works of which we

---

[3] E.g. Pl. *Phdr.* 271d–272c; Arist. *Rh.* 2. 12; cf. *Rhetorica ad Alexandrum* 7. 4–6.

[4] The development of oratory itself contributed to the sophistication; and note Dover's remark (*Greek Popular Morality* (Oxford, 1974), 35) that the social class of jurors may have been normally higher in the late 4th century than in the 5th.

know this to be true: much of Isocrates, Antiphon's *Tetralogies*, Gorgias' *Helen* and *Palamedes*, not to speak of the Latin examples, most of the *Verrines* and the *Second Philippic* of Cicero. Later Greek rhetoric is represented for us much more by declamations—i.e. model school-exercises—than by speeches with an actual occasion, and the precepts of the rhetors are directed primarily to this kind of composition. The techniques of *ēthos* are very largely common to the 'real' speech and to the shadow; and our judgement of the skill with which they are applied, given our lack of external evidence concerning the historical circumstances of many 'real' speeches, must be based on similar criteria.

I have selected five speeches for examination: two forensic, one deliberative, one (in essence) epideictic, and one declamation. This will I hope show how the portrayal of personality, the speaker's and that of others, is a dominant factor in all kinds of oratory, and at all periods of Greek literature.

II

Let us begin with a well-known speech about which it is possible to argue whether or not it is in any sense 'real'. This is Lysias 24, an acknowledged minor masterpiece by the orator who was reckoned in antiquity as the leading model of character portrayal (ἠθοποιΐα).[5] An 'invalid' defends his claim to a small pension, which has been challenged at his annual examination (δοκιμασία); to be entitled to such an allowance, he would need to show that he was disabled for work and had no other adequate means of support; the opponent calls both qualifications in question. Neither the speaker's nor the challenger's name is given. Even stranger (19–20), the claimant has a trade, but does not tell us what it is, though his words exclude perfumery, hairdressing, and shoemaking.[6] Nor does he tell us precisely what his disability is; but it is evident to the eye ('I am such as you see me', 14), and affects his mobility ('I use two sticks when others use one', 12).

---

[5] S. Usher, 'Individual Characterization in Lysias', *Eranos*, 63 (1965) 99–119. For an ancient account of this aspect of Lysias, Dion. Hal. *Lys.* 7–8 cannot be bettered.

[6] *Pace* Bizos in the Budé edn. of Lysias, ii (Paris, 1955), 101. Perhaps he was a money-lender?

Let us briefly consider how the character of the speaker is brought out.

The process begins with the first words, which are always crucial. He is grateful to the challenger for giving him an opportunity to 'give an account' of his way of life. Here is no cringing pauper, but a man proud of what he is. At the same time, his disability deserves pity (2), but he draws attention to this, not to win sympathy, but to underline the unnatural wickedness of the opponent, who displays envy (φθόνος) where pity would be in place. On the contrary, he takes pride in the way his character has surmounted his physical handicap. The prooemium, where *ēthos* must first be established, thus shows us a man of spirit. It is difficult not to be reminded of Socrates' alleged 'big talk' (μεγαληγορία), as Plato and Xenophon represent it.[7] He then, somewhat condescendingly, addresses the charges that he is not qualified as an invalid and has a profession which gives him a living. We are told (5) what the grounds for these assertions were: he rides a horse, and he keeps company with men of means. To answer them, he first tells his story, prefacing it by saying that everybody knows him. There is no false modesty about the man. When he gives his family background (6), in standard form, the point he emphasizes is his dutiful care of his mother in her old age (γηροτροφία), and his own lack of children to keep him in old age. The second charge, that he rides a horse (10–12), is met by ingenious sophisms. The speech-writer evidently sees no incongruity in attributing a good deal of rhetorical artifice to his client, and this is interesting: either the ἠθοποιΐα is not very realistically carried out (contrast, for example, Lysias 1 or Demosthenes 55, and note the absence of the common topos protesting lack of skill in speaking) or else the individual really was something of an intellectual. A similar impression is made by the rebuttal of the accusation of ὕβρις (15). Not only does the speaker use the regular contrast of wicked rich and honest poor (Blass[8] thought that this topos came from Lysias' supposed handbook of arguments, *Paraskeuai*), but he suggests (18) that his opponent

[7] Esp. Xen. *Apol.* 1, who say that every writer who has attempted it has succeeded in capturing his μεγαληγορία, though not the preference for death which alone made sense of it.

[8] *Die Attische Beredsamkeit,*[2] i (Leipzig, 1887), 382, 638.

cannot be serious but is saying these things only to make fun of him—which of course would be grossly discourteous to the court. Again, in the reply made to the charge that he gathers spendthrifts and criminals in his place of work (19–20), there is an oddly feeble and sophistical argument. To make such a charge, he says, is to blame his visitors and not him; and, since all Athenians habitually congregate in someone's shop or workplace, it is implicitly to condemn a familiar feature of the social scene. Anyway, this is, he says (21), a trivial point. In the peroration (21–7) comes the serious issue. It would, he claims, be quite wrong to deprive him of the privilege granted long ago. He is a good decent democrat, now old and ill, who emigrated to Chalcis in the time of the Thirty, though he could have safely stayed at home.

Let us set this remarkable little speech against the key text in rhetorical theory, Aristotle's account of *ēthos* as a mode of 'proof within the art' ($\pi\iota\sigma\tau\iota\varsigma$ $\check{\epsilon}\nu\tau\epsilon\chi\nu o\varsigma$):

> There are three kinds of proofs ($\pi\iota\sigma\tau\epsilon\iota\varsigma$) provided by means of speech. Some are based on the character ($\check{\eta}\theta o\varsigma$) of the speaker, some on putting the hearer into a certain frame of mind, and some on the speech itself, in virtue of its power of proving or seeming to prove something. We have proofs based on character when the speech is spoken in such a way as to make the speaker worthy of credit: we give credit to the good ($\epsilon\pi\iota\epsilon\iota\kappa\epsilon\hat{\iota}\varsigma$) more completely and more speedily whatever the subject, but especially where there is no clear certainty but divergence of opinion. This must be achieved through the medium of the speech, and not because there exists a previous judgement that the speaker is of a certain sort. Some teachers of rhetoric do not include the speaker's goodness as part of the art, on the ground that it makes no contribution to persuasiveness. The contrary is true: the most effective proof resides in *ēthos*. (*Rh.* 1. 1356[a]1 ff.)

In our speech, the speaker does indeed try to show throughout that he is $\epsilon\pi\iota\epsilon\iota\kappa\eta\varsigma$. It is clearly something that was not obvious. He has to rebut suggestions that he is violent and keeps bad company. He stresses in return his family loyalties and his sound democratic behaviour. On the other hand, there clearly was a 'previous judgement' concerning him present in the hearers' minds before he ever opened his mouth. It consisted in his visible deformity and, evidently, in a reputation for being a difficult character. Lysias has to take account of this and use it.

Eccentricity, bad manners, and dubious repute are transformed into a sort of independent self-respect (one might call it μεγαλοψυχία) which is thought of as acceptable. At the same time, the speech clearly does not tell the whole story. In particular, he conceals his trade, though all the court knew it. It must have been something indefensible.

It is the unusual individuality of this speaker that convinces the reader that he must have been a real person. Whether or not he delivered the speech remains an open question. It could well bear no more relation to the actual proceedings than the *Apologies* of Plato and Xenophon do to the trial of Socrates.

III

I turn next to a speech which is certainly 'real', and reveals an exceptionally delicate technique. Despite Dionysius' view that Isaeus' artifice was such that his clients' lies would never be believed,[9] it is impossible not to admire the skill with which the litigants in his testamentary cases contrive to convey, not indeed individuality, but acceptable ἐπιείκεια, and to do so in the course of telling what seems at first sight a bald story.[10]

In Isaeus 2 an adopted son has claimed the estate of the man who adopted him, Menecles. Challenged by Menecles' brother, he had persuaded his father-in-law, Philonides, to give evidence that the adoption was valid and not made under pressure. Philonides is then prosecuted for false witness, and the speech that Isaeus writes is that delivered in these proceedings by the claimant to the estate in his father-in-law's support. Thus it is not the *ēthos* of the defendant Philonides that is in question, but the claimant's own and that of Menecles and his family. The charge to be answered is that Menecles acted under the undue influence of his young wife (the claimant's sister) or when not in his right mind.

The prooemium is skilful. The opening words display straightforwardness and honesty: 'If anyone was legally adopted, I was sure I was.' Family solidarity appears in the detail of calling the opponent 'uncle'. At first, the words are

---

[9] Dion. Hal. *Is.* 16.
[10] W. Wyse's great edn. (Cambridge, 1904) offers a subtle and properly sceptical commentary on much of Isaeus' argumentation.

mild: 'uncle, in my judgement, was ill advised'—but then comes the sting, sharpened by sentimentality—'in trying by every means to make his dead brother childless'. To prove the case, the whole family history is set out, lucidly so far as it goes, but no doubt not very honestly. The speaker's father, Eponymos, a friend of Menecles, had two sons and two daughters. After his death, the sons gave one of their sisters in marriage to Leucolophos, with an adequate dowry, and, three or four years later, the younger sister to Menecles, whose wife had died not long before—but long enough, it is made clear, to make a second marriage decent (4). This sister also had a dowry, and evidence is called to prove this (5). In all this, the family appears as acting very properly: 'we knew there was no one my father would rather have had his daughter marry than Menecles'. Next (6) the two brothers set off as mercenaries under Iphicrates; it appears later (12) that one of them continues in this way of life. This is not in itself very respectable, unlike service in the citizen army. The speaker therefore adds that they 'got some credit and made something out of it' before returning home. There they found their younger sister still childless. Menecles then approached them, and spoke very well of his wife, but said he did not wish to take advantage of her by letting her grow old with him childless: 'it was enough for him to suffer' (7). He therefore proposed that she should be given, with his consent, to a younger husband. All this passage is so written as to bring out Menecles' resigned self-sacrifice, the goodness of his young wife (who is at first very unwilling to leave him) and the general harmoniousness of the family in these embarrassing circumstances. The girl does remarry, and her former husband is generous in the matter of her jewellery and clothing. Some time after—the chronology is very vague, doubtless designedly—Menecles feels sorry for himself and looks for someone 'to keep him in old age, bury him when he dies, and do the expected things thereafter'. We note again the pious and moralizing tone. His own brother has one son. Why should he not adopt him? Again, his considerateness is marvellous: it would be a disgrace to deprive his brother of his only male child. (No untruth is told here, but it emerges later (23) that the brother has daughters.) He resolves instead to take one of Eponymos' boys, his divorced wife's brothers. One of them, a

rolling stone, declines the honour. It is the speaker who is
adopted. The adoption was made by a healthy man, in sound
mind (14). He was certainly not under the influence of the wife
he had divorced, for she was now married again with two sons
of her own, whom she could have put forward if she had had
the power. And no complaint was made at the time, nor at any
time in the twenty-three years which Menecles survived after
the act of adoption. If we are to believe this, the family relationships were ideal. Menecles then urged his adopted son to marry
(18), and generally treated him as a father should treat his own
son, to be rewarded by all the care and respect a natural father
would expect.

The main narrative ends here. An attentive reading of it and
the rest of the speech makes it clear that Isaeus has done well by
his client, not only by *suppressio veri* but by a consistent portrayal of ἐπιείκεια, culminating (46–7) in an unctuous peroration, in which his opponent is said to want to deprive his dead
brother of all future honours and ritual. It is not difficult to see
how a quite different gloss might be put on the whole story. An
old and perhaps imbecile husband, who parts with a young
wife and then adopts her brother, could equally well be represented as the victim of a family of blackmailers. It is not for us
to know the truth, only to admire the orator's art.

IV

Forensic oratory is naturally the most significant area for the
display of character, whether that of the speaker or of the persons of whom he has to speak. But it is not out of place in the
other branches either. Let us, by way of example, consider from
this point of view Demosthenes' first great deliberative speech,
the *First Philippic*. It is true, of course, that the arousing of emotion is more prominent than the mere portrayal of character.
Demosthenes wants the Athenians to sense the danger and to
act, not rashly indeed, but in the heat of anger. He is angry,
indignant, and alarmed himself. But, from the rhetor's standpoint, there is much in common between *ēthos* and *pathos*; it is
significant that Quintilian's discussion treats both as species of
adfectus, constituting between them the orator's most important
field of effort. The main difference is that *ēthos* (for which, as he

206 · 	 D. A. Russell

observes, the Romans have no proper translation) stands for
the gentler emotions, whose expression persuades and con-
ciliates, and *pathos* for the violent ones that dominate and dis-
turb.[11] The terms were indeed puzzling by Quintilian's time;
but his discussion reminds us that this whole psychological
dimension of oratory is really one. In the *Philippics*, *ēthos*,
though subordinate to *pathos*, is an essential element. It makes
sense to analyse the whole speech in terms of the way in which
it rests on the characteristic qualities of the three parties concerned: the orator, his Athenian audience, and the enemy
Philip.

(i) The presentation of the orator as good adviser begins with
1. He would not be speaking if the situation did not compel. He
is not self-assertive. But we soon see him (10) to be a man of
high sentiment, the kind of man to enunciate the γνώμη:
'Shame is the strongest compulsion on free men.' Yet (14) he
gives practical counsel, for we cannot change the past or put
things right overnight. His advice is detailed (20), and he
believes in it well enough (29) to volunteer to sail with the
troops if things go ill. Confident as he is, he knows he must not
conceal disagreeable truths (38) and reminds us (again senten-
tiously, in the true adviser's mode) that in war it is no use
following events, you have to be ahead of them. Finally (51) he
closes with a clear recommendation of himself on grounds of
ēthos: he has never before spoken simply to please (πρὸς χάριν),
and does not do so now. He is quite frank and open. Of course
things may not go well; human uncertainty must always be
accepted. So he closes, in character, on a modest but encourag-
ing note.

(ii) What everyone remembers best about Demosthenes'
treatment of his audience in the *Philippics* is his scathing attack
on the Athenians' slowness, laziness, and lack of serious commitment (εἰρώνεια) (7, 8, 11, 35-7) and his satirical references
to their love of gossip and rumour (10, 49). But this does not
appear until after he has both established his own character
and spoken of Philip's. Moreover, he normally includes himself:
these weaknesses are 'ours' not 'yours'. They are indeed vividly
portrayed; especially masterly is the imagined conversation at

---

[11] Quint. 6. 2. 8-24.

10—'"Is there any news? ... Is Philip dead?" "No, but he's ill"'—and the massive period at 35 contrasting the pains taken with ceremonial processions with the carelessness over preparations for war.

(iii) Finally, Philip. He is of course a paradigm of activity (5) and a shameless and wicked aggressor (9); but he has his enemies at home (8), he is drunk on success (49), and his very strength can be seen to turn in the end to his opponents' advantage.

In one passage in particular (38–42), it seems to me, these three *ēthē* come together to define the whole situation. The honest and moral adviser reproaches his people, who have the means but not the skill—they respond to Philip's every move like bad boxers—and rescues them from despair by pointing to Philip's fatal flaw, his inability to rest content with what he has.

Such an analysis is of course incomplete. To say nothing of the *pathē* (fear, indignation), it does not discuss the rhetorical economy of the speech or the actual situation. But it seems to me to set out with sharpness what many readers feel to be the essentials of the matter.

V

Epideictic oratory, the oratory of praise and ceremonial, also has scope for the portrayal of character. The credentials of the speaker must be established. Even in the case of a simple personal encomium, impartiality and standing have to be proved. It is best *laudari a laudato viro*. In the many diverse and complex varieties of epideictic speech that were developed especially in the Roman period by the 'sophists', there is often room both for the speaker's *ēthos* to be defined and for many incidental pieces of character indication. Dio Chrysostom begins his *Olympicus* (*Or.* 12), which is mainly concerned with the statue of Zeus and our knowledge of God, with an elaborate definition of his own position as a latter-day Socrates, a plain owl whose wisdom is worth more than the peacocking of sophists. In what is perhaps his most famous speech, *Euboicus* (*Or.* 7), which is essentially an encomium of the life of the poor and an attack on luxury and vice, there are both deliberative and forensic features, though the whole must be classed as epideictic. There is so much *ēthos*

in it, of all kinds, that a brief analysis seems a good way of showing how this element in oratory became even more significant
in the literary and rhetorical circumstances of this later period
than it had been in the classic age of the Attic orators.

The audience, indeed, is not much characterized. We see
that they are supposed to have an interest in philosophy and
poetry, to recognize allusions and welcome information. Dio
appeals to this characteristic when there is a risk of their
becoming bored (81, 128). Somewhat more weight lies on the
ēthos of the speaker. Dio characterizes himself (it is his regular
stance, not something assumed for the particular occasion) as a
wanderer, who has many tales to tell, and has had first-hand
experience, during his years of exile, both of the hardships of
poverty and of the security that it gives (1, 8–9). He also claims
to be a philosopher, and he takes pains to explain that the dis-
cursive, unoratorical economy of this allegedly extemporized
speech (102) is the legitimate philosophical pursuit of an argument, not mere idle garrulity. But it is the skill with which Dio
conveys the characters of the persons occurring in the narrative
(1–80) that sets this speech among the masterpieces of this art.
Everything is cleverly directed to making the main moral
point. The hunter whom Dio encounters after his shipwreck on
the coast of Euboea is recognized by his physical appearance
(4), talks as an honest countryman, and tells his own simple tale
(10 ff., a *narratio* closely modelled on classical forensic speeches).
There follows (22 ff.) a story within the story, the narrative by
the hunter of what befell him on his one visit to the neighbouring city. He speaks as a man who has never seen such things
before, describing the works of man in terms of natural features,
the theatre as a sort of ravine and the noise of the crowd as a
storm at sea. Two orators appear, one harsh and uncompromis-
ing, accusing the hunter of growing rich off public land he does
not pay for, the other (33) ἐπιεικής, a quiet speaker with a practical and generous proposal. Their speeches are clearly differentiated. The hunter himself speaks in his own defence (42 ff.),
winning sympathy by his *naïveté*. When his accuser speaks of a
'talent', he thinks he means a measure to weigh meat, not a sum
of money (44). He triumphs over his opponent (62–3). This
story ended, Dio resumes his account of his own encounter with
the hunter's family in their remote huts. It is a pretty idyll of

two young people in love and about to marry according to the simple ways of the countryside. It all goes to point the moral: these ways are better than the sophistications and disputes that spring from the marriage contracts of the rich (80). It would be hard to find in Greek a more skilful deployment of this kind of *ēthos* (in speeches, in description, and in action), here directed at no practical end save that of a moral sermon. The latter part of the speech (81–152) is very different; it is a powerful, but sometimes confused, stretch of direct moral invective and preaching. There is, however, much in it that relates to the traditional characterization of types and professions which we find in the orators. Dio wants to explain what honest work the urban poor could do. He does not agree with orators who abuse their opponents for being children of hired labourers, schoolmasters, or children's attendants (παιδαγωγοί) (114). These are occupations which poor men perform but which are not disreputable in themselves. Real disgrace, on the other hand, attends the luxury trades: actors, auctioneers, lawyers, and especially prostitutes. Some of this again rests on rhetorical tradition (we recall Demosthenes' attack on Aeschines' life as an actor), some on philosophical tradition; some at least is Dio's own reflection on the evils of the time.

VI

Our last example comes from the rhetorical schools of late antiquity. It is only from this period that we have complete specimens of declamation (μελέται) in Greek; but the techniques are old, and the language classical, based on imitation (μίμησις) of the orators.[12] The fifth-century rhetor Sopatros (*Diaereses Zetematon*, 8. 315 W) gives a brief note on the following exercise:

'The discoverer of treasure pays a thousand drachmas tax. A miser finds five hundred drachmas, and pays the thousand. He asks for the death penalty.' The miser's object is to recover his thousand drach-

---

[12] Significantly, one of the main contributions made by ancient rhetors to the study of *ēthos* is to be found in two treatises specifically designed to correct faults in declamation: Ps.-Dionysius, *Ars Rhetorica* 10–11; see D. A. Russell, 'Classicizing Rhetoric and Criticism: The Pseudo-Dionysian *Exetasis* and *Mistakes in Declamation*', in *Entr. Hardt*, xxv. *Le Classicisme à Rome* (Geneva, 1979), 113–34. The author tries to distinguish between the 'philosophical *ēthos* of the various characters, which depends on 'nation, origin, age, principles, fortune, profession'.

mas. He asks for death in order to win the court's sympathy and get his money back. The subject is full of *ethos* (ἠθικόν): the quality of the miser and the distress to him of having given the money demand this treatment. It is this distress that makes him ask to die, and this is how you can give the speaker *ēthos*.

This case belongs to a familiar class of rhetorical fictions, in which it is supposed that anyone who finds life no longer worth living can apply to the court for a death sentence and a dose of hemlock to put him out of his miseries.[13] It is worked in full by Libanius (*Declamation* 31), from whom Sopatros may have taken it, though it is noticeable that Libanius employs certain arguments which Sopatros does not state. The speech does of course rest on the *ēthos* of the speaker, though that of the court has also to be taken into account.

The process of presenting the miser naturally begins with his first words: 'You have got the five hundred, that marvellous treasure trove, and as much again from the unhappy finder's previous fortune.' He soon tells how he fainted outright when the money came to light; he nearly died, and wishes he had: let his wish be granted now!

The narrative, in regular form, comes next (5 ff.). It begins, as so often in 'real' speeches, with a family history. The speaker had a thrifty father, who taught him that he must never let himself be poor, and he has dutifully followed his example. He married a woman more rich than beautiful, and they had a very modest wedding. He lets his wife wear gold jewellery, because it is a good investment, but deprecates expenditure on consumables. He keeps no horse, because an ass does as well. Since he is speaking to the representatives of the state, and has to consider how they will react, he must of course make it clear that he pays his taxes (17), though reluctantly and at the cost of the family's diet. He is also at pains to represent himself as a pious man. He sacrifices to the gods, but on a modest scale. There is of course good warrant in popular philosophy for the value of the humble offerings of the poor (21). This pious discourse leads to the account he gives of the vision which disclosed to him the site of the treasure; his hopes and bitter disappointment are vividly portrayed (40).

---

[13] A common scenario: D. A. Russell, *Greek Declamation* (Cambridge, 1983), 35–7.

The narrative concluded, the speech (like many similar declamations) resolves itself into a series of answers (λύσεις) to imagined objections (ἀντιθέσεις). It will be said that he has not suffered in body sufficiently to justify permission to die. Yes, but the loss of wealth is to him, given his nature and upbringing, worse even than the loss of health. It will be said that the law required the tax, and it is unreasonable to complain. Yes, but it was not the intention of the lawgiver to penalize trivial gains. At this point (37), Libanius provides an example of a device regularly associated with the portrayal of *ēthos* and *pathos*, a *prosopopoeia* in which the speaker imagines himself going to the lawgiver's tomb and asking for an interpretation; the lawgiver replies from his grave that he never imagined that so small a sum as 500 drachmas would be regarded as a treasure trove falling under his rule, but adds—with an eye to the court's reaction—'The people (δῆμος) has good sense, and will understand a point which escaped me.' Thirdly, it will be said that he might have tried again, and asked Fortune for another find. Yes, but suppose that had been smaller still! 'What I had before my discovery was enough for me: I am like the camel in the fable who lost what he had by looking for more.'[14] Fables traditionally 'lend charm', just like proverbs; so it is appropriate for the miser to use one to gain sympathy.

The speech ends with an adaptation of the common pathetic pleas of defendants to the peculiar circumstances of the miser:

Let someone fetch my children. Why are you crying and howling? If it is for the thousand drachmas, you are quite right, and it is a credit to the training you had from me. But if it's because I am going away, that's not sensible. If anything like this happens to you, make the same application to the people yourselves. Do not disgrace your parentage by bearing loss easily ... So what is my advice to you? Precisely what I have always given, nothing new. Regard bread and water as food enough. Rejoice when you receive, weep when you give. Do not discredit my life by avoiding its ideals. So long as you have money, pay no attention to those who mock you. Let a small mound be my grave, and the clothes I am wearing my shroud. (51–2)

These passages show that the main use of *ēthos* in the orator's

---

[14] The camel asked Zeus for horns, but Zeus responded by docking his ears (Halm 184).

armoury is to conciliate or to raise a smile, not to rouse emotion—at least, not any very strong emotion. Rhetorical theory generally makes a sharp distinction between the aims and techniques of *ēthos* and those of *pathos* ('passion'). Quintilian is an exception. He must indeed be fundamentally right in viewing these two psychological elements of oratory under the single head of *adfectus*, however much they differ in gravity or vehemence. But the common view was not this. Anger, deep disgust, and pity are passions. They are to be roused by a range of techniques different from those appropriate to *ēthos*: in the epilogue, rather than in the prooemium or narrative; by rhetorical questions, anaphoras, hyperbata, and grand language rather than by the devices of ecphrasis, reported conversations, or homely turns of phrase. The consequence of this separation—or perhaps rather the cause of it—is a way of viewing literature which pervades much ancient criticism. It is well seen in Longinus' famous comparison (9. 11–15) between the two Homeric epics, in which the *Iliad* is characterized as full of passion and action, and the *Odyssey* as essentially a comedy in which *ēthos* is dominant. This association of *ēthos* with comedy and *pathos* with tragedy is a constant one. Ordinary people, the characters of comedy, do not have grand passions. Ordinary people, too, are, as a rule, the characters of forensic oratory. It is concerned with the tensions and malice of everyday life. If there are strong feelings, the orator and the jury tend to look on them with a tolerant and worldly eye. Given their task, it is natural that the orators, and those who claimed to give them instruction, should have devoted such care and study to the 'types' that can be seen in the court-room. The result, for us, is that we possess, in the speeches of the Attic orators and their successors, a marvellous collection of character-types, and a carefully planned technique by which they can be displayed. Though the two main functions of *ēthos* in oratory—conciliation and the characterization of other parties—are distinct, they have in common a requirement of realism and good humour. The masters of this art, from Lysias to Libanius, have much to teach us both about literary skills and about the common conditions of civilized humanity.

IO

Childhood and Personality in Greek Biography

CHRISTOPHER PELLING

I

Everybody notices when a great man dies; it is more difficult to notice when one is born, or when one is growing up. It is not surprising that ancient biographers often faced a dearth of reliable material on their subject's childhood and youth; and, for writers of a certain sort of biography, the temptation to fill this gap with the telling, fictional anecdote was difficult to resist. This is clear in biographies of literary figures:

> When Pindar was a boy, according to Chamaeleon and Ister, he went hunting near Mt. Helicon and fell asleep from exhaustion. As he slept a bee landed on his mouth and built a honeycomb there. Others say that he had a dream in which his mouth was full of honey and wax, and that he then decided to write poetry. (*Vita Pindari* 2, trans. Lefkowitz[1])

Similar tales were told about Plato, Homer, Hesiod, Lucan, Ambrose, and others.[2] Or stories could be less supernatural: stories, for instance, of Homer's travels as a young man to Ithaca, or of his studying poetry with a schoolteacher named Phemius; or of Sophocles' magnificent appearance in the

This paper was originally written for the Corpus Christi College, Oxford, Classical Seminar on 'Childhood in Antiquity' in Feb. 1985; since then versions have been inflicted on audiences in Manchester, Liverpool, Rome, Harvard, and Lexington, Va. My thanks to all for kindly hearings, and especially to Thomas Wiedemann, Robert Garland, Michael Reeve, Christopher Gill, Tim Cornell, Judith Mossman, and Mansur Lalljee for reading and commenting on earlier drafts.

[1] Cf. M. R. Lefkowitz, *The Lives of the Greek Poets* (London, 1981), 59, 155–6.

[2] Homer: Lefkowitz, *Lives*, 24. Plato: A. S. Riginos, *Platonica: The Anecdotes Concerning the Life and Writings of Plato* (Leiden, 1976), 17–21. Hesiod and Lucan: Suet. *Vita Lucani*, pp. 178–9 Rostagni. Ambrose: Paulinus, *Vita Ambrosii* 3. 2–5 (a reference I owe to Mr Wiedemann). Others: Riginos, *Platonica*, 19 and n. 39; cf. Lefkowitz, *Lives*, 59 n. 12.

chorus celebrating the victory of Salamis.[3] Some philosophers were similarly embroidered, though they tended to become interesting when a little older, at the stage of adolescence when they were ripe for conversion. Epicurus, for instance, turned to philosophy in disgust at a schoolmaster who could not explain the meaning of 'chaos' in Hesiod; Metrocles was so embarrassed when he farted during a declamation that he tried to starve himself to death, until Crates visited him and won him over by dropping a casual fart himself. (He had thoughtfully prepared himself by eating some lupins.)[4] Admittedly, even literary figures do not always get this sort of elaboration: it is remarkable how little is told about the early years of Socrates, for example, given his central importance for the development of biography. But there are still a fair number of such stories to be found.

It is unclear how many of these stories were made up by the biographers themselves, and how many figured in the tradition—often oral—which the biographers were using. Either way, a remarkable feature of ancient *political* biography is how little of this anecdotal elaboration one gets.[5] Of course, literary biographies are peculiarly susceptible to such embroidery, where influences and inspiration can be engagingly rephrased in anecdotal terms. Still, it was political biography that more often favoured the 'cradle-to-grave' form, in which awkward childhood gaps would be more visible; and more was usually known of the adult lives of political personalities, including their private lives, and there were correspondingly more qualities which one could, if one wished, retroject into childhood. We do occasionally find something of the kind:

---

[3] Homer: Lefkowitz, *Lives*, 13, 20–2, 140–1. Sophocles: ead., 77, 160; cf. 93–4.

[4] Epicurus: Diog. Laert. 10. 2, Sex. Emp. *Adu. Math.* 10. 18–19. Metrocles: Diog. Laert. 6. 94 (cf. 6. 96 on his sister Hipparchia). On stories of the young Plato, see Riginos, *Platonica*, 39–52.

[5] This distinction between 'literary' (or 'cultural' or 'intellectual') and 'political' biographies must be understood roughly. Leo's distinction in terms of generic form has long been recognized as imperfect (cf. e.g. A. Momigliano, *The Development of Greek Biography* (Harvard, 1971), 87–8; J. Geiger, *Cornelius Nepos and Ancient Political Biography* (Hist. Einzelschr., 47; Stuttgart, 1985), 11–19); and men such as Cicero and M. Aurelius are both cultural and political figures. 'Cultural' biographies themselves straddle a large range, from propagandist tract to curious gossip. But it will emerge that certain important distinctions of content can still be made, affecting such central points as style of presentation, focus of interest, and degree of truth or mendacity: so, rightly, Geiger, *Cornelius Nepos*, 18–29.

Alexander hearing of Philip's successes, and saying in vexation to his friends that 'my father will leave nothing for me to do'; or Cato being held out of a window by a playful Poppaedius Silo, but still refusing to say that he would ask his father to support the citizenship proposals.[6] And many stories were told of the young Alcibiades, for instance the tale of a wrestling-match when he bit his opponent's arm to get out of a hold. 'Alcibiades, you're biting like a girl', said the indignant opponent; 'No,' said Alcibiades, 'like a lion.'[7] Indeed, it seems that material on childhood featured quite prominently in that fifth-century precursor of political biography, Stesimbrotus of Thasos: he evidently had a considerable amount to say about the youth and education of Themistocles, Cimon, and probably Pericles, not without a tinge of malice.[8] That was in keeping with the tradition of invective, which often concentrated on childhood and family background: we can indeed see that the childhood of all three of those fifth-century figures was already the subject of partisan controversy.[9] But it seems that Stesimbrotus' lead was rarely taken up, and later writers and audiences found the childhood of political figures much less interesting—particularly outside Athens, away from the democratic tradition of vigorous invective.[10]

---

[6] Plut. *Alex.* 5. 4; *C. Min.* 2. 1–5.

[7] Plut. *Alc.* 2. 2–3; other stories scattered through 2–9, discussed by D. A. Russell, 'Plutarch, "Alcibiades" 1–16', *PCPS* 12 (1966), 38–42.

[8] *FGrH* 107, esp. frs. 1, 4, 6. He was evidently interested in Pericles' private life (frs. 10–11), and some of Plutarch's material on Pericles' youth may also derive from him: cf. P. A. Stadter, *A Commentary to Plutarch's* Pericles (Chapel Hill, 1989), introd. On the character of his work, cf. the contrasting views of F. Schachermeyr, 'Stesimbrotus und seine Schrift über die Staatsmänner', *Sb. Oest. Ak. Wiss.* 247/5 (1965), and K. Meister, 'Stesimbrotus' Schrift über die athenischer Staatsmänner', *Hist.* 27 (1978), 274–94.

[9] Invective: below, p. 217. The youth of Cimon and Pericles was clearly the subject of contemporary exchanges: cf. Plut. *Cim.* 4. 4, 4. 6–9, with 15. 3; and the attacks on Pericles' 'educators' Damon and Anaxagoras (*Per.* 4. 3–4, 32, etc.). For Themistocles, cf. Plut. *Them.* 2. 6, 2. 8, 3. 2, with the comm. of F. J. Frost (Princeton, NJ, 1980). As Frost emphasizes, the controversy lasted into later generations: cf. Xen. *Mem.* 4. 2. 2; *P. Oxy.* xiii. 1608 (Aeschines Socraticus).

[10] Theopompus (*FGrH* 115) and Idomeneus (*FGrH* 338) wrote 'on the Athenian demagogues', perhaps consciously following Stesimbrotus. Schachermeyr, 'Stesimbrotus', 20–1, claims that they showed a considerable ethical interest in *paideia*, and suggests that Stesimbrotus was similar. Yet no particular concern with education is visible in Theopompus, *FGrH* 115 frs. 85–100; Idomeneus perhaps had more (*FGrH* 338 fr. 13, on Aeschines' education; cf. fr. 2 on his mother, and fr. 15 on Phocion's father), but this is a natural consequence of his use of material drawn from invective (cf. e.g. frs. 9, 12), and nothing suggests that he was really judging politicians 'mit schulmeisterlichem Stirnrunzeln' (Schachermeyr).

Plutarch is a very useful guide here, for we can tell that he *was* very interested in youth and education. When he has the material, he does make a great deal of it—in *Alexander*, for example, or *Demosthenes*, or *Philopoemen*, or *Cato Minor*:[11] clearly, there were no generic rules to outlaw such material; but remarkably often he obviously has none. He has no childish squabbles of Romulus and Remus, usefully though they might have prepared the fratricide; no schoolboy infatuations of Antony with any schoolgirl Cleopatra; nothing on Camillus or Flamininus to match the material about their pairs Themistocles and Philopoemen. And it is not simply his Roman biographies— nothing on Nicias (how he was frightened by an eclipse in his youth, perhaps? It is the type of story one might expect to be made up); no stories of the young Agesilaus bending truth and justice to help a good-looking friend; nothing, or hardly anything, on Pelopidas or Lycurgus or Lysander or Timoleon or Eumenes or Phocion. Plutarch himself does not fabricate to fill the gaps; but this is also revealing about his sources, for it is not likely that Plutarch is suppressing anything here, nor that there was a mass of material that escaped his notice: he was too well informed for that. This sort of anecdotal tradition simply did not exist for him to know.

Nor, indeed, did it really exist in Roman biography. Why *don't* we find stories of Augustus hearing of Caesar's conquests in Gaul, and dreaming of similar glory for himself? And one could do so much with stories of Caligula's youth—how he got on with his sister Drusilla in the nursery, for example. (Suet. *Cal.* 24. 1 has a story of their being discovered in bed together by their grandmother Antonia, but by then they were in their late teens.) Why not a few colourful stories about the most colourful emperors, Elagabalus or Gallienus? But what we mostly find is generalizations about youthful promise or excess; or a routine collection of omens, portents, or prophecies of greatness. The emperor whose youth is treated most extensively in the Scriptores Historiae Augustae is Marcus Aurelius: that *Life* gives quite a full treatment of the various instructors and

---

[11] In such cases we can often offer specific explanations for the material's availability. *Phil.*, for instance, is informed by Polybius' encomium (below, p. 218); *Alex.* both by encomium and by works such as that of Onesicritus (ibid.); *Dem.* perhaps by literary biography; *C. Min.* by the martyrological tradition.

the honours he paid them, and tells for instance of his early penchant for sleeping on the ground and wearing a rough cloak.[12] It seems to be the affinity with literary biography, and Marcus Aurelius' status as an intellectual as well as an emperor, which makes the difference. We also have something on Commodus' youth, where the point is rather the converse—Marcus did all he could to educate him, and it did no good at all; and on the Gordians, where the size of the library features heavily.[13] It was intellectual figures, or at least figures where the intellectual register was appropriate, which stimulated this interest: political figures usually did not.

This is the more remarkable because there were neighbouring genres which elaborated politicians' childhoods in precisely the ways which biography eschewed. Among the closest genres to biography were, first, encomium and its inverse counterpart invective, and secondly, the biographical novel on the model of Xenophon's *Cyropaedeia*.[14] These genres treated public men more often than literary figures;[15] and they certainly encouraged attention to childhood, describing it in very predictable, and often fictional, ways. In the *Cyropaedeia* Xenophon lays great emphasis on Cyrus' youth, and it is full of elaboration: 1. 3 is especially telling, the sequence of precocious (and utterly infuriating) remarks he made when first brought to Astyages' court. Invective again favoured tales about its victim's youth, this time of course scurrilous ones:[16] Aeschines helped his father in the schoolroom and his mother in her initiation rites (Dem. 18. 258-9, 19. 199), Demosthenes was called 'Batalos' because of his lewd habits (Aesch. 2. 99), Alcibiades once ran off with one of his lovers (Antiphon fr. 66), Cicero handled filthy clothes in the family laundry (Dio 46. 5. 1). Encomium tended not to develop such specific material, and

---

[12] SHA *M. Aurel.* 2-3; cf. 4. 9-10.

[13] SHA *Comm.* 1; *Gord. I* 3; *Gord. II* 18; cf. *Anton. Geta* 3-4.

[14] Cf. esp. Momigliano, *Development*, ch. 4.

[15] Not of course that literary figures were immune: the attacks on Epicurus and Aristotle, for instance, have much in common with the exchanges of Aeschines and Demosthenes. (Epicurus too was attacked for assisting his father in his school for a paltry fee; he apparently retorted that Aristotle took to soldiering and selling drugs after squandering his patrimony: Diog. Laert. 10. 4, 8.)

[16] Cf. R. G. M. Nisbet's comm. on Cicero, *In Pisonem* (Oxford, 1961), 194; K. J. Dover, *Greek Popular Morality* (Oxford, 1974), 32-3.

hence was less anecdotal;[17] but it equally dwelt on its subject's youth. We can already see this in Isocrates' conventionalized picture in *Evagoras*,[18] and Polybius' later encomium of Philopoemen 'explained who his family were and described his training when young ... setting out clearly the character of his education':[19] that work has evidently left its mark on Plutarch's *Philopoemen*.

Encomium, invective, and the biographical novel were familiar genres in the Hellenistic age. There were various works on Alexander and his successors, for instance, which seem to have been modelled on Xenophon's *Cyropaedeia* (though it is true that we know very little about them):[20] in particular, perhaps, Onesicritus' work *How Alexander was Brought up*, which Diogenes Laertius specifically connects with the *Cyropaedeia*.[21] That work's extravagant qualities are clear; less is known about Marsyas of Pella who wrote *On the Education of Alexander*, or of Lysimachus' *Paideia of Attalus*.[22] Such works presumably did not *confine* their interest to childhood: like Xenophon, Onesicritus carried the story some way past his subject's youth, and the emphasis on *paideia* embraced 'culture' as well as 'education'. It was he, for instance, who told the story of Alexander keeping the *Iliad* by his bedside, and the exchanges with the Gymnosophistae.[23] But childhood was surely central to the theme, and it is no surprise that some romantic material has filtered into the early chapters of Plutarch's *Alexander*.[24]

Yet such *Lives* as *Alexander* and *Philopoemen* remain exceptional. With encomium, invective, and the biographical novel all developing this interest in childhood, we might have ex-

---

[17] Cf. S. Halliwell, above, pp. 56–7.

[18] Isoc. *Evag.* 21–2.

[19] Polybius' own description of the work, 10. 21. 5–6. Cf. esp. Plut. *Phil.* 3–4.

[20] Geiger, *Cornelius Nepos*, 48–9, though he is perhaps too cautious.

[21] *FGrH* 134 T 1 = Diog. Laert. 6. 84.

[22] *FGrH* 135–6, 170: cf. Momigliano, *Development*, 82–3.

[23] *FGrH* 134 fr. 38 = Plut. *Alex.* 8. 2; fr. 17 = Strabo 15. 1. 163–5, Plut. *Alex.* 65. On Plutarch's use of Onesicritus, cf. esp. J. R. Hamilton, *Plutarch*, Alexander: *A Commentary* (Oxford, 1969), xxxi, liii, lvi–lvii.

[24] Cf. esp. Hamilton, comm., liii, lvi–lvii. Not all of course will come from Onesicritus: Eratosthenes is cited at 3. 3, Hegesias of Magnesia at 3. 6, Aristoxenus at 4. 4. But some may well be specifically Onesicritus, esp. on Alexander's education in 5. 7–8. 5 (cf. Hamilton on 5. 7); possibly 6 (cf. fr. 20 = *Alex.* 61; T. S. Brown, *Onesicritus* (Berkeley and Los Angeles, 1949), 20); 8. 2 = fr. 38. The important point is the more general one, the traces in Plutarch's material of this encomiastic and novelistic *tradition*.

pected to find similar material with other figures too; but on the whole we do not. Even with such men as Demetrius and Pyrrhus, figures who might well have inspired such encomia or novels, Plutarch's early chapters do not really suggest that he knows this type of material. He dwells on Pyrrhus' unprepossessing appearance, for instance, and an early military failure of Demetrius (*Pyrrh.* 3. 6; *Dtr.* 5), not very tactful themes for the encomiast or novelist. And there remain those other figures who seem clearly to have remained unembroidered—some of an earlier age, Nicias, Lysander, or Agesilaus for instance, but some more recent, Timoleon, Phocion, and Eumenes. This is not the place to enter the controversial debate on the history of political biography in the Hellenistic age;[25] perhaps *Lives* of Nicias or Eumenes were being written, but their authors eschewed such fictional childhood material; more likely, political biographies were not really being written at all, and even the novelistic and encomiastic traditions were not so rich or extensive as we might have expected.[26] Either way, the interest in politicians' childhoods remained stunted; and Plutarch, when he came to write genuine political biography, chose to do it in a style which, in this as in other ways, contrasted with those neighbouring genres.

Why should there be this difference in treatment between cultural and political figures?

First, there genuinely seems a difference in the attitude to truthfulness: in political biography no tradition of systematic mendacity seems to have developed. This needs to be emphasized, for Momigliano argued that 'the borderline between fiction and reality was thinner in biography than in ordinary historiography'.[27] Yet that dictum is truer of some sorts of biography than of others, and Plutarch, the only Greek political biographer we can really discuss, is really rather scrupulous

[25] See most recently Geiger, *Cornelius Nepos*, 30–65, with whose sceptical approach I sympathize.

[26] Timoleon is an especially interesting case: despite his glorification by the historian Timaeus, there was apparently no serious attempt to embellish his childhood in the manner of encomium or the novel, and nothing suggests that he was the subject of any political biography. Cf. Geiger, *Cornelius Nepos*, 55 n. 89.

[27] Momigliano, *Development*, esp. 56–7; cf. id., 'Marcel Mauss and the Quest for the Person in Greek Biography and Autobiography', in M. Carrithers, S. Collins, and S. Lukes (edd.), *The Category of the Person* (Cambridge, 1985), 87–8.

about fabricating material. Extravagant anecdotal fiction is simply not in his style, and nothing suggests that his generic predecessors (if he had any) were more cavalier. That point is fundamental;[28] but it remains a point about political biography, the narrative genre, and that takes us only so far. If audiences had been interested in politicians' childhoods, the stories would still have been made up, and, as we have seen, there were other genres to transmit the gossip; anecdotes could readily have survived in oral tradition, too. On the whole, that did not happen; that illuminates the taste of the public as well as of the biographers; and that public taste invites discussion.

A second explanation goes deeper. It is striking that interest in childhood was almost confined to interest in education; given that limitation, then *of course* the most intellectual figures were likely to be the most embellished. Even Plutarch helps to illustrate this: so much of the material he does have focuses on the teachers of Pericles or Themistocles or Philopoemen, for instance, or Alcibiades' relations with Socrates, or Cicero's or Lucullus' early intellectual prowess;[29] and focuses on those themes in a fairly unimaginative way, as we shall see. Youthful *behaviour*, the development or prefiguring of later traits, features largely in modern biography, and can be telling with unintellectual figures too—even politicians. In the ancient world this receives much less anecdotal embellishment: it is not wholly neglected—there are the stories of Cato or Alcibiades, for instance—but on the whole such points tend to emerge in a much less colourful way, with vague generalizations about early promise, or early concern for justice or glory.

One further reason for modern biographers' interest in childhood is the element of social mobility in modern society.[30] It is fascinating to muse on one Prime Minister (Mrs Thatcher) being a grocer's daughter, or another (Lord Wilson) being photographed on the steps of No. 10 as a lad; or on a pop star being just an ordinary boy in Form 3B, getting into all the usual scrapes and not getting very good marks. The ordinari-

---

[28] Too fundamental to develop fully here: I discuss it in an essay on 'Truth and Fiction in Plutarch's *Lives*', to appear in D. A. Russell (ed.), *Antonine Literature* (Oxford).

[29] *Per.* 4–6; *Them.* 2; *Alc.* 6; *Cic.* 2; *Lucull.* 1. 4–8, 44 (1). 4; cf. below, pp. 232–5.

[30] I owe this point to Dr Cornell.

ness gives the reader a strange *frisson* of intimacy: such paradoxical success could have happened to people like ourselves. In the ancient world ordinary people did not on the whole become politicians, but they did sometimes become literary figures. And—a related point—ancient politicians did not feel the same need as their modern counterparts to play on the public's interest in their youth, and conspire in creating a sort of mythology of their own childhood. A striking example of that is Churchill's famous description of his first Latin lesson.[31] He *cared* about portraying himself as an early dullard, knowing that his audience would love it. Ancient political audiences were not so bothered about such things, and the politicians were less concerned to create this feeling of intimacy. They had no use for such myths.

This has brought us on to *self*-portrayal, and indeed in ancient autobiography we can see a similar, but more elaborate, contrast.[32] Egyptian and Near Eastern dynasts might talk about their childhoods, sometimes in a very individual way: thus the Egyptian Amen-hotep II (c.1447–1421 BC) wrote proudly of his youthful horsemanship, how he trained the best steeds of Memphis, how he was charmed by his visits to the pyramids; and the Assyrian Assurbanipal (668–626 BC) described his schooldays with enthusiasm—the difficulties of learning division or multiplication, or the way he was made stupid, even perhaps 'addled' (the reading is admittedly uncertain), by the beautiful script of Sumer or the obscure Akkadian.[33] Greek and Roman politicians were more

---

[31] *My Early Life* (London, 1930), 24–6.

[32] Ancient self-portrayal is treated magisterially by G. Misch, *A History of Autobiography in Antiquity* (Eng. trans., London, 1950); more recently, cf. K. J. Weintraub, *The Value of the Individual* (Chicago and London, 1978) chs. 1–2; G. W. Most, 'The Stranger's Strategem', *JHS* 109 (1989), 114–33.

[33] J. B. Pritchard, *Ancient Near Eastern Texts* (3rd edn., Princeton, NJ, 1969), i. 244–5; D. D. Luckenbill, *Ancient Records of Assyria and Babylonia* (Chicago, 1927), ii. 378–80. In general, Eastern texts developed a greater interest in politicians' childhood, as Momigliano stresses in *Development* and in 'Marcel Mauss' (though, elaborating a thesis of Helene Homeyer, he builds too much on the very special case of Cyrus I): this can be traced, for instance, in the Persian material collected by D. Gera, 'The Dialogues of the *Cyropaedia*', D. Phil. thesis (Oxford, 1987), app. 2. Such an interest may well have influenced Xenophon's portrayal directly, and through him the later Greek tradition of biographical novels. Its influence on biography itself was probably less than Momigliano suggests.

reticent.[34] It is notable, for instance, that Plutarch knew little of Aratus' youth and virtually nothing of Sulla's, though he probably knew both men's autobiographies. 'Annos undeuiginti natus ...' ['When I nineteen ...'], begins the *Res Gestae*; and though Augustus certainly said more of his youth in his *Autobiography* than he did in the other work—he did discuss his family, and seems to have mentioned Cicero's dream that he would one day be Rome's salvation—he was still well into the complicated history of 44 by book 2.[35] Political autobiography does seem to have been largely *res gestae*, the record of a man's *achievements*, with all the limitations that suggests: that was the way politicians wished to be remembered.

Literary self-portrayal came to strike a different note. At first the tone is similar enough: Plato's *Seventh Letter* begins with events when Plato was in his twenties.[36] Isocrates' *Antidosis* has a great deal to say about the value of his form of *paideia*, defending his role as a moulder of the minds of the young, but of his own youthful development he says not a word. Such works are still distinctively *apologies*, defences of a man's career: childhood material would not have sat very comfortably here (just as both Aeschines and Demosthenes attack each other's childhood with specific charges, but defend their own with brief, dignified generalizations).[37] By the Augustan period Nicolaus of Damascus was fuller, including the admiration of his contemporaries for his remarkable educational prowess (*FGrH* 90 fr. 131. 1)— not that there is much individuality in such conventional self-praise: it is indeed very similar to his account of Augustus' childhood in the *Vita Caesaris*, or to Josephus' portrayal of him-

[34] Rutilius Rufus' Latin autobiography was possibly an exception: certainly, Cicero was suspiciously well informed about his education (cf. *R-E* Ia. 1270; H. Peter, *Historicorum Romanorum Reliquiae*, i² (Leipzig, 1914), cclvii). But even here Cicero probably did not know enough to infer his age correctly (*Lael.* 101; cf. Vell. 2. 9. 6; *R-E* Ia. 1269); and it anyway seems likely that Rutilius presented himself as a philosopher as well as a politician (cf. e.g. Sen. *Ep.* 24. 4).

[35] Frs. 3, 4, 7 M; Suet. *Aug.* 8. 1 suggests that little was known of his life before his late teens. In *Vita Caesaris* Nicolaus was perhaps writing 'on Augustus' paideia' in the manner of the *Cyropaedeia* and Onesicritus (cf. Jacoby on *FGrH* 90 frs. 125–30, introductory n.); but, although he clearly knew the *Autobiography*, he could still find little more than a page to write about Augustus' youth (4–11).

[36] Riginos, *Platonica*, 39, comments on Plato's reticence about his youth throughout the dialogues.

[37] Attack: above, p. 217; defence: Aesch. 2. 146, 167; Dem. 18. 257. On autobiography as self-defence, cf. esp. Most, 'The Stranger's Stratagem'.

self in his *Autobiography*.[38] But Nicolaus adds some anecdotes
about his various early wise remarks, and those are a little more
distinctive: about Aristotle and the Muses, for instance, or
about 'education being like a journey through life' (fr. 132.
2–3). In later authors the individual note becomes more
marked. Lucian, with whatever degree of seriousness, tells of his
early skill at wax-modelling, and how it let him down when he
was apprenticed as a sculptor.[39] Galen goes further, not merely
representing himself as a singular figure but also introducing an
element of analysis and explanation: he talks of his luck in
being educated by a father who was skilled in communicating
mathematics and grammar, then at fifteen led him to philosophy, then allowed him at seventeen to switch his talents to
medicine when warned to do so by a dream; and he can analyse
what exactly he learnt from philosophy, and comment on the
value of that early mathematical training in saving him from
Pyrrhonian scepticism.[40] Galen's analysis recalls Horace's
tribute to his father (*Serm.* 1. 6. 67–92); and that is one of
several 'autobiographical' Latin poems (if that is quite the right
word) which leave very personal pictures of schooldays. Just as
Horace strikingly recalls the school where the sons of centurions
swung their satchels (*Serm.* 1. 6. 72–3), so Ovid tells how he
tried to write prose, and the words naturally fell into verse (*Tr.*
4. 10. 23–6). Once again, Marcus Aurelius seems to fill a special
position, and his 'autobiography'—if, once again, that is the
right term for the εἰς ἑαυτόν—finely describes those early days
and early influences, as he analyses precisely what he owes to
his great-grandfather, grandfather, parents, and various tutors,
and finally to the gods:

Thanks to Diognetus I learnt not to be absorbed in trivial pursuits; to
be sceptical of wizards and wonder-workers with their tales of spells,
exorcisms, and the like; to eschew cock-fighting and other such dis-
tractions.... It was the critic Alexander who put me on my guard
against unnecessary fault-finding.... Alexander the Platonist cau-
tioned me against frequent use of the words 'I am too busy' in speech
or correspondence.... To the gods I owe it that the responsibility of
my grandfather's mistress for my upbringing was brought to an early

[38] Nic. Dam. *Vit. Caes.*, esp. 4–6 (cf. above, n. 35); Jos. *Vita* 7–9.
[39] Lucian, *Somnium* 1–3.
[40] Galen, *Libr. Ord.*, p. 88; *Libr. Propr.*, p. 116.

end, and my innocence preserved. (εἰς ἑαυτόν 1. 6, 10, 12, 17, trans. Staniforth)

Marcus really analyses the formation and development of his character. That is some way from a Josephus or even a Nicolaus;[41] this is an individuality which probes the mind, analyses the ways it is different (not merely superior), and seeks to *explain* the differences. One begins to feel some intimacy with someone who writes like this, just as one later comes to know St Augustine, with his pictures of the miseries of his schooldays, or his reading Virgil and weeping for the woes of Dido, or his robbing a pear-tree, or his engaging habit of setting on passersby and turning them on to their heads, or the profound effect when he read Cicero's *Hortensius*.[42] But such self-revelation and self-analysis is developing a tendency which is already visible in Marcus, even in Lucian and Galen, and indeed in Horace and Ovid too—and of course in the poets' case in a way which goes far beyond the explicitly autobiographical poems. There is no hint that *political* autobiography was anything like so personal or so intimate, and childish stories and influences would have sat far less well with its dignity, its *gravitas*. And this note of intimacy gives an important contrast with political biography, not just autobiography. This intimacy of psychological portrayal, this revelation or analysis of the 'real person', is not something which became part of the generic tradition, any more than it became conventional to invent a fund of early anecdotes.

II

So far we have been exploiting Plutarch for what he can tell us about the biographical tradition; if he did not include childhood material, we have been provisionally assuming that the stories did not exist for him to know. That assumption is a fair one, but only because Plutarch was both extremely well informed, particularly about Greek heroes, and extremely

---

[41] As Misch, *Autobiography*, 479–80 rightly stresses. Nic. Dam. and Jos.: n. 38 above.
[42] *Conf.* 1. 8–9, 13, 2. 4–8, 3. 3–4. Augustine's interest in childhood was not confined to his own: cf. his fine portrait of his mother Monica, with her youthful weakness for wine-bibbing (9. 8).

interested in childhood and education.[43] We can indeed often
see him making the most of whatever slight information he *does*
know—in the *Sulla*, for instance, where he strains to extract
large inferences from two insubstantial anecdotes; or in the
Gracchi, where (despite an extreme paucity of material) he puts
great stress on the influence of the mother Cornelia, emphasizing that the *paideia* she gave the boys was even more influential
than their inherited nature in forming their characters (1. 7); or
in *Lysander* and *Agesilaus*, where again he has little information,
but tries hard to relate both men's personalities to their
Spartan training. The precise qualities thus explained are
admittedly very different: it is Lysander's 'ambition and contentiousness' (2. 4), but Agesilaus' 'common touch and kind-
liness of manner' (1. 5); but at least Plutarch's interest in the
subject is clear and insistent. That prompts further questions
about his technique. These examples already suggest that he
was concerned to explain character-development; elsewhere he
stresses that such development is normal with all individuals.[44]
But how effectively does he trace that development? What sorts
of points does he try to extract from childhood? Does he even *try*
to investigate the 'real person', in the way that Augustine and
Marcus and even Horace reveal themselves and analyse their
debts to others? Evidently, we shall find some differences; and
here it may be interesting to explore Christopher Gill's distinction between 'character' and 'personality', in particular his
suggestion that Plutarch's approach is typified by an interest in
'character', whereas modern writers more usually adopt the
viewpoint of 'personality'.[45] Childhood is a promising area to

---

[43] His interest in education scarcely needs exemplification: see esp. *De Profectibus in
Virtute, An Virtus Doceri Possit?, De Audiendis Poetis,* and (for more details of the psycho-
logical process) *De Virtute Morali.* For education as a civilizing and restraining force in
the *Lives,* see esp. *Cor.* 1. 4–5; *Mar.* 2. 2–4; *Them.* 2. 7; *Numa* 26(4). 10–12; B. Bucher-
Isler, *Norm und Individualität in den Biographien Plutarchs* (Noctes Romanae, 13; Berne and
Stuttgart, 1972), 21, 24, 49, 67–8.

[44] *Mor.* 392b–e; cf. e.g. 28d–e, 37d–e, 76d–e, 82b–c, 83c–f, 450 f, 453a, 551c–552d,
584e. Inherited nature was of course important too, as those passages show. Cf. esp.
A. Dihle, *Studien zur griechischen Biographie* (Göttingen, 1956), 81; Bucher-Isler, *Norm und
Individualität,* 47; C. Gill, 'The Question of Character-Development: Plutarch and
Tacitus', *CQ,* ns 33 (1983), 469–87.

[45] Ibid. He further explains his distinction of these two 'viewpoints' in this volume:
see esp. pp. 1–9. For some reservations, see C. Pelling, 'Plutarch: Roman Heroes and
Greek Culture', in J. Barnes and M. T. Griffin (edd.), *Philosophia Togata* (Oxford,
1989), 231.

test that distinction, for modern biographers so typically exploit childhood influences and experiences in explaining their subject's personality; and they are characteristically both *individuating* their subject, isolating the ways in which he or she is different from other people, and trying to *understand* and *explain* those differences. That certainly fits Gill's 'personality-viewpoint'; in what ways is Plutarch's approach different?

The most usual sort of item we find is what one could call 'the routine generalization'.

> Romulus seemed to be more intelligent and politically shrewd than Remus; in his encounters with his neighbours in the countryside he showed that he was more a leader than a follower . . . (*Rom.* 6. 3)

> Aemilius was rather different from many of his contemporaries: he had no time for judicial oratory, and the greatest distaste for demagogic techniques; it was not that he could not do such things, but that he preferred to seek a reputation for bravery, justice, and good faith—in which he immediately outshone everyone. (*Aem.* 2. 5–6)

> Cyrus had from his early youth a sort of vehemence and extreme intensity, whereas the other one [Artaxerxes] seemed gentler in everything and naturally less violent in his impulses. (*Artax.* 2. 1)

Such generalizations are indeed so routine that we can surely sense Plutarch's own hand: he is simply retrojecting aspects of the men's later careers. And in these cases at least, Plutarch is not *fabricating*, even if no such material stood in his sources. He is simply inferring what sort of youth it must have been who grew up into the man he knew: this is 'imaginative reconstruction', not fiction.[46]

Sometimes the reconstruction is more elaborate. It may make negative points: Marcellus was basically a soldier, but he 'had enough enthusiasm for Greek *paideia* and literature to make him respect and admire those who excelled in them, though he himself had never had the leisure to study or learn these subjects as much as he would have wished' (*Marc.* 1. 3). Once again, that is surely no more than an inference from Marcellus' later career: this was the man who enthusiastically carried off the Greek treasures from Syracuse, but had to devote most of his life to Rome's perpetual wars (1. 4–5); and

---

[46] For an elaboration of the distinction, see my comm. on Plutarch, *Antony* (Cambridge, 1988), 33–6; and 'Truth and Fiction'.

he also showed some of the weaknesses which Plutarch associates with the uneducated soldier, in particular a lack of self-control.[47] Or the reconstruction may be fairly circumstantial, even though it is not anecdotal. Agis had been brought up in luxury by his mother and grandmother, but even before he was twenty 'he tore off all the bodily decoration and adornment that suited his beauty, and stripped himself of all extravagance and escaped from it, priding himself on the rough cloak, and went on in search of the Spartan food, baths, and way of life' (*Ag.-Cl.* 4. 1–2). Plutarch knew of the famous ladies (cf. 7. 2–4, 19–20) and of the prominence of female wealth in this degenerate Sparta (6. 7, 7. 5–7); it was clear that Agis did pride himself on his rough Spartan cloak (14. 3–4); at some time he must have abandoned foppery for asceticism; and it would surely have been in adolescence. Further circumstantial reconstruction is found in *Coriolanus*, where we hear of the envy of his youthful rivals, 'so that they excused their inferiority by attributing it all to his physical strength' (2. 2). Similar envy emerges later in the *Life*, and it seems that this again is part of an extensive retrojection.[48]

Coriolanus is indeed interesting here. There are other occasions when Plutarch dwells on his heroes' relationships with their mothers—in the *Lives* of Agis and the Gracchi, as we have seen, and also Sertorius and Demosthenes. One does not want to make Plutarch into a mantic pre-Freudian, and his treatment does not normally go very deep; but the perspective of *Coriolanus* is more enterprising.

Marcius set himself to surpass his own record in courage. And since he was always eager to attempt fresh exploits, he added one deed of valour to another and heaped spoils upon spoils ... But while other men displayed their courage to win glory for themselves, Marcius' motive was always to please his mother. The delight that she experienced when she saw him crowned, the tears of joy she wept as she embraced him—these things were for him the supreme joy and felicity that life could offer. (Epaminondas was very similar ...) It was his mother's will and choice which dictated his marriage, and he continued to live in the same house with her, even after his wife had borne his children. (*Cor.* 4. 5–8, trans. Scott-Kilvert)

---

[47] I discuss *Marcellus* more fully in 'Roman Heroes'.
[48] So D. A. Russell, 'Plutarch's Life of Coriolanus', *JRS* 53 (1963), 21–9 at p. 23.

As Russell has brought out,[49] this is an unusually rich opportunity to analyse what Plutarch was doing to his sources, for he is clearly dependent on Dionysius of Halicarnassus; and here we can see how thoroughly he has recast Dionysius' picture. From Dionysius he knew that Coriolanus was an orphan (8. 51. 3–4); that his wife and mother seemed to share the same house (8. 40. 1 etc.); and that in the final scene he collapsed before his mother's pressure. That was enough, and this extensive psychological reconstruction seems to be his own—and it produces a very different mother from the much limper woman portrayed by Dionysius.[50] Nor, indeed, is this a particularly unrespectable or uninteresting thing to be doing. Erikson's influential biography of Martin Luther, for instance, is not playing wholly different games: he is reconstructing Luther's early relationship with his father rather than his mother, and admits frankly that his method is to start from later events and read back what the childhood relationship 'must have been' like.[51] It is vastly more elaborate than in Plutarch, with its extensive Freudian psychoanalytic apparatus; but not, perhaps, conspicuously more convincing.

Such an analysis leads us back to Gill's distinction of 'character' and 'personality'. In this case it is surely hard to deny Plutarch a considerable interest in 'personality': is Plutarch not really trying to get inside Coriolanus' skin, to work out why he acted in a way which was so distinctive, and to relate it to what was individual in his personal background? It indeed demonstrates Plutarch's capacity to draw an exemplary moral from a very individual case, for at *Cor.* 4. 1 he has already distinguished an easily quenched and a more stable form of ambition; these are evidently types which will recur in others, but the genesis *within* Coriolanus of this type of firm, stable ambition is related not merely to his nature but also to his individual circumstances and motives. *Alcibiades*, too, develops an intensely individual figure.[52] It is true that Plutarch initially

---

[49] Ibid.

[50] Cf. esp. 8. 51. 4: I discuss this instance more fully in 'Truth and Fiction'. For other reinterpretations of Dionysius' material, see Russell, 'Plutarch's Life of Coriolanus'.

[51] E. Erikson, *Young Man Luther* (New York, 1958), 37, 47, 50, 65.

[52] Though 'individual' in a way which requires further definition, and which shows some differences from modern approaches and assumptions. Cf. below, p. 236–7.

describes Alcibiades' character in a disappointing way, as
embodying 'the desire for honour and to be first in the state'
(2. 1)—as Russell says, 'one of the commonest passions in Plutarch's repertoire'.[53] So far that suits 'character', subsuming to
an exemplary class and inviting ethical judgement rather than
identifying what is individual and different. But ancient
authors often begin by stating a truth in a very general way,
then gradually correct and complement and redefine, so that
we are finally left with a subtler picture. And as *Alcibiades* progresses the man becomes much more singular: no one else could
behave with this charming outrageousness, or with such versatility and flair. Here we clearly have the *individuation* which one
associates with a 'personality'; as we also do in, say, *Lysander*,
where the man gradually emerges as an extremely un-Spartan
figure, running counter to normal expectations in several interesting ways.[54]

Whether in these cases we quite have the psychological *understanding* is a different point; we shall return to that. But there
are other portraits where the psychological register is surely
present. Consider for instance the *Theseus*. The impact on
Theseus of Heracles, whose heroics were so recent, is immediately made a psychological point. Theseus was related to
Heracles, and this, he felt, put a special burden on him;
Heracles' successes would not let him sleep; the desire for such
glory 'inflamed' him; he learnt from Heracles how to make a
punishment fit the crime or the criminal ... (6. 8, 8. 2, 11. 2). If
one compares earlier treatments of this relationship, Isocrates
for instance only talks of Theseus doing things 'that were fitting
to their kinship';[55] it seems to be Plutarch who moves into the
psychological register, and helps us to understand Theseus'
own view of his debt. Similarly in *Cleomenes*: it is Plutarch who
reconstructs the effect on the young Cleomenes of marrying
Agis' widow. 'He would ask her often about what happened,

[53] 'Plutarch, "Alcibiades" 1–16', 38.
[54] I discuss the characterization of Lysander in 'Aspects of Plutarch's Characterization', to appear in *ICS*; cf. below, p. 236.
[55] Isoc. 10. 23; cf. D. S. 4. 59. 1, and other passages listed at *R-E* Spb. xiii. 1204. The
absence of anecdote is here especially striking; contrast the pleasing Hellenistic story of
Paus. 1. 27. 7 (= *FGrH* 607 fr. 4; cf. *R-E* Spb. 1058), which he may well have known.
The seven-year-old Theseus met Heracles over dinner; Heracles took off his lion-skin,
and everyone else thought it was a real lion and fled. Theseus stayed.

and listen carefully as she told of Agis' plans and purposes . . .'
(*Ag.-Cl.* 22 (1). 3). In Cleomenes' case that was combined with
the influence of the shrewd philosopher Sphaerus (23 (2). 3–6).
As with Theseus and Coriolanus, we have a very individual set
of circumstances and influences, and an analysis of the external
pressures on the men: all this fits Gill's category of 'personality',
with the individuation, the psychology, the concern to understand. Exemplary morals can doubtless also be drawn, but we
have already noticed Plutarch's capacity to use individual cases
to point general ethical truths.

But Gill does of course have a case, and we may still feel Plutarch's analysis does not go very deep, that it takes disappoint-
ingly little empathy to understand a Theseus or a Cleomenes.
The men's youthful circumstances may be singular; the men
themselves, less so. Take another aspect of the *Theseus*. Plutarch
knew something about Theseus' early erotic adventures: he
mentions one at 29. 1, his rape of a girl called Anaxo when he
was still at Troezen, and adds that he tended to rape all the
daughters of the monstrous figures he killed. Theseus' weakness
for women will become an important theme later in the *Life*,
and will in fact be the climactic point in the epilogue compar-
ing him with his pair Romulus. Theseus carried off Helen too
when she was just a girl, he had this disturbing tendency to get
involved with Amazons, and so on. Had Plutarch wanted to
sketch in as much as possible of Theseus' personality at the
outset, he would certainly have found room for those early
rapes; that is what a modern political biographer would do, if
he happened to find himself writing a *Life* of Theseus. Plutarch
preferred to hold it back: he thought it artistically superior to
begin by dwelling on Theseus as a great hero, then gradually
introduce the various darkening shades to fill out and qualify
the picture. Again, it is the technique of gradual redefinition,
which means that ancient writers often hold back important information till later than a modern would expect.[56] Here he
wants to collect all the shady ladies together towards the end of
the *Life* to prepare the path for the final downfall. We can see

---

[56] This is in fact a refinement of the basic narrative technique discussed briefly by
Fraenkel in his comm. on Aeschylus, *Agamemnon* (Oxford, 1950), app. A; for related
techniques in other authors, cf. e.g. C. F. Russo, *Aristofane, autore di teatro* (Florence,
1962), 57–65.

something similar in the *Elder Cato*. When Plutarch first introduces Cato's proud hostility to Greek culture, he does so in
rather appreciative tones. It is only later, after he has established the grander and more impressive aspects of Cato's
personality, that he will revert to this, and begin to trace how
this attitude had weaknesses as well as strengths, and in important respects Cato was diminished by such antihellenism.[57] All
that is certainly still an interest in personality: these are individual figures, and one comes to comprehend them fairly well.
But it means that, in the early chapters, Plutarch is not pulling
out all the stops all the time to help us to understand people.
That is not his only concern, and other literary considerations
may carry more weight.

That said, one often feels that Plutarch is simply not doing as
much as he can to understand people anyway—it is not just a
question of holding things back, but of not doing it at all.
Indeed, we are now close to the real paradox of his technique.
For all his stress on education and character-development,
Plutarch's own presentation of the childhood of particular
heroes is often extraordinarily banal: so banal, indeed, that distinguished critics can claim that he gives no idea of development at all[58]—an overstatement, but an understandable one.
Antony, for instance, is one of the *Lives* which generates a real
interest in psychology, as Antony's mental torment becomes so
clear. *Given his make-up*—that blend of susceptibility, simplicity,
bluffness, and nobility—we can certainly understand why he
was so peculiarly vulnerable to Cleopatra, and then so agonized and torn; it is once again an individual portrait, a
'personality'. But Plutarch makes no real attempt to explain
why Antony came to have that particular make-up: that is precisely what a modern biographer would regard as the first
priority. Influences are indeed a major preoccupation of a

---

[57] Cf. Pelling, 'Roman Heroes'.
[58] 'The hero is there, all in one piece': V. Cilento, *Transposizioni dell' antico* (Milan,
1961), 109, quoted with approval by Russell, 'On Reading Plutarch's *Lives*', *GR* 13
(1966), 145; Russell's own discussion (144–7) is here especially interesting. Cf. also
Misch, *Autobiography*, 291; Bucher-Isler, *Norm und Individualität*, 61. The more precise
formulation of Gill, 'Character-Development', 476, is very fair: 'even when the author
regards the theme of character-formation as relevant to his narrative (as Plutarch
clearly sometimes does), the actual process of personal development is very lightly
sketched'.

modern biographer; Plutarch too is interested, as we saw when
he related traits of Lysander and Agesilaus to the Spartan educational system. But the way he introduces the point in *Lysander*
is eloquent. 'His ambition and contentiousness he derived from
his Spartan education, *and we should not greatly blame his nature for
this*' (2. 4). The point, it seems, is not introduced *primarily* to
explain: the explanatory force is a means to an end, to guide
our moral judgement and dissuade us from too hasty a condemnation. Similarly, in *Marcellus* it is important to know that
Rome was so beset by wars, but mainly so that we should not be
too harsh on Marcellus for neglecting his literary education: explanation is again the handmaiden of ethical assessment. The
treatment of family, too, is uneven. Sometimes the analysis of
family background can genuinely illuminate hereditary traits
(*Antony*, *Brutus*) or important aspects of youthful environment
(*Gracchi*, *Cleomenes*, *Coriolanus*); but just as often the treatment of
γένος is simply casual and curious, as in *Fabius*, *Pyrrhus*, *Phocion*,
or *Aemilius*.

Nor is the quest for understanding pursued insistently elsewhere. Given Plutarch's capacity for imaginative reconstruction, he might so easily have built a picutre of Lysander's first
reaction to seeing foreign luxury, a mixture perhaps of inner
contempt and ruthless determination to exploit it for Sparta's
interests. Elsewhere too we can easily identify psychological re-
constructions it might have been interesting to make. What
would the country boys Marius or the elder Cato really have
felt when they first met those smooth men of the city? How
must Demosthenes have reacted when his mother denied him
the chance to study (4. 4)? What must it have been like for
Artaxerxes to have an elder brother like Cyrus? What was the
mental effect on Themistocles of his illegitimacy? Plutarch
could make that sort of psychological reconstruction—we have
seen that from *Theseus*, *Coriolanus*, and *Cleomenes*—but, usually,
that was not his way.

Even the crucial aspect of education is presented rather than
explored. Only very rarely does Plutarch analyse precisely *what*
a figure has derived from his particular tutors or particular
philosophical school.[59] It is in fact most typically when educa-

---

[59] This is another central point which cannot be elaborated here; see 'Roman
Heroes'.

tion is deficient—in *Coriolanus*, for instance, or *Marius*,or even *Marcellus*—that the point really helps us to understand their personalities, for it then helps to explain their distinctive flaws. But *Pericles* is particularly interesting here, for this is one of the few cases where Plutarch does try to discriminate what his hero learnt from his tutors. Anaxagoras specifically taught him to be above superstition, for instance (6), and how to include impressive natural philosophy in his rhetoric (8. 1). Still, even here all his educators tend to be *telling him the same things*, in particular guiding him towards a specific political style: Anaxagoras gave him 'a majesty and φρόνημα that was too weighty for demagogy' (4. 6); Zeno then defended that dignified public demeanour (5. 3); Damon at least encouraged and guided his political ambitions, and was suspected of helping him towards tyranny (4. 3, 9. 2). That gives a hint of Plutarch's reasons for developing the theme so fully. It matters a lot to him that Pericles had so good an education, but only because with so many good tutors he must have developed a particularly high intellect and character, φρόνημα. It does not go any deeper than that: but this was itself deep enough to land Plutarch in terrible difficulties over his characterization. It was a great trouble to him that in his early years Pericles adopted various disreputable popular techniques to establish his position; and Plutarch comes up with the uncomfortable judgement that Pericles' behaviour was 'contrary to his own nature, which was not at all democratic' (7. 3).[60] He does not seem to have faced the question whether this was really compatible with his admiration for Pericles' integrity and greatness of spirit.[61] It is not that Plutarch did not

[60] *Aem.* 30. 1 provides a particularly interesting parallel. Aemilius authorized the enslavement of 150,000 men and the devastation of 70 cities. That presented Plutarch with similar problems, for Aemilius too has been presented as a distinctively cultured figure: so 'this in particular ran counter to his nature, which was reasonable and noble'. So also with the well-brought-up Gracchi, eventually led astray 'contrary to their nature' (*Gracch.* 45 (5). 5). It is figures like this whose lapses are felt as particularly problematic. Cf. Gill, 'Character-Development', 478–81: 'his analysis [of apparent character-change in *Sulla* and *Sert.*] depends on his view of good character (fully developed, reasoned excellence of character), and his conviction that it guarantees emotional continuity regardless of circumstances' (481). As Gill stresses, it is precisely *paideia* that imparts this 'fully developed, reasoned excellence of character'.

[61] P. A. Stadter, 'The Rhetoric of Plutarch's *Pericles*', *Anc. Soc.* 18 (1987), 251–69, acutely illustrates the rhetorical problems which this stage of Pericles' career presented, and the importance of this 'out of character' analysis to Plutarch's narrative strategy; but the criticisms levelled by A. W. Gomme (*Historical Commentary on Thucydides*, i

have a perfectly good model to use, that of the youthful leader
of the people who becomes more moderate as he grows older:
there is a certain amount of that in *Caesar*, *Pompey*, and even
Cleomenes. But it will not do here simply because Pericles was so
thoroughly educated, and hence *must have* developed a character which was above genuine demagogy at an early stage.
The analysis is not really very profound, and tends to regard
education simply as something you have either had or not had,
rather like a vaccination: if you have had it, then you ought to
be immune from certain dangers for ever. Here, as so often,
Plutarch's preoccupation with education is disquietingly superficial. Pericles' education created the problem for Plutarch's
characterization; but the analysis was too shallow to solve or
even illuminate that problem at all satisfactorily.

Take *Alcibiades*, too. Plutarch makes a fair amount of his
growing up in Pericles' house, and of his relationship with Socrates. But the interesting thing about it is simply that, despite
all his flair and excesses, he was still the sort of man to listen to
Socrates; there is no attempt to explore *what* Socrates might
have told him about the Athenian democracy, for instance, or
the admirable aspects of Spartan military culture. How much
more he could have made of the relationship with Pericles, too.
He has an anecdote where Alcibiades hears that Pericles is
thinking out a speech in which he would submit an account of
his magistracy to the Athenian people; Alcibiades promptly reflects that it would be 'better to think out how to *avoid* giving
accounts to the Athenians' (8. 3). But that is all. Consider the
following passage:

Alcibiades was inspired by Pericles' power, which he saw around
him every day; but he was deeply disillusioned by the ingratitude the
Athenian *dēmos* showed him. He considered where Pericles had perhaps made mistakes: perhaps his haughtiness was out of keeping with
a younger generation, perhaps more affability and charm was
needed. He also saw what Pericles had achieved, and determined that
he too, one day, would have a great achievement that would be his
own, and he would make Athens indeed prince of Greece.

(Oxford, 1956), 65–6) and W. R. Connor (*Theopompus and Fifth-Century Athens* (Washington, DC, 1968), 114) still have some force. This particular narrative strategy was an
uncomfortable one, but Pericles' education forced Plutarch to adopt it.

But Plutarch did not write that, I did. He had the wherewithal to make that sort of psychological deduction, but he had enough to say about Alcibiades if he simply *described* the peculiar flair and glamour of his political style. Trying to *understand* what made him the sort of politician he was could, in this *Life*, be discarded. Understanding people was just one among several things which he was trying to do; it was not always the priority. And that is a fundamental difference between Plutarch and modern biography.

III

This is largely because, for ancient biography, there was less in the *adult* personality to understand. Plutarch individuates his personalities; he has a rich and differentiated vocabulary for describing traits;[62] but it remains true that he, like most or all ancient writers, has an extremely *integrated* conception of character, and that his figures are consequently individual in a way which we find oddly limited.[63] The differing elements of a character are regularly brought into some sort of relationship with one another, reconciled: not exactly unified, for a character cannot be described with a single word or category, and is not a stereotype; but one element at least goes closely with another, and each element predicts the next. Antony has his simplicity, his ἁπλότης or 'oneness,'[64] which leaves him so vulnerable to flatterers or more powerful personalities (Curio, Fulvia, Cleopatra); that helps to explain why he is so passive. The simplicity goes well with his soldierliness too, and the rumbustious sense of fun he shares with his men—and then goes on to share with Cleopatra, so that the same qualities both build and destroy his greatness; the soldierliness and the leadership then go well with the nobility, which he shows for instance in honouring the fallen Brutus at Philippi (22. 6–7); that nobility goes closely with his capacity to be inflamed by Roman values and duty,

---

[62] See esp. Bucher-Isler, *Norm und Individualität*.

[63] For similar remarks, see R. B. Rutherford, 'The Philosophy of the *Odyssey*', *JHS* 106 (1986), 149–50 and n. 31. N. Rudd, *Lines of Enquiry* (Cambridge, 1976), 160–2, has a stimulating and cultured discussion to which I am indebted, though perhaps he underestimates the distance between ancient and modern assumptions. Cf. also Dihle, *Studien*, 76–81; n. 70 below.

[64] *Ant.* 24. 9–12; cf. my comm. ad loc.

and therefore to feel his shame intensely at the end—the head-in-hands scene as he sails from Actium (67), the Roman suicide (76), the fine dying words, 'a Roman, by a Roman valiantly vanquished' (77. 7). It all fits together very tightly: not as a stereotype, for these are all distinct traits; but they are closely *neighbouring* traits, and we are not surprised that Antony shows them all. In modern terms, his personality exemplifies a 'syndrome' of traits which are independent but which one naturally finds in combination (rather than a set of characteristics which are all deducible from a single original 'source-trait').[65]

This is typical.[66] Lysander's ruthlessness, deviousness, and unscrupulousness all combine readily with his personal ambition and pride. He belies all the natural expectations of a Spartan, even a travelled one—both the conventional Callicratidas and the corrupt Gylippus are developed as his foils—and is certainly individuated; yet those characteristics still bind together tightly. The younger Cato's high principle and resolution go with his Stoicism,[67] and that in its turn goes with his determination to feel shame only at the truly shameful: that explains his scruffiness, his strange but (to him) logical treatment of his women, perhaps even his drunkenness (cf. 6. 1-4); but this singleness of purpose also goes with a disabling lack of political insight and flexibility. In describing Aratus, Polybius dwelt on the paradox of his personality, his *unpredictable* blend of timidity and daring (4. 8); Plutarch turns him into a much less peculiar

---

[65] For terms and discussion, see e.g. R. B. Cattell, *The Scientific Analysis of Personality* (Harmondsworth, 1965), chs. 3-4. 'Source-traits' do not work for Plutarch's characters (*pace* e.g. A. Garzetti, *Plutarchi Vita Caesaris* (Florence, 1954), xliii-xlix): so, rightly, Bucher-Isler, *Norm und Individualität*, 60, though at 82 she oddly thinks that this detracts from their cogency as individual personalities.

[66] Much useful material can be gleaned from Bucher-Isler, *Norm und Individualität*, 25-46, though her approach is austerely lexical. Her pp. 39-45, exemplifying 'Gleichzeitiges Vorkommen gegensätzlicher Tugenden' might be expected to provide counterexamples: but in fact many of of the 'virtues' are not particularly 'contrary' (e.g. ἀνδρεία does not combine at all uncomfortably with αἰδώς, ἀπάθεια, γνώμη, δεινότης, δικαιοσύνη, or ἐγκράτεια, to take only her first six cases); and in some cases where the combination is more surprising Plutarch himself explains why the grouping is an easy one (e.g. it was natural that someone of Marcellus' period, education, and tastes should become πολεμικός, σώφρων, and φιλάνθρωπος (*Marc.* 1. 2))..

[67] This formulation may help to explain why Cato's Stoicism is allowed more explanatory force than most heroes' education or philosophy (a point noted but not explained in my 'Roman Heroes'). Stoicism more distinctively explains Cato's lack of concern for conventional opinion, and that is important in relating the scruffiness, for instance, to the high principle.

mixture. There is a particular 'sort of cleverness and understanding' which now explains his apparent inconsistencies, and
is represented as a regular feature of human nature (*Arat.* 10.
4–5).[68] Even Alcibiades' 'many-sidedness' is not the sort of
complexity we find in a modern counterpart, any more than,
say, Homer's Odysseus is 'many-sided' in quite our sense.[69] It
still requires only a rather limited list of categories to capture
an Alcibiades or an Odysseus: each trait still predicts the next,
and the reader swiftly gets the idea. Such characters are arrest-
ing, not intriguing: this is a very different sort of complexity
from what we shall see in, for instance, Strachey's General Gordon. The same really applies to Sulla, even though Plutarch
goes out of his way to stress his 'inconsistency' (*Sulla* 6. 14–15).
And Caesar's ambition, determination, and ability are the
traits which control that *Life*: we would bring out the man's
many-sidedness in a different way—one which in fact is closer
to Suetonius, whose rapidly shifting categories lend themselves
to such protean complexity.

Plutarch's 'integrated personalities' are nothing unusual in
the ancient world, though it is arguable that his integration is
peculiarly thorough and complete, as those comparisons with
Polybius and Suetonius suggest; but his characters are clearly
very different from the more complex figures which modern
writers like to develop.[70] He would indeed find it rather difficult to cope with some of the quirky combinations so familiar to
our popular awareness: the maharaja with four Rolls-Royces
whose only ambition is to compete at Wimbledon, the England
fast bowler whose delight is writing poetry, the distinguished
philosopher with an amazing knowledge of the workings of the

---

[68] I discuss *Aratus* at greater length in 'Aspects of Characterization', and try to show
how this difference in approach leads Plutarch to recast the emphasis and detail of
Polybius' narrative.

[69] Cf. esp. Rutherford, 'Philosophy'. The same goes for Tacitus' Licinius Mucianus
(*Hist.* 1. 10) and Horace's Tigellius (*Serm.* 1. 3. 1–19), *pace* Rudd, *Lines of Enquiry*, 161–
2. Such ancient figures are, in Aristotelian terms, 'consistently inconsistent' (*Poet.*
1454^{a}27–8)—and much more *predictably* inconsistent than modern counterparts.
Mucianus' inconsistency, influenced as it is by Sallust's Sulla and Catiline (*BJ* 95, *BC*
5), is indeed stereotyped rather than singular (cf. J. Griffin, *Latin Poets and Roman Life*
(London, 1985), 39–40). Plutarch's Sulla too has something in common with this type.

[70] For most interesting treatments of ancient and modern assumptions, cf. Dihle,
Studien, 76–81, which I discuss in more detail in 'Aspects of Characterization', and
S. Halliwell, *Aristotle's Poetics* (London, 1986), 149–52.

British telephone system. And the more developed portraits of
formal biography tell the same story. Lytton Strachey's 'New
Biography' is in some ways a special case as his work was so
consciously iconoclastic, but it makes the point particularly
plain. Stratchey is always straining for the *un*expected. Here we
are presented with personalities whose traits do not sit at all
comfortably together, whose combination in a single individual
is paradoxical: Gordon earnestly tracing the location of Old
Testament sites around Jerusalem, Bible in hand; but also
approaching military operations with vigour and dynamism;
but also hiding himself from his troops and staff for bouts of
brandy and soda; but also, when coolly sober, bombarding the
Ambassador in Cairo with utterly contradictory telegrams
about the military situation, sometimes thirty a day. Dr Arnold
towers darkly in his gown and religion; he also finds it humanly
difficult to get out of bed in the morning; he also cavorts with
his children on the hearthrug; he also suffers from a strange
hypochondria. When *Eminent Victorians* was published, Virginia
Woolf wrote to Strachey about his Gordon:[71]

> My only criticism, which I ought to hesitate to give until a second
> reading, is that I'm not sure whether the character of Gordon alto-
> gether 'convinces'. I felt a little difficulty in bridging the gulfs, but I
> rather think this is inevitable from the method, which flashes light
> and dark this side and that . . .

These 'gulfs' capture something quite important. One may dispute whether Strachey does make Gordon convincing; but if he
does, it is a great tribute to his art, and it is indeed a primary
task of a biographer in this genre to bring together such almost
random, sometimes conflicting, traits in a single individual
personality. And the only thing that brings them together is
that single individual: Gordon may have combined all those
traits, but there is little in the traits themselves to predispose us
to expect their combination.
    This contrast naturally affects the characters' exemplary
quality. Even with Plutarch's most individual figures, we can
still naturally talk about what may happen to '*a sort of person like*
Antony' when he encounters a '*a sort of person like* Cleopatra':

    [71] Letter of 28 Dec. 1917: Virginia Woolf and Lytton Strachey, *Letters*, ed. L. Woolf
and J. Strachey (London, 1956), 68.

such figures will certainly not recur often, but at least their traits combine so readily that a recurrence is conceivable. One would not talk of 'a sort of person like General Gordon', for so paradoxical a combination must be unique. It would of course be a mistake to think that this was Plutarch's *reason* for the integration, to believe that he characterizes in this way to make the extraction of morals more straightforward.[72] That is to start from the wrong end, as if our modern assumptions were unquestionably right or natural, and Plutarch's different approach required explanation. In fact, this taste for the quirky is very much a modern fad. Plutarch's characterizing technique rests on assumptions which he inherited and saw no reason to question, and, indeed, which few other cultures fundamentally questioned until the nineteenth century (though it is true that few cultures integrated quite so thoroughly as the Greeks).[73] Similar points—and similar modern comparisons—can so easily be made with other Hellenic genres, epic, historiography, or drama: it makes much more sense to talk of 'a sort of person like Odysseus' or Hector or Pericles or Orestes than 'a sort of person like Pierre' or Anna or Churchill or Hamlet—or even less dominating figures such as Masha or Nina in *The Seagull*.[74]

[72] The integration does not even invariably aid the moralism. One of his ethical interests is the demonstration that human nature is very varied, and can produce *people like this* (cf. esp. *Cim.* 2. 5; *Ag.-Cl.* 37 (16). 8), an insight which should encourage rather than impede an interest in idiosyncrasy.

[73] Shakespeare's characters strike us as more individualized than their ancient counterparts (see J. P. Gould, 'Dramatic Character and "Human Intelligibility" in Greek Tragedy', *PCPS*, NS 24 (1978), 46–8); but Dr Johnson praised them differently: 'In the writings of other poets a character is too often an individual: in Shakespeare it is commonly a species' (Preface to his 1765 edn. = *Dr Johnson on Shakespeare*, ed. W. K. Wimsatt (Harmondsworth, 1960), 59). Johnson's tastes were those of his day. Cf. M. C. Bradbrook's discussion. *Themes and Conventions of Elizabethan Tragedy* (Cambridge, 1935), 50–4.

[74] The nearest ancient parallel to a modern 'complex personality' is perhaps afforded by divine 'personalities'. Gods do often combine a multiplicity of traits or associations which do not group naturally, most clearly Apollo and Hermes, and arguably Artemis: that, doubtless, partly springs from the amalgamation of the associations of discrete local cults (see e.g. C. Sourvinou-Inwood, 'Persephone and Aphrodite at Locris: A Model for Personality Definitions in Greek Religion', *JHS* 98 (1978), 101–21). The treatment of childhood is consequently more varied: the Homeric Hymn to Hermes, for instance, does introduce that range of different qualities, all pointed by anecdotes about the god's first days—not merely the inventiveness (making the lyre), the mischief-making (the stealing of Apollo's cattle, both on his first day alive), and the charm he exercises on both Zeus and Apollo himself, all qualities which could be held to be neighbouring, but also the flair for beguiling song, which seems less naturally

The integrating assumptions clearly went very deep, and it would be facile to derive them from a straightforward interest in the exemplary. The integration certainly goes well with the drawing of exemplary morals, and in some cases will have encouraged or facilitated that process; equally, the taste for morals reinforced the assumption of integration; but the causal relation of the two was surely delicate and tangled—and, of course, wholly unconscious.

This fundamental difference between ancient and modern has its impact on the treatment of childhood. Plutarch can give that telling anecdote or generalization prefiguring the 'sort of person' that Alcibiades or Cato or Aratus is going to be. It is not going to be a paradoxical combination of divergent traits, any or all of which might be usefully prefigured. And Plutarch can develop his technique of gradual refinement: the traits he is going to develop will not *wholly* call into question those which we know from the beginning, they will just sharpen and complement them. Contrast Strachey on Florence Nightingale:

> What was that secret voice in her ear, if it was not a call? Why had she felt, from her earliest years, those mysterious promptings towards . . . she hardly knew what, but something very different from anything around her? Why, as a child in the nursery, where her sister had shown a healthy pleasure in tearing her dolls to pieces, had *she* shown an almost morbid one in sewing them up again? (*Eminent Victorians* (London, 1918), 120)

One can tell how Plutarch would have used the story of the dolls: a straightforward, and not very imaginative, foretaste of her later concern for healing. Strachey is very different: now the elder sister takes 'a healthy pleasure' in tearing the dolls apart, while Florence's behaviour is 'almost morbid': 'it was very odd; what could be the matter with dear Flo?' Strachey brings out how paradoxical and unexpected the behaviour is: it still prefigures the later person, who is demoniacal in her pressure for work, driving more passive assistants into early graves, but it prefigures those more individual traits in a distinctly

---

related. This contrast of divine and human raises interesting points: for instance, an unusually singular combination of human traits is presented by Achilles in the *Iliad*, and one wonders about the relevance of his divine parentage. But that cannot be pursued here.

more individual way. Still, elaboration need not guarantee success, and this is not good writing. The anecdote stretches credibility ('it is difficult to think of dainty Parthe "tearing up dolls",' wrote an indignant family friend[75]); the psychology is dark but forced. Plutarchan simplicity and restraint might after all have been fairer.

Childhood anecdotes also prefigure the clashing elements in a personality. It is distinctive of Strachey's Cardinal Manning that his ability and ambition are more weighty than his piety, though the piety is real enough; and the clash of these elements leads to psychological strain, which Manning is powerful enough to cope with—again, we notice how *singular* a person this is, and how un-Plutarchan it is to have such conflicting tensions. So in his childhood we have the piety, in a very evangelical household. At the age of four he was told by a cousin of six that God wrote down everything we did wrong, and for some days his mother found him sitting under a kind of writing-table in great fear. 'I never forgot this at any time in my life, and it has been a great grace to me', wrote Manning later—and Strachey notes it, with a typical, slightly malicious hint of the self-righteousness as well as the piety. 'Yet', Strachey goes on, 'on the whole he led the unspiritual life of an ordinary schoolboy', and more noticeable was 'a certain dexterity of conduct'. At Harrow

he went out of bounds, and a master, riding by and seeing him on the other side of a field, tied his horse to a gate, and ran after him. The astute youth outran the master, fetched a circle, reached the gate, jumped on to the horse's back and rode off. (*Eminent Victorians*, 6)

It is a much less expected story for a future Cardinal, and yet it prefigures something more important than the piety. So childhood anecdotes are here used to focus two conflicting traits, and the paradoxical one carries the greater weight. The whole technique is more complex, and the characterization again incomparably more singular, than in Plutarch.

With so much more to understand in the adult figures, there

---

[75] Mrs Rosalind Nashe, in an entertaining article in *Ninteenth Century*, 103 (1928), 258–65 (cit. C. R. Sanders, *Lytton Strachey: His Mind and Art* (Port Washington and London, 1957), 203. For other criticisms of the passage, see M. Holroyd, *Lytton Strachey: The Years of Achievement 1910–1932* (London, 1968), 287–8.

is therefore more to prefigure; we might expect there to be more
for the child to develop, too, and more that could be related to
specific influences. Here we can trace a growing interest
through Strachey's *œuvre*. A few points are traceable even in
Eminent Victorians: Manning's evangelical home, or Nightingale's closeted childhood in the Derbyshire country house,
carry some explanatory force; or there is the more delicious
point about Arnold:

> It is true that, as a schoolboy, a certain pompousness in the style of his
> letters home suggested to the more clear-sighted among his relatives
> the possibility that young Thomas might grow up into a prig; but,
> after all, what else could be expected from a child who, at the age of
> three, had been presented by his father, as a reward for proficiency in
> his studies, with the twenty-four volumes of Smollett's *History of
> England*? (*Eminent Victorians*, 183–4)

But it is left at that, and there is no clear interest in tracing in
detail how particular influences shaped a child's development.
Most of the 'understanding' is to be reached by considering the
man himself or the woman herself, not their society; that is still
in the Plutarchan tradition. And indeed, there is comparatively
little development to trace: Manning is already showing the
same tensions as later.

By *Queen Victoria* that has changed. We have a chapter on
'Antecedents' as well as one on 'Childhood', and Strachey is
very concerned indeed to depict the importance of the uneasy
atmosphere in the royal family. Her christening, for instance,
provoked a marvellously embarrassing scene;[76] that does reveal
something about the uncomfortable background against which
she grew up—the background which finally erupted in a public
tirade against Victoria's mother, the Duchess of Kent, delivered by William IV before 100 embarrassed guests at a birth-
day dinner, again a story in which Strachey reveals. He is
concerned to point influences, too: of governesses, of her uncle
the king of Belgium, of her father's political sympathies and
associations, and of the lack of robust masculine friends—'It
was her misfortune that the mental atmosphere which sur-
rounded her during these years of adolescence was almost
entirely feminine'—which may explain why she was so mes-

merized when young handsome male cousins, including the youthful Prince Albert, visited. Then in *Elizabeth and Essex* Strachey points Elizabeth's 'seriously warped sexual organization', crucial for understanding the way she handled English noblemen and foreign kings. This is explained by 'the profound psychological disturbances of her childhood'—the early beheading of her mother, the bewildering sequence of stepmothers, finally the extraordinary sexual attention of Catherine Parr's later husband Thomas Seymour, with his engaging habit of bounding into her room, tickling her in bed, and slapping her bottom. The Freudian influence by now is clear, and this detailed tracing of influences takes us some distance from Plutarch.

This preoccupation with influences and understanding is of course what we now expect. It is particularly clear in Erikson, but for instance Emil Ludwig's *Bismarck* is also similar—the bad relations with his distant, theatrical mother, always too busy to have him home, which led to his neurosis, cynicism, and 'refractory and unequable nature';[77] no wonder he came to despise the liberal ideas his mother espoused, and no wonder his reaction was so ambivalent to the harsh, whipping, military school his mother sent him to. Tickling, bottom-slapping, and whipping tend to be less typical of the more regular genre of political biography, less highly wrought than Strachey, less self-conscious and artistically pretentious, distinctly more respectful, and in some ways closer to the grave, dignified genre of multi-volume Victorian biography which Strachey was striving to replace. But this preoccupation with influences and understanding remains dominant. Almost at random, one could take Philip Williams's fine book on Hugh Gaitskell.[78]

There are in fact some surprising similarities with Plutarch. Williams too is concerned with education, though the points are made in greater detail. The Dragon School was 'a highly unorthodox and notably unconventional preparatory school ... masters were known by their nicknames'. Later, his public school Winchester was 'much less philistine than most of its contemporaries. Intellect was not despised as at Rugby or Harrow.' There is often the routine generalization, more

[77] Emil Ludwig, *Bismarck* (Eng. trans., London, 1927), 29.
[78] *Hugh Gaitskell* (London, 1979).

pointed than in Plutarch but showing rather the same flavour: 'at prep school, Winchester, and Oxford alike, he was unusually unpossessive and behaved as a "natural socialist", treating everyone as equal and everything as held in common'. One wonders exactly what that means, and what really lies behind it: surely a measure of retrojection from later years? And there is the telling anecdote, too, which one suspects is not always subjected to rigorous historical criticism: 'he once startled a strange lady in the street by chanting to her from the pram: "Soon shall you and I be lying | Each within our narrow tomb"'. But what is different here is that perpetual quest for understanding, clearly the author's first priority. The chapter is headed 'Seeking Something to Fight For'—the psychological register which Plutarch sometimes moves into, but generally eschews. There is the interest, again, in isolating influences: 'to his mother he owed the gaiety and friendliness . . . the strong Burma connections had—surprisingly—no apparent influence on his life, outlook, or policy. Separation from his parents possibly did have such an influence'; 'Winchester's heavy emphasis on self-restraint helped Hugh to keep under firm control the strong emotions that seethed beneath a placid surface.'

What would Plutarch have made of all that? It is quite alien to his manner, even in the passages where he is trying to understand: we are moving into a quite different register when we seek to isolate such broad influences. Plutarch would have been perplexed; and he would also have felt the irony that he is now regarded as the man with the taste for fiction, while the moderns regard themselves as reconstructing truth. Williams's reconstruction of these influences is much more moderate and cogent than those of Strachey, Erikson, or Ludwig; but all rest on a very slender foundation. Winchester was like that, and Gaitskell was like that too; Bismarck's mother and Luther's father were unsatisfactory, and Bismarck and Luther turned out the way they did; Thomas Seymour was sexually peculiar, and Elizabeth was arguably a bit peculiar too; hence there *must have been* a causal connection. Plutarch would have thought all this a new, peculiar brand of imaginative reconstruction; and I am not sure that he would have been too impressed.

11
Conclusion

CHRISTOPHER PELLING

We must not gloss over the point. Just as the Greeks failed to develop a genuine discipline of historical research, so also they were unable to grasp the true nature of a human being. The observer always remained detached, when he should have been placing himself in the other man's soul. Instead of understanding, he praises or blames. And always he regards a man as something complete and entire, never as anything that develops. How could they have understood the contradictions that are found in every soul of any richness, and whose unification alone creates a person's individuality? Only their tragedians (for Menander's comedy certainly fell short of it) had the capacity to create whole persons of the sort where we can sense how they must have become the way they are, through life's experiences and despite life's experiences. And then, of course, there was Plato: but Plato at least potentially burst through virtually all the limitations of the Greek spirit. I do not here discuss how the Greeks came to be like this: in the sixth and fifth centuries there was the potential for a quite different development. But, since they did develop in this way, we must suppose that they grasped little, and conveyed less, of genuine human individuality. The universal culture and the later philosophies, all aimed at normal humans, reduced this to its own level. How different it was with the Romans of the same period! (For the later Hellenizing culture of the Roman empire again imposed its own level.) One cannot stress their superiority enough. We hear of Lucilius, and know of Horace, how poetry became the revelation of the poet's self: and then there is Cicero, all of whose works breathe his rich individuality, despite all the rhetoric. That is a whole person. His Greek contemporaries were, at best, professors.

So wrote Wilamowitz in 1907.[1] Much of this volume could serve as an extended critique of that text.

Greek audiences did not always shy from the particular: any narrative page of Herodotus or Thucydides shows that, and

---

[1] *Internationale Wochenschrift für Wissenschaft, Kunst und Technik*, 1 (1907), 1109–10 (= *Kleine Schriften*, vi (Berlin and Amsterdam, 1972), 124).

anyway one has only to consider the plots of tragedy. No doubt the audience reaction to a fine play would involve pity and fear, as Aristotle thought (*Poet.* 1449ᵃ27, 1453ᵃ2–7), and no doubt an important ingredient in that response was a self-regarding feeling of 'it could happen to me'—or, as Aristotle defines 'pity' more carefully in the *Rhetoric*, a feeling that 'it, or something like it, could happen to me, or someone close to me'.[2] But what precisely would that 'it' be? The events of a tragedy are most peculiar, reflecting circumstances which could not remotely recur in a straightforward way in the audience's own lives. After all, how often are we likely to find ourselves having to murder our mother, or marry her, or defy an edict to bury our brother? The precise way in which the audience developed their response may be elusive: perhaps we should speak simply of unreflective emotional sympathy, a capacity of an audience to empathize even with such massive figures in such extraordinary tales; but some at least may have intellectualized, drawing exemplary morals from the most individual of cases. If even the greatest of men is as vulnerable as Oedipus, how much more vulnerable must they be themselves; if a disordered great house can produce such dreadful doings and dilemmas, then even their own house might provide its less extravagant analogies—and they could feel that without exactly fearing that their wives might all turn out to be Clytemnestras, or (if women were present) their husbands to be Jasons. Either way, the extraordinariness of the circumstances did not impede the empathy or the moralism.

Yet that extraordinariness was not extended to characters: circumstances are highly particular, characters highly normative. Not types, perhaps, or at least not exactly: we shall discuss that in a moment. But it is hard to disagree with Malcolm Heath's assessment:

such Sophoclean characters as Electra or Philoctetes carry great dramatic conviction, because their individuality has been worked out in the details of the text; but the individuality that is thus worked out is not in itself detailed or subtly nuanced: it consists of a few basic traits, clearly and consistently delineated.[3]

---

[2] *Rh.* 1385ᵇ13–20; cf. 1386ᵃ1–3, 23–39.
[3] *The Poetics of Greek Tragedy* (London, 1987), 119.

Sometimes those basic traits are very few indeed, with Lycus in *Heracles*, for instance, or Jason, or Tecmessa, or Alcestis, or even Creon in *Antigone*; but even in more developed portraits, even where a figure is demonically abnormal or agonized by inner torment, the characteristics are still very broadly sketched: Clytemnestra, Pentheus, Hecuba, Phaedra, Hippolytus, Ajax, Medea. Not that the simplicity detracts from the power: indeed, the contrary is often the case, as the same points insistently impose themselves on the audience's consciousness. But there is not much *delicacy* here—not at least in the choice or grouping of traits, though there may well be in the techniques and language by which they are conveyed—and we are far removed from modern drama. The contrast between circumstances and characters is neatly pointed by John Jones's comparison of Orestes and Hamlet:

> while Hamlet is extraordinary, his situation is commonplace in that many men—men of unremarkable capacities—could have handled it efficiently. Contrast the Aeschylean Orestes, whose situation is anything but commonplace . . . Orestes has a task which only he can perform, while Hamlet has a task which almost anyone but him can perform.[4]

Strength and simplicity of characterization need not exclude 'placing oneself in the other man's soul', in Wilamowitz's phrase: as Halliwell, Easterling, Goldhill, Griffin, and I all emphasize, that is often exactly what authors invite their audiences to do, even if the psychology required is sometimes rather shallow for our tastes. But whatever be the case with the authors or audiences of drama, it is striking that figures within the plays themselves are so bad at this sort of empathetic understanding. Odysseus in the *Ajax* may manage it, but that is remarkable, and felt as such.[5] When we ponder a figure in everyday life, we are often aided by our discussions with others who have closer or different knowledge of the person; similarly, a familiar scene in modern drama consists of two people discussing an absent third, with comments that may not always be unimpeachably accurate, but which still guide and deepen an audience's insight. Such discussions come naturally to modern

---

[4] *On Aristotle and Greek Tragedy* (London, 1962), 42–3.
[5] Cf. also Gill, pp. 20–1.

Western culture; indeed, psychologists often refer to the so-
called 'actor–observer effect', whereby 'in general, we tend to
perceive our own behaviour as occurring largely in response to
various situational factors, but that of others whom we observe
as stemming primarily from internal dispositions or characteristics'[6]––and do so increasingly as we develop to maturity. In
other words, we explain our own conduct by relating it to the
circumstances which provoked it––we justify it, in fact––but like
to explain others' behaviour by analysing their characters.
There is some evidence that this 'effect' varies from one culture
to another––that in Hindu culture for instance, where the concept of a person is more holistic and assumes a greater dependence on social context, the opposite tends to be found:[7] there
adults are far readier to categorize both deviant and socially
commended behaviour of others in terms of circumstances
rather than dispositions. Greek literature aligns more closely
with the Hindu than the Western experience. As Gill remarks,
we are in fact inured by Greek drama to expect 'the person concerned to explain her acts by reference to her beliefs and
desires, and . . . the mode of explanation by external causes to
be used by an outside observer'[8]––that is, the very opposite of
the Western actor–observer distinction. There are exceptions,
of course: Gill's own example of Achilles and Diomedes in *Iliad*
9 is one.[9] But the generalization is surely right, and it *is* peculiarly bizarre and exceptional when Eteocles accepts an external chain of causes as if it were his own motive. So often what
analysis we find comes from the principals themselves, reflecting on their own behaviour. To understand a Phaedra, a
Hippolytus, a Medea, or a Clytemnestra, we must start from
the figures themselves, from their actions, and what they say
about themselves and their thoughts. Of course, we do find
observers too commenting on actions, especially the chorus, but
their first response is often to relate them to some wider pattern
of human experience; and when they do explain them in terms

---

[6] S. T. Fiske and S. E. Taylor, *Social Cognition* (New York, 1984), 64. I am here most
grateful to Mansur Lalljee for references and discussion.
[7] J. G. Miller, 'Culture and the Development of Everyday Social Explanations',
Journal of Personality and Social Psychology, 46 (1984), 961–78.
[8] p. 23.
[9] p. 14.

of the characters, it is strikingly rare that their remarks show any depth or perspicacity. They much more often appal us with their crassness: tragedy so regularly explores the failures of communication and understanding among figures who are closely linked, and in an ordered world should be harmonized. The chorus of *Antigone* sing of *erōs*, and Goldhill is surely right that this is highly relevant to the action:[10] it does illuminate what might typically be expected of an ephebe or a *parthenos*, and points a normal human pattern. But it is far from clear that they are displaying any fundamental *insight* into the abnormal Antigone, or even Haemon. As so often, the remarks of observers fail to deepen our understanding; or if they do, it is only because they clash with it, and bring out how strange, unexpected, and easily misconstrued the events and figure really are.

This in itself assumes we have 'constructed' a character, in Easterling's phrase, which we can then measure against others' comments. The problems in such construction are clear. There is the need to readjust for the differing perceptions, values, and assumptions of a Greek audience: Goldhill is again clearly right, they would *not* quite love and hate as we do, and the assumptions of appropriate or disquieting behaviour for a virgin, or a mother, or a son, or simply a citizen may be far removed from our own.[11] Such imaginative cultural leaps may not be different in type from those we make every day, in seeking to engage sympathetically with people of different ages, cultures, and moral or religious values, but they are very different in degree. There are also the barriers imposed by Greek dramatic conventions, as Gould in particular has stressed:[12] the form and rhythm of a confrontation scene, for instance, or the distinctive registers of lyric monody, stichomythia, or rhesis. Again, our adjustments do not differ in type from those we make in adapting to the conventions of any theatre, including our own; but again they may differ in degree. Still, the adjustments can be made. One of Gould's principal examples was the confrontation of Phaedra and the Nurse in *Hippolytus*, certainly

---

[10] pp. 101–5.

[11] p. 105. Goldhill's own book *Reading Greek Tragedy* (Cambridge, 1986) is a fine illustration of the analysis required to make the necessary cultural shifts.

[12] J. P. Gould, 'Dramatic Character and "Human Intelligibility" in Greek Tragedy', *PCPS* 24 (1978), 43–67.

a sequence moulded by generic expectations, and certainly also
a case where 'love' (*erōs*) is in point; yet many will find Griffin's
analysis of this scene persuasive:[13] we are invited to enter into
Phaedra's inner consciousness (a point which Gould would
allow, but not emphasize[14]), and we respond most effectively.
Another of Gould's examples was the later confrontation of
Theseus and Hippolytus, formally a more regular ἀγών, in
which this time 'hate' is not far away. Yet it is important that
we feel this as a *travesty* of an ἀγών, one in which the issue is pre-
judged; and what renders it a travesty is not a formal or structural feature, nor even just the intricacies of the plot. It is the
nature of the two men involved, and their utter lack of
understanding—that crassness where there should be harmony, in fact. This is a matter of their characters, their *ēthē*, and
we can sense it well enough. True, we cannot use every statement as a character-marker in quite the way we would with a
modern play. To take one of Gould's examples, when Hippolytus wishes 'that I could stand opposite and view myself, to weep
for my own misfortune' (1078–9), it would be rash to draw
large conclusions about a taste for self-contemplation and self-
worship:[15] this rather points to the objective fact that Hippolytus is dying isolated, and dying for the lack of a friend to witness for him (1022)—'witnessing' has indeed been a vital theme
of the play. Now Phaedra's body is the only, decisive witness
(972), securing that testimony to her noble acts which she
always sought (403–4). There is no one to speak or weep for
him, any more than there is anyone but Antigone herself to
weep for her as she goes to her death:[16] in both cases, it is the
objective fact of isolation that the audience senses, more than
Hippolytus' self-righteousness or Antigone's emotional collapse. We must be careful, then, which character-markers we
use, but the clash of characters remains basic to the scene; and
we can understand it.

   In everyday life we try to understand people all the time:
why he is underperforming, why depressed, why bumptious,

[13] pp. 133–5.
[14] 'Dramatic Character', 56–7.
[15] R. P. Winnington-Ingram, 'Hippolytus: A Study in Causation', in *Entr. Hardt*, vi.
Euripide (Geneva, 1958), 186–7; contrast Gould, 'Dramatic Character', 57–8.
[16] R. A. S. Seaford, 'The Last Bath of Agamemnon', *CQ*, NS 34 (1984), 253–4.

why insecure; how she can possibly like Wagner, horror films, or pot noodles; why he is so irritatingly cheerful this early in the morning. Typically we are concerned with *patterns* of behaviour, and we are seeking some general statement about the individual's circumstances and psychic make-up which will make those patterns more intelligible, and possibly reversible. One distinctive difference in the ancient literary genres, especially drama, is their natural concentration on particular actions or decisions, and their exploration of character in the context of those decisions. It is no longer patterns of behaviour for their own sake that we are trying to penetrate, but patterns that serve as backgrounds for a particular agonizing choice: should Orestes kill his mother, should Oedipus accept Polynices' supplication, should Ajax relent, should Phaedra give in to the Nurse, should Odysseus kill the suitors, should Achilles go back to the fight, should Socrates try to escape execution? No wonder so much of the complexity we do find centres on psychic conflict, on the peculiar agonizing which attends a dilemma; and no wonder so much of the modern discussion of Homeric psychology has centred on the 'divided soul' which seems to be implied by the way such decisions are reached. Here Halliwell's discussion seems cogent:[17] even to describe Odysseus as 'speaking to *his* soul' does imply a concept of self, however stylized the manner of its articulation;[18] and the variation of function applied to the individual elements of the body implies that this is a convenience of language much more than a literal biological construct.[19] What does *not*, surely, follow is the claim that 'in such a psychology as this the idea of "decision" is unlikely to be important':[20] on the contrary, we seem to have a clear, if stylized, way of expressing—precisely— *decisions*; and the choice of language implies a self which, from the beginning, carries its own intimations of complexity.

But this sort of 'complexity' is not quite what we regularly mean by the term: we are closer to Wilamowitz's 'contradictions

[17] pp. 36–42.

[18] Cf. P. F. Strawson, *Individuals* (London, 1959), 96–7.

[19] Cf. G. Lienhardt, in M. Carrithers, S. Collins, and S. Lukes (edd.), *The Category of the Person: Anthropology, Philosophy, History* (Cambridge, 1985), 148–50 (similar language phenomena among the African Dinka).

[20] A. W. H. Adkins, *From the Many to the One* (London, 1970), 23.

that are found in every soul of any richness'—a complexity of *trait*, rather than of decision-making or of mental
geography. Wilamowitz's remark recalls that of Pirandello,
quoted by Silk:[21] 'each one of us believes himself to be a single
person. But it's not true ... each one of us is many persons.'
And it is interesting that, in their different ways, Brecht,
Strindberg, Pirandello, and even Strachey present fragmented,
discontinuous personalities[22] (though Strachey more clearly
implies an underlying unity—Wilamowitz's 'unification' which
'alone creates a person's individuality'); but they present that
discontinuity as itself reflecting an important aspect of reality,
either the reality of the individual figure or that of the fragmented world in which he lives. The discontinuous, 'imagist'
characterization which Silk finds in Aristophanes seems rather
different, less a refraction of reality than a flight from it. Silk's
analysis in some ways recalls the points made by Griffin about
the *Iphigeneia in Aulis*, where again we 'contemplate and experience a kaleidoscopic succession of emotions, only loosely
attached to particular persons';[23] but the differences between
comedy and even this most discontinuous of tragedies are much
more striking, and illuminate some of the questions about
'mental background' which Silk raises in the final pages of his
essay.[24] Griffin rightly insists that, even in the *Iphigeneia in Aulis*,
'enough of a psychological explanation is given to allow us to
find the events humanly intelligible': even if it is unimportant
to fill in any specific mental background, it still remains vital to
that intelligibility that a background *could* be filled in, if we or
the poet chose. It is just that the background would not be particularly interesting or distinctive, and its sketching is not central to his, or our, concerns. It is hard to think that this is true
with a Mnesilochus or a Xanthias. In their case it is plausible to
think that we 'switch mentalist assumptions on and off like a
tap', in Silk's phrase, and are unconcerned when an 'imagist'
passage fails to fit the assumptions another passage encouraged;
or at least that we construct mental backgrounds for particular
actions without trying to build them into an organic whole.

---

[21] p. 166.
[22] For Brecht and Strindberg, see Silk, ibid.; for Strachey, my chapter, pp. 238–43.
[23] p. 145.
[24] p. 172.

The terms on which we credit Agamemnon or Achilles or Iphigencia with a mind seem rather different: not exactly non-realist, but with a conspiratorial agreement between poet and audience that here the mind is not the focus of interest.

Brought up on post-Romantic assumptions and literature, especially the nineteenth- and twentieth-century novel, we may find that surprising. We do indeed expect our characters to be much more idiosyncratic, and share Wilamowitz's expectations of complexity and contradictions. We have this belief in the unique and unrepeatable nature of any individual whom we are required to take seriously, and we have correspondingly more interest in *development*, seeking to explain how so singular a mix of traits could have formed—another concern Wilamowitz thought disablingly absent from the Greeks. (An overstatement, this, as Halliwell and I both argue; but a fairly natural one.) This hankering for the idiosyncratic is a strange and recent prejudice, and in itself it is easily discardable, for we quickly grasp that the characters of tragedy (at least) do not behave in that sort of *uniquely* distinctive way. But it is important to distinguish 'idiosyncratic' from 'individual';[25] if we are left with a strong feeling of the individuality of each of (say) Sophocles' heroes, despite the lack of idiosyncrasy,[26] the nature of that residual individuality is not easy to determine or describe. Easterling has stressed Sophocles' skill in seizing on circumstantial detail, his ability to make us feel what it must be like to be in the position of a Philoctetes or an Oedipus or an Ajax. That is partly the consequence of Sophocles' peculiar gift for communicating, for instance, the pure tactile sense of Philoctetes' festering wound or Oedipus' filth; but, more generally, we can understand that someone confronted by an accusation he knows to be false might indeed omit certain crucial questions, and launch certain wild accusations; the ambiguities we might feel, the perplexity over which interpretation of Antigone's conduct we choose, again reinforce our feeling of a real consciousness behind her words and actions; and the peculiar power of Philoctetes' poetry again conveys a particular

---

[25] P. E. Easterling, 'Character in Sophocles', *G & R* 24 (1977), 121, 124 (= E. Segal (ed.), *Oxford Readings in Greek Tragedy* (Oxford, 1983), 138, 140–1); cf. Goldhill, pp. 101–2; id., *Reading Greek Tragedy*, 174.

[26] Easterling, 'Character in Sophocles', 124 (= *Oxford Readings*, 140–1).

and individual impression of his lonely plight, and the intensity
of his response. A feeling of reality in the development of events,
then, produces a strong sense of involvement with the action
and its characters: the 'human intelligibility' of the scene dis-
tracts us from seeking arcane explanations in terms of individual, distinctive motives. When we see Agamemnon
persuaded to walk on the tapestries, we need not infer any
motives peculiar to him, but rather ones which we find intelligible in wider human terms: we are content to be convinced
that 'someone of such-and-such a type would naturally react
like this'.[27]

That seems to be right, but we can still ask how differentiated
the concept of 'such-and-such a type' really is: do we mean
simply *any* human at all who was so prosperous? Or any human
with a wife like Clytemnestra? Or any human with a natural
hubristic streak, or a weakness of stature, or even a certain
gentlemanliness or tiredness? We can easily find ourselves rephrasing the conventional questions in these slightly different
terms. And what of Sophocles' central figures? Certainly their
heroic isolation and intransigence show some similarities—
Ajax, Antigone, Oedipus, Philoctetes, Electra—but it would
surely be inadequate to regard these as straightforward repeti-
tions of a single 'type'. As Easterling began by saying, we do
have a clear idea of them as different people, and this does not
rest simply on the fact that their stories are different, that they
are implicated in different 'humanly intelligible' scenes. My
own emphasis on the idea of an 'integrated' character plays on
the same question.[28] The playwrights combine in their characters traits which group naturally, and do not furnish any
paradoxical or unique combinations; in that sense they are far
removed from those we are accustomed to find in modern
works. But that in itself does not render these characters 'types':
Oedipus' energetic intelligence in the *Oedipus Tyrannus* groups
perfectly naturally with his other traits, as does Ajax's strong
adherence to an exaggerated Homeric ethic, or Antigone's

---

[27] The phrase 'human intelligibility', often used and discussed in recent articles,
owes its currency to Easterling's discussion of 'Presentation of Character in Aeschylus',
G & R 20 (1973), 3–19, in which Agamemnon's behaviour is the principal example.
Heath's exegesis (*Poetics of Greek Tragedy*, 119–20) is also particularly helpful.

[28] pp. 235–44; cf. Silk, p. 157, on 'character-traits as a continuum'.

single-minded harshness to her sister. These are not reducible to a single 'Sophoclean hero', but in each case the new trait combines very readily with the old ones. This is not an idiosyncratic character-mix, then, but one which might readily recur in another human being or dramatic creation; yet in each case we have an individual, grasped and realized as distinct and different, none the less. Not that such 'integration' is universal: Pentheus' endearing kindness to the aged Cadmus, for instance, does come as rather a surprise after his earlier stridency and harshness (*Bacchae* 1316 ff.);[29] the defendant of Lysias 24 presents himself as having some interesting angularities, as Russell shows;[30] and Polybius' Aratus (but not Plutarch's) is another clear counter-example.[31] But these really are exceptions; integration was the rule.

'Instead of understanding, he praises or blames', wrote Wilamowitz: and if we move to other genres, there is no doubt that the taste for the ethically exemplary can impede an interest in individual differences. Halliwell brings this out clearly with the *Evagoras*, and Russell with the orators;[32] I touch on something similar with Plutarch—though I am anxious to insist that the exemplary should not be seen as the primary taste, conditioning the assumptions of 'integration': the two rather reinforce one another.[33] Gill similarly assimilates both ethical evaluation and a normalizing tendency to his 'character-viewpoint', without regarding either as primary.[34] In his book on the *Poetics*, Halliwell also shows how Aristotle's treatment of *ēthos* rests on very different assumptions from anything we would mean by 'character': *ēthos* is closely tied to action and to moral choice, and determines the ethical qualities of those actions and choices, 'that in virtue of which we say the actions are of a certain sort' (*Poet.* 1449^{b}38 f.). Halliwell writes:

Character (*ēthos*, or commonly the plural *ēthē*) is a specific moral factor in relation to action, not a vague or pervasive notion equivalent

[29] Cf. Heath, *Poetics of Greek Tragedy*, 117. It comes as less of a surprise after various other ploys to recover audience sympathy, for instance the increasing stress on his youth; but that is a different sort of point.

[30] pp. 200–3.

[31] pp. 236–7.

[32] pp. 42–59; 198–9.

[33] pp. 238–40.

[34] pp. 2–9.

to modern ideas of personality or individuality—least of all to individuality, since *ēthos* is a matter of generic qualities (virtues and
vices).[35]

Jones similarly stresses that *ēthos* lacks the *inclusive* quality we
associate with 'character' or 'personality'. In no way does Aristotle assume that *ēthos* will sum up all the relevant facts about a
person, and he certainly does not share the modern prejudice
that the function of action is to reveal character:

> Revealing a moral choice means, for Aristotle, declaring the moral
> character of an act in a situation where the act itself does not make
> this clear. Reader and spectator are appraised of the ethical colour of
> the action at this point of the play. To our sense of characteristic
> conduct Aristotle opposes that of characterful action.[36]

So far so good, and it is certainly right to draw attention to
the normative tendency in such a treatment of *ēthos*: and such
ethical characterizing of an action will often be in terms of
virtues or vices. Still, it is perhaps premature to move, as Jones
does, to talk of Aristotle's interest in 'types' and 'type-
definition'.[37] We should not speak as if there were no middle
ground between the modern cast of individual and the generalized 'type', nor assume that this view of 'characterful action'
need necessarily be hostile to a fair measure of individuation.
For one thing, in a drama we always see a series of moral
actions and choices, not only one (what Aristotelian 'unity of
action' demands is a rounded and causally related *sequence* of
events). Antigone has to decide, not merely to bury her
brother, but to react to Ismene in the way she does, and to
adopt a particular stance in her confrontations with Creon;
Oedipus has to decide not merely to hunt down the culprit, but
to reject Teiresias, to suspect Creon, to take the line he does
over oracles, to blind himself, to seek to avoid returning into the
house; and so on. All those actions are revealing of, or informed
by, *ēthos*, but we would describe that *ēthos* rather differently in
each of the moral choices. None of the actions or choices are at
all difficult to reconcile with one another, but their combina-

---

[35] See S. Halliwell, *Aristotle's Poetics* (London, 1986), ch. 5; the quotation is from p.
151.
[36] See Jones, *On Aristotle and Greek Tragedy*, 32–40: the quotation is from p. 33.
[37] Ibid., esp. 40–2.

tion serves to discriminate someone who need not be a 'type', even though he is not an idiosyncratic individual in a modern sense.

Secondly, it may be wrong to think that this ethical characterization of action need *always* be in terms of virtues or vices, or at least that these virtues or vices may always be as undifferentiated or 'typed' as we naturally assume: we would indeed find it hard to categorize some of those choices of Antigone and Oedipus in straightforward 'virtue-or-vice' terms. In the *Poetics*, it is true, Aristotle talks of these generalized qualities rather crudely as virtues and vices;[38] but it is clear that his ethical treatment must be set against the wider analysis in the *Nicomachean Ethics*, and there his 'normative' elements are interpreted more widely. He is concerned not merely with how to be virtuous or just, but with how to live: in *EN* 4 he can discuss how not to be sullen and bad-tempered (δύσκολος, 1126ᵇ11 ff.), or how to be versatile (εὐτράπελος) in relaxed conversation (1127ᵇ33 ff.); he talks of the need to avoid blushing too much (1128ᵇ10 ff.). Elsewhere he describes talking and walking at the same time as suggesting a 'brash and boorish' *ēthos* (*Rhet.* 1417ᵃ23–4), and Theophrastus is only a breath away. These aspects which we might associate with, in Gill's terms, 'personality', Aristotle would view rather as a combination of different character-habits (*hexeis*) or in the case of the blushing a symptom of distinctive experiences (*pathē*).[39] Those *hexeis* can themselves then settle into a determinate *ēthos* which could, in its turn, inform moral choices. Such a treatment seems to leave room for a considerable differentiation of figures: if they are 'types', they are at least a rather singular brand of type, and our notions of 'virtue' and 'vice' may be inadequate (as, indeed, they often are with Theophrastus). What sets the limit on individual variations is in fact less the concept of *ēthos* itself, or the view of 'characterful action', than the range of actions or *ēthē* open to tragedy. The serious man (σπουδαῖος), who in Aristotle's view ought to be tragedy's subject, will be less

[38] And, for that matter, in the *Rhetoric* (cf. 1388ᵇ34). See esp. Halliwell, *Poetics*, 158–9.

[39] This point was made by Martha Nussbaum in discussion of Gill's paper at the colloquium: I have taken over several of her examples from the *Ethics*. I am also grateful to David Wiggins for discussion.

variegated: for instance, Aristotle knows that human preferences for different pleasures vary immensely—but the σπουδαῖος, he thinks, will not be prey to such variations (*EN* 1176ᵃ10–15). Nor will he have much opportunity to show his versatility in relaxed conversation, or the way he talks while walking: the public and dignified texture of tragedy will rule this out. Still, it seems clear that a considerable range of individual behaviour is left open. Aristotle would indeed admit that in certain circumstances right conduct could vary according to the individual concerned (τὸ μέσον τὸ πρὸς ἡμᾶς, e.g. 1106ᵃ36 ff., 1152ᵇ25–31), something that encourages alertness to individual differences even among the virtuous.

The question of ethical moralism is more far-reaching, and perhaps we ought to be looking for a different sort of moral, and stressing a different aspect of individuality. In encomium or invective the moralizing will centre on the focal figure, with the evident danger that he may be reduced to a crude concatenation of virtues or vices. Tragedy is subtler: its moralism is more often descriptive than protreptic, exploring ethical truths of human nature rather than producing simple examples to imitate or avoid. The moral import of the *Oedipus Tyrannus* centres more on the fragility of human nature than on Oedipus' virtue or vice; and in such a case it matters that Oedipus is the sort of person he is, but only in the sense that *even so great a man as he* can be vulnerable. We can extract a moral from that for ourselves, but it is not obvious that Oedipus himself *needs* to be conceived in especially normative terms, any more than we need feel that his extraordinary circumstances or fate could recur in our own life. Aristotle certainly demands that a hero be 'like ourselves', but that must be taken in a subtle and qualified sense. What is necessary is 'that the characters should not stand at an ethical extreme, but should be such that an audience can experience a sympathetic moral affinity with them';[40] just as in oratory the audience can be conciliated or disarmed by a speaker's *ēthos* in order to draw the right conclusions about him,[41] and that can be done by a figure as singular as the speaker of Lysias 24, even if the usual range of types is less dif-

---

[40] See Halliwell, *Poetics*, 159–61: the quotation is from p. 160.
[41] Cf. Russell, p. 198.

ferentiated. The audiences of tragedy were perfectly able to ponder general issues on the basis of unique cases. If the uniqueness attends the circumstances more than the characters, that does not arise from the taste for moral exemplification, but rather springs from the non-idiosyncratic, integrating assumptions we have already noticed. We have also seen that these need not exclude that limited measure of individuality: it is the individual's role within the whole work, not his simple virtue or vice, that matters for the moralism.

This is even clearer outside tragedy, in the larger canvas that epic or historiography can allow. Herodotus is evidently interested in a pattern of tyrannical behaviour, yet all the tyrants are different, if only in limited ways—Cyrus with his peculiar ability and drive, Cambyses with his madness, Darius with his insight, Xerxes with his vacillation and even a bizarre weakness. It is indeed peculiarly pointed to see how these individuals, no matter how hard they try or how much they know, cannot avoid falling into the same patterns of events. Their individual differences thus become part of the ethical pattern which Herodotus explores: their limited individuation is not merely allowed by the moralism, it is integral to it. Similarly with Thucydides: it is now the interplay of individuals and a democracy which becomes absorbing, and is used to suggest exemplary truths. Not, of course, that it was inevitable that figures with the precise individual traits of Nicias and Alcibiades would come to play a part in Athens' downfall, any more than it was inevitable that that downfall should come from the particular sequences in Sicily or at Aegospotami. What was inevitable, arguably, was that Athens was one day doomed to destroy herself: and this was for reasons that might apply in the future to any similar imperialist democracy. In this sense her fate was exemplary; but exemplary in a way which allowed for significant variations in particular circumstances (3. 82. 2 clearly brings out Thucydides' view of such qualified 'cycles'). Once again, a general moral can be extracted from very particular cases, and reapplied to particular cases in future; the normative does not exclude the singular, but interweaves with it. And one of the reasons for Athens' fall was, precisely, the emergence of figures who were more *individualistic* as well as individual: men who not merely showed a distinctive style, but also pursued their own instincts and interests rather than the common good (cf. esp. 2. 65. 7, 5. 16). And that again might recur—not necessarily in the exact way of an Alcibiades or, differently but just as significantly, a Nicias; but in some way. For Pericles, the individual's talents were most wholly fulfilled at Athens, but there was also a strong sense in which his interests should be wholly submerged in the state (2. 37, 60. 3–4, 61. 4); the unease of that argument may already be felt. For Alcibiades, the individual is more concerned with gratifying his own pride and ambitions; what Pericles had attributed to the city—its worthiness to rule, its exposure to envy and hate, its expectation of everlasting fame—he now transfers to himself.[42] He may argue that the state will benefit (6. 16. 3), but the events themselves tell a different tale. Sicily is very much his show; and when such individual shows go wrong they desperately endanger the city, though eventually Nicias (no less disquietingly concerned for himself, 7. 48. 3–4) should take as much of the blame as Alcibiades; nor of course is the city itself guiltless. This interaction of individual and community is most complicated, and what matters is not merely the distinctiveness of the individuals but also their egoism; it is individualism, as well as individuation, which is now vital to Thucydides' theme. It is, indeed, an ethical theme, provided we recognize that ethics is as concerned with pointing truths of human behaviour as with preaching about their value or awfulness.

Nor are such interests novel to Herodotus or Thucydides. A closely related theme is there at the beginning in Homer's Achilles, who sees things in so distinctive a way, and whose individuality sets him at odds with the values of his community, to his comrades' peril and his own catastrophe. As so often, the worlds of Homer and Thucydides emerge as curiously close to one another. Plato too has much to say about the role of a Socrates within a state: an individual figure in behaviour and in insight, for whom the state has no room, to its loss. Tragedy too has its parallels: its figures are public men, with social responsibilities—but Ajax too shows a distinctive, exaggerated ethic, one which does not embrace those responsibilities but

---

[42] 6. 16. 1, with 2. 41. 3 (cf. 1. 73. 1, 75. 1); 6. 16. 5, with 2. 37. 2, 64. 5. Cf. C. W. Macleod, *Collected Essays* (Oxford, 1983), 75, 86.

comes to run counter to them. The public quality of the figures need not always impair their individuality; it can rather render it more problematic, and create tensions which are peculiarly rich in tragic potential. An Alcibiades, an Achilles, an Ajax, or a Socrates is still not idiosyncratic, of course, and we may not even find them especially challenging to understand. Their many-sidedness is not ours, and each trait still largely predicts the next;[43] we still have only that small number of characteristics, powerfully drawn. But such figures fundamentally belie the natural expectations of their milieu; they have a distinctive style or ethic, and the resolve to remain true to it; their contemporaries find them bemusing, even if the reader does not. That is individuality, in a strong sense, and it is part of the authors' point. It does not militate against an exemplary purpose, it is central to it. Nor is it sufficient in such cases to claim that the characterization is simply subordinate to the plot. In such cases theme and characterization interweave so intimately that they virtually merge.[44]

And this reverts to the most basic point of all, one fundamental to all the chapters in this volume. Characterization cannot simply be detached from the works as a whole: theme and characterization perpetually interact, and character is only one part of 'the total image of human existence' that a literary work presents.[45] This has long been common wisdom about tragedy, and some of the other chapters in this volume suggest how readily the point can be extended to other genres. Homer's Agamemnon can only be gauged if we consider his function in the poem as a whole; an orator's characterizing techniques and interest will vary according to his case; Plato's characterization, like his tone, ranges widely according to his theme and argument; even in biography, pre-eminently a genre where theme and characterization coalesce, Plutarch's interest in understanding his heroes varies according to the other themes of a life. All this might suggest that a collection of essays on characterization is itself a flawed project, suggesting a detachability that is simply impracticable. But though authors would

---

[43] Cf. my remarks on Plutarch's Alcibiades and Homer's Odysseus, p. 237.
[44] See Goldhill's discussion of Barthes, p. 112; id., *Reading Greek Tragedy*, 174.
[45] Gould, 'Dramatic Character', 62.

vary their practice from one work to the next, they varied it only in a certain range, within limits set by the everyday assumptions of their audience as well as by the conventions of their genre. To illuminate that range and those limits has been our concern.

I. Index of Passages Discussed

II. Index of Names

Modern scholars are included only when their views are discussed *in extenso*, or recurrently in several of the chapters.

III. Index of Themes and Concepts